R| ‖‖‖‖‖‖‖‖‖‖‖‖‖‖‖‖‖
D0732681

"In her own inimical way, Marsha Shearer has addressed many of the actions of Donald J. Trump that have been the cornerstone of his presidency. Her essays characterize his issuance of outrageous tweets as both creating daily chaos and stoking hatred and fear. While clearly a foe of this President's actions, Shearer focuses her attention on the declining participation in elections and advocates revisionist thinking for both political parties to provide voters with better candidates to lead America's future. BRAVO!!!"

—Douglas Hughes, Trade Association Executive and Lobbyist (Ret). Instructor on the U.S. Constitution and the Founding Documents.

66

"In this book, Shearer chronicles her intellectual and emotional response as she comes to grips with the enormity of the Trump presidency. These essays shine a light on significant issues and offer hope as well as suggestions for their remediation. In sum, this book puts into perspective the dangers posed by Trump's behavior; by allowing them to pass unchallenged risks them becoming the 'new normal.' Shearer's essays provide that challenge."

—Roger F. Cooper, Author of *Impressions*, Doctor of Psychology, former President of National Psychologists in Management.

REVIEWS

❝

"Future historians will debate and judge the long term effects of the Trump presidency on the nation and the world; in this series of essays, Marsha Shearer offers a provocative early contribution to that debate. Her analysis and arguments are thorough, well-considered, cogently argued and cover a wide range of policies, actions and decisions, ultimately passing a devastating critique on President Trump and his administration. Whether one agrees with her conclusions or not, these essays set a high bar for both supportive and countervailing analyses of the Trump years.

—Dr. Mark D. Welton, S.J.D., Professor Emeritus, Department of Law, United States Military Academy

❝

These vivid, insightful set of essays by a clearly gifted writer are truly remarkable. Shearer's marvelously detailed and engaging entries chronicle the time just prior to the 2016 election through much of the first three years of Trump's administration. The universal appeal of these essays stems from its riveting blend of the particulars of life during the Trump era while living in Trump country; the result is that reading these well-written and engaging essays serves as a cathartic experience for the rest of us.

—Sue Dubman, Brown University; Bioinformatics, Cancer Research Specialty Vice President and Senior Director Positions at the National Cancer Institute and the University of California-San Francisco (Ret.)

REVIEWS

❝

I have enjoyed reading Shearer's opinion pieces for the past several years; now she has expanded them and turned them into a series of essays on the Trump Administration outlining her serious concerns. The clarity of her writing is only surpassed by her clarity of thinking. She says she wrote so she would not forget. I hope as you read them you will not forget the events of the Trump Presidency. After 30 years in the US Army, I cannot understand how any military officer can support this Commander in Chief.

—Colonel Brian P. Mullady, (Ret.), Soviet Foreign Area Officer, Chief of Staff of the Defense Department charged with conducting the START, INF, Chemical weapons and other treaties in the former Soviet Union. Senior American, United Nations Iraqi Weapons Inspectors

❝

This is a work that sorely needed to be written. Sorely in the sense we need to be reminded just how mind-numbing the cascade of insults to rationality, common sense and decency has rendered the body politic. Everyone needs to read this book, which catalogs stunning political malfeasance, as a reminder of just how ordinary extraordinary pathological behavior at the highest level has become.

— James R. Ukockis, Phd, Senior Economist, U.S. Department of the Treasury (Ret.)

AMERICA IN CRISIS

ESSAYS ON THE FAILED PRESIDENCY
OF DONALD J. TRUMP

MARSHA SHEARER

Bulk copies are available by contacting: America.in.Crisis.Book@gmail.com

Cover design: GoMyStory.com/John W Prince

Page design & typography: GoMyStory.com /John W Prince

Cover Photo: iStockPhoto

First Edition

Library of Congress Control Number: 2019918029

Printed in the United States of America

Marsha Shearer, The Villages, Florida

America in Crisis: Essays on the Failed Presidency of Donald J. Trump

ISBN 978-1-951188-01-6

DEDICATION

FOR STEVE, RICK AND JEFF
AND IN MEMORY OF
JOSEPH S. FLYNN, SR
- RABBLE ROUSER EXTRAORDINAIRE

TABLE OF CONTENTS

Prologue
Self-Medication in a World Gone Mad 1

04 September 2016
The Fundamental Problem with American Politics 4

24 October 2016
The Election Conundrum of 2016—and Your Choice of Evil Is... ? 9

28 November 2016
Donald J. Trump is President. What the Hell Have We Done? 14

11 January 2017
The Trouble with Donald (Spoiler Alert: He's Seriously Nuts!) 19

28 January 2017
Tick Tock... Trump's First Week 23

22 February 2017
We Have Met the Enemy... 28

20 March 2017
For Trump Voters: What Will it Take? 31

06 April 2017
A Problem of Their Own Making 37

30 April 2017
The First One Hundred Days 42

10 May 2017
The Only Logical Reason for Firing James Comey 47

27 May 2017
Trump's Budget—The Con Man Cometh 50

10 June 2017
The Comey Hearing 54

14 June 2017
A Time to Reflect... On Guns 58

23 July 2017
"It's Mueller Time" 61

26 August 2017
What Will it Take (Part II) 64

14 September 2017
Shelter from the Storm—A Question of Empathy 69

15 October 2017
Looking for Profiles in Courage 73

09 November 2017
Uncovering the Truth—It's Not Easy 77

02 December 2017
The Assault on Truth 81

28 December 2017
Donald J. Trump: The Avatar of American Corruption 85

13 January 2018
And the Winners Are... 89

27 January 2018
Why a booming Stock Market and a Growing Economy Isn't Enough 93

11 February 2018
Now it's Our Turn 97

22 February 2018
Only in America: Straight Facts About Guns 101

10 March 2018
Enough Is Enough 105

17 March 2018
Background Check—Trump Would Have Failed 109

25 March 2018
The Second Amendment—Dissected: Then and Now 114

30 March 2018
The Kids from Parkland 118

07 April 2018
Teachers Say "No More" 122

14 April 2018
Well, What Do You Know—It Really Is All in the Mind 126

28 April 2018
Making a Case for a Third Party—Or— 130

09 May 2018
Truth Matters: But Not to Donald 134

19 May 2018
Fire, Ready, Aim—"The March of Folly" 138

26 May 2018
This Is Not Normal. He Is Not Normal. 142

04 June 2018
"Witch Hunt"—A Primer 148

09 June 2018
Q: Who Are We? A: A Nation of Immigrants. 152

19 June 2018
How to Reduce the Influence of Money in Politics 155

28 June 2018
A House Divided—Trump's Fondest Wish 159

03 July 2018
Scott Pruitt: Swamp Creature Extraordinaire 163

17 July 2018
Trump and Putin... WTF? 168

25 July 2018
Trump's Tax Cut—Promises Revisited 170

29 July 2018
One Month Into the War: News from the Front Lines 175

05 August 2018
Tell Me Again—Who are the "Takers?" 179

22 August 2018
How to Prevent Another Trump—Lessons Learned 184

29 August 2018
In Support of a Presidential Election Commission 188

06 September 2018
The Elephant in the Room 192

13 September 2018
Trump's Undermining of the Press 196

19 September 2018
What Will it Take? (Part III) 200

30 September 2018
The Kavanaugh Hearing 204

13 October 2018
The Politics of Division 208

28 October 2018
Words Matter. Trump's Incite Violence. 212

08 November 2018
An Open Letter to Republicans 215

18 November 2018
The 2018 Election Postmortem 218

25 November 2018
The Gaming of U.S. Foreign Policy 223

03 December 2018
A Scorecard for Scoundrels 227

22 December 2018
Trump's Lump of Coal in the Taxpayers' Stockings 231

25 December 2018
Donald's Very Bad, Most Awful, Worst Week Yet 234

31 December 2018
2018: A Review of the Year and Implications for the Future 238

07 January 2019
Not a Great Start to the New Year 243

10 January 2019
Immigration and the Government Shutdown 247

15 January 2019
The Manchurian President? 252

25 January 2019
The Walls Close In and the Plot Sickens 257

05 February 2019
A Legend in His Own Mind 262

17 February 2019
To Impeach or Not to Impeach: The Tragedy of Trump 267

26 February 2019
Ever Feel You're Living in an Alternate Universe? 270

05 March 2019
The Meltdown—A Loser Surrounded by Failure 274

18 March 2019
Question: Who Are We? Answer: To Be Determined. 279

28 March 2019
Victory Lap—Uh, Not So Fast 283

15 April 2019
He's Getting Worse 287

24 April 2019
The Mueller Report 292

19 May 2019
Too Many Pots; Too Much Heat 298

01 June 2019
A Cure for What Ails Us 302

05 June 2019
The Impeachable Offense is —A Lack of Defense 307

13 June 2019
Trump in a Nutshell—With So Much Left Over 311

27 June 2019
Trump's Progress Report 315

04 July 2019
America: The Fourth of July 2019... 321

15 July 2019
Two Plus Two = Russia... But Who Gives a Damn? 327

24 July 2019
Meet Donald Trump: Racist, Xenophobe, Despot and... 333

30 July 2019
He's Getting Worse—Again! 337

03 August 2019
America's Vote Hijacked 341

07 August 2019
Guns + Trump = A Toxic Brew 346

18 August 2019
So Much Success 351

28 August 2019
A Seat on the *Titanic* 358

03 September 2019
Heroes and Villains 364

12 September 2019
What Went Wrong? 370

16 September 2019
Impeachment—The Only Option 376

It's Almost Over. Now What? 382

How to Make a More Perfect Union 387

Epilogue
The Final Act—Starts With *Though* and Ends With the Answer to *Why*. ... 394

Acknowledgments 399

About the Author 401

PROLOGUE

SELF-MEDICATION IN
A WORLD GONE MAD

"Our lives begin to end the day we become silent about the things that matter."—MARTIN LUTHER KING, JR.

"We don't just forget things because they don't matter, we also forget things because they matter too much."—PHILIP ROTH

I love politics like others love baseball. Or chess. Or any of the other strange and wonderful passions that help define us. For me, everything in the public sphere is political, because everything in politics affects the public sphere. Politics is the perfect example of a 'push me, pull you' reciprocal relationship—for better, or worse.

The Trump Presidency is an example of this in the extreme. It has affected, for worse, everything from personal relationships, to foreign policy, to our place in the world.

This book, which began as opinion editorials for a local online paper, morphed into a series of essays. When I stopped writing for them, I started writing for me. I wrote to help me process what was happening. For me, it's personal. Call it self-medication in a world gone mad.

I wrote to be sure I didn't forget.

These essays were written in real time and are presented in chronological order. They provide documentation and commentary from just prior to the 2016 election through much of Trump's third year. I haven't gone back and modified content based on new information; they are one person's reflection of that event at that time.

I wrote to be sure I didn't forget.

Ben Bernanke, former Federal Reserve Chair, said "The enemy is forgetting." But with Trump, that enemy comes with the territory. Day after day, he does so much damage, he instigates such turmoil and disaster, and he lies so continually, he creates such chaos—and all almost non-stop— that it's easy to forget today what he did yesterday because today is so much worse. The problem is that tomorrow we'll be saying the same thing.

So, I wrote to be sure I didn't forget. And, I wrote in hopes the reader won't either.

My goal is to present one person's interpretation of the worst and most consequential presidency in the history of this country. The events I chose struck me, at the moment, as important to remember.

My imaginary audience are citizens, disturbed and angry by what Trump has done to the people, our country, and its institutions. There are lessons here as well for future generations. I hope that my grandchildren and theirs will study what happened, and view this time in our history as a warning about how easy it is to lose our way when we allow anyone to play to our worst fears and instincts, rather than 'the better angels of our nature.'

There's nothing special about me; I have no professional political credentials. Because of that, maybe you and I are alike. We're citizens, and like you, I take that responsibility seriously.

My background is in educational administration. I've written and published professionally in my field, but I'm not a journalist or politician—although I wish I had been both—or either. But, I am a voter and an American, sickened by events. Perhaps that's all the *bona fides* required.

Maybe these essays are nothing more than a therapeutic exercise, trying to grasp and process what's happening, and one person's attempt to deal with it.

Maybe the reader will be prompted to remember, helped by this written record, so that mistakes made aren't forgotten. Or repeated.

Maybe the people, through the government that represents us, will put corrective measures in place to assure norms and requirements, previously taken for granted, are codified in law or regulation, so that a person as flawed and lacking in humanity as Trump, can never again run for president. The penultimate essay addresses some of these ideas.

When the Trump Presidency is over, the divisions he manufactured, prodded, poked, and magnified will need to be addressed. The last essay in the series presents some ideas that might help the healing process and bring us closer together.

We are, after all, still and so far, the *United* States of America.

04 SEPTEMBER 2016

THE FUNDAMENTAL PROBLEM
WITH AMERICAN POLITICS

"Politics is the gentle art of getting votes from the poor and campaign funds from the rich by promising to protect each from the other." — OSCAR AMERINGER

What a weird campaign season this has been. According to polls, the majority of Americans aren't enamored with either Presidential choice; unfavorable ratings for both are at record levels.

Voters feel disillusioned, that government isn't listening to them and can't be trusted. This may be the first time in recent history where there is so much divisiveness and undiluted anger in the country, and within the body politic.

Yet, even with all the angst, there seems to be a growing consensus in both parties on one particular issue. Voters from all sides are rebelling against the establishment—against 'typical' Washington politicians... 'typical' meaning, well, all of them.

Candidates are going to extremes to tout their lack of

governmental experience. Just think about that. In what other career is lack of experience seen as a plus? When Trump voters are asked what appeals to them, a frequent response is, "He's not a politician." And, what they dislike about Hillary is that she is. What they're really saying is, "I want someone who works for me."

Voters, and even a few politicians, are proposing term limits to counter the effects of the lifelong incumbent. We rightly rail against those who enter Congress, firmly in the middle class but somehow, inexplicably, leave government as millionaires.

Let's put aside the fact that our do-nothing Congress is, in large part, the result of refusing to consider or vote for anything that's supported by President Obama. There is another reason for this inertia, and it will exist long after President Obama leaves office. That reason is money. The workings (or nonworkings) of our government are based on the principle of legalized bribery, and it begins with the decision to run for office.

In 2012, the average cost to win a Senate seat was $10.5 million; the average for a House win was $1.7 million. There are a few self-funders, but that's no solution. In fact, the idea that only the ultra-rich could run for office would be an anathema to the Founding Fathers.

Running for office costs money—there's no denying that. But, big checks come with at least the perception of big expectations, and the odds for corruption increase. Those may sound like a harsh words, but the Founders defined it, in part, as putting private interests above the public good.

A few candidates are taking steps, on their own, to

disavow private influence by refusing to accept money from big corporations and Superpacs. Bernie Sanders did it, and proved he could still be competitive. But when opponents don't do the same, it creates an uneven playing field. It should be the contrast of platforms, ideas, promises, and priorities that determine who wins, not the amount of money in the bank account.

From the day winners take office, they have to raise money for the next election. It's estimated that newly elected members of the House have to raise $10 thousand per week, in order to defend their seat two years hence. They average 10 hours per week on the phone, begging for money for the next race, and even more time schmoozing with prospective donors. And, that's time not spent working for constituents. The exchange of big money is just that—an exchange—for influence, for access, for *quid pro quo*. I give you this; you give me that.

After our newly minted politician is sworn in and on-the-job, the serious bribery begins. Let's say our new Congressman came to office with a promise to work to lower the cost of prescription drugs. Or provide ways to refinance student loans. Or alter the tax code so that corporations pay their fair share. In 2011, there were *23 registered lobbyists for every member of Congress.*

They represent every industry, group and concept imaginable... the good, the bad, and the ugly. Assuming the public good (lowering drug prices, helping lower interest on student loans, or fair taxation) doesn't match the goal of private interests, (keeping drug prices high, more money for banks and corporations), there are lobbyists, paid to ensure that their boss's private interests come before the public good.

So, now our newbie Congressman is besieged from all sides—from constituents who want promises fulfilled, to the lobbyist threatening to fund an opponent in the next primary. There is a push and pull between the public good and private interests. Politicians have to decide between the two. Too often, the result is to do nothing at all. This year, Congress spent more time in recess than in session, accomplishing little, while drawing a nice paycheck at taxpayer expense. No wonder voters are pissed!

That's the problem with politics in America. Until the influence of money is eliminated or seriously reduced, nothing will change. Congress will continue to remain in the doldrums with 10 percent approval. And citizens will continue to view politicians as self-serving and untrustworthy. This is the overriding issue. The influence of money in politics is preventing a truly responsive government by, of, and for the people.

But there are solutions. Zephyr Teachout, Associate Professor of Law at Fordham University, in her book *Corruption in America,* provides some ideas.

- Congress can pass legislation banning former members from becoming lobbyists. At this point about 50 percent of Senators and 47 percent of House members make that their next career move. By eliminating this possibility, we might get candidates more interested in serving the public than themselves.
- Allow only public funding for presidential elections by providing a tax credit up to a certain amount to

spend on the candidate or party of their choice.

- End Citizens United and Superpacs which allow unlimited campaign contributions.
- Disallow contributions by corporations to any federal, state or local campaign, and set a maximum of, say, $300 for an individual contribution to any one candidate.
- Ban all contributions of any sort, at any time, from registered lobbyists.
- Bust those trusts! We are heading for an oligarchy, if we're not already there. Reducing the number of massive corporations that have essentially become monopolies will reduce their influence and go a long way toward reducing corruption.
- Ask candidates at all levels what they are prepared to do to end the influence of big money in politics and to promote campaign finance reform.

Voters, regardless of party, instinctively know that government should be about promoting laws and actions that support the public good—however each candidate chooses to define that. And, we also recognize the corrupting influence of money. Unless we take this problem seriously, it will destroy our Republic from within just as surely as any foe from without.

24 OCTOBER 2016

THE ELECTION CONUNDRUM OF 2016

— AND YOUR CHOICE OF EVIL IS... ?

"We are free to choose, but we are not free from the consequences of our choice."—ANON.

If the most ardent Hillary and Trump supporters were given truth serum, they would admit their candidate is seriously flawed. Each comes with a background and history; a record of achievement as well as lousy performance and poor judgment. On that, if we're honest, we can agree. So, now what?

The easiest thing is to retreat to our partisan corners. We fall back on considerations like appointments to the Supreme Court and other excuses to vote the party ticket. But, as each day brings new accusations on both sides, ignoring them becomes equivalent to sticking our collective heads in the sand.

Being partisan, without acknowledging the candidate's characteristics we've come to know and hate, is truly the definition of putting party before country.

Given what's just been said, I thought long and hard—

over a period of months—about what to do. I was, and still am, a committed Bernie supporter. It has been agonizing, especially given what was suspected, and now known, about the Democratic National Committee's actions to sabotage his candidacy. It hasn't been proven definitively, but it's hard to believe those actions took place without the knowledge and approval of the Hillary campaign and Hillary herself. So yes, that upsets and angers me. It reinforces my greatest areas of concern; her lack of honesty, trustworthiness and transparency. I don't like her. Yet given all that and more, I voted for her. And I'll tell you why.

Never in Donald Trump's long and privileged life, is there a record that he has given a single day to public service. He never ran for or held a local office. He avoided military service using bone spurs as an excuse. He never volunteered at a soup kitchen or an animal shelter, never read to kids in kindergarten, never mentored high school students in an inner city.

He's never taken one step to correct a problem that didn't affect him directly. Think about that. Take as an example a problem he identified as a national priority and which he could have taken personal and total control: every item manufactured under his name is made elsewhere, including much of the steel used for his hotels. He admits importing foreign workers on a regular basis. He doesn't have to do this.

He could have used his money to show that quality products can be manufactured here, even if they might cost more. He chose not to. He could have provided precious jobs for local workers, even if it meant paying more. He chose not to. He says he wants to help America. He bemoans our educational system, our roads and highways, our rail and airports as 'third world,' yet this multibillionaire apparently chooses to pay nothing in federal income taxes for years on end. Because he can. He could have chosen not to take full advantage of a tax system he bemoans, but he didn't. This being said, confirmation will await release of his tax returns, and that won't happen voluntarily.

He has never led positively by personal example. He says he's given millions to charity, but there's no way to substantiate that, because he refuses to release his tax returns.

He's not intelligent. An intelligent adult, among other things, speaks in full, grammatically correct sentences, has a vocabulary that surpasses a 4th grader, can speak using nuance, can think and express ideas logically, can stay on topic, and doesn't need to rely on the same adjectives and clichés in conversation.

He's mean and miserly, and he's rich enough to get away with it. There are too many documented examples of refusing to pay the full price, or any price, for work done. And, when contractors complain, his response is, 'Sue me.' So much for ethical business practices.

He worked hard to delegitimize the Presidency of Barack Obama and never apologized for those actions, or any actions, that turned out to have been a mistake. The Central Park 5 case is a horrendous example.

In his personal and business life, he treats people as objects, as pawns in a chess game—well, checkers maybe. He hasn't the mental capacity for chess. And, he has enough money to assure he always wins. He's a manipulator and a bully.

Then there are The Women issues. And The Black issues.

And The Inner City issues. And The Hispanic issues. And The Anti-Semitic issues. And The Religion issues. And The Muslim issues. And The Scapegoating The Press issues. And, the_____, fill in the blank. And repeat. He has been endorsed by the KKK and more than one White Supremacist hate group—they say he supports their principles. They should know. He seems to lack concern or awareness of other people and their feelings; his lack of empathy is stunning.

His current top tier advisors and campaign heads include Steve Bannon, the former chair of Breitbart News, the voice of the Alt Right. David Bossie is next in line. He's the former president of Citizens United, the case that ended up in the Supreme Court, opening the door to unlimited and anonymous campaign contributions—the personification of 'rigging the system'—against the little guy and for special interests and lobbyists.

Even the most ardent Trump supporters see that he isn't much interested in pursuing a deep understanding of policies or issues. His guidance will come from people who hate the current system: the Breitbarts of the world, who are happy to tear down what is left of the Republican Party and this country, and rebuild both in their image.

Staff members complain they can't keep him 'on message,' and that he has an attention span of a flea. How do they think any of that will change once he's in the White House?

Trump supporters say they like him because 'he speaks his mind.' That's not a measure of a person. What comes out of his mouth, is. They say they like him because he's a billionaire. That's not a measure of a person. How he earned the money and what he does with it, is what should be measured.

These may be the ultimate questions to ask before voting—"Is this the person I want representing me and my country? Is this the person I want my grandchildren to look up to and emulate?" Actually, that is already happening; teachers are calling it the 'Trump Effect'—the recent increase in bullying, name calling and racism. The man is unfit for public office. Period.

Donald Trump is a very frightening man. The country he envisions is one that results from stoking anxiety, hatred and fear. He encourages and reinforces bigotry. If elected, he will destroy this country and our standing in the world. He says, "Elect me. I'm the only one who can fix this." Those are the words of a dictator. For him, this election has always been about him, not about the country. Not about us.

So no, I voted early and had no qualms voting for Hillary. The conundrum is resolved. For me, the goal is to defeat Trump and everything he stands for.

Regardless of Hillary's faults, and she has many, I know we will still have a Republic at the end of her term. And, we may have even solved some problems and made things better along the way.

For me, given the alternative, that is enough.

28 NOVEMBER 2016

DONALD J. TRUMP IS PRESIDENT.
WHAT THE HELL HAVE WE DONE??

"It's too easy to dismiss Trump as a buffoon ...but to do so is to make light of a very serious threat."—SADIQ KHAN

It's finally over. The electorate has spoken and in a few short weeks, the 45th President of the United States will be inaugurated. The most ill-prepared, inexperienced person in the history of the Presidency has been chosen to lead us. The voters wanted change. And change is what we're getting. So, let's review what Trump has done, since his election, to prepare himself for this enormous responsibility, and to deliver the change he promised.

He attended two Daily Briefings about the state of the world and our national security; that's two out of about 26—so far. One would hope his interest in the topics might be piqued, but, apparently not.

He is in the midst of appointing advisors and cabinet officials. While he promised his supporters he would 'drain the swamp,' it appears he's populating it with vast numbers of alligators and other miscreants. He chastised Hillary for her close associations with Goldman Sachs, but thus far has appointed a number of key people with significant ties to G.S. and Wall Street—whom he blamed for the "tremendous economic problems and who rolled over the working class." Key appointments also come from Congress (presumably part of the DC swamp) in the form of Jeff Sessions and Tom Price, with more to come. Millionaires and billionaires all.

And, we should all be worried about the number of generals in leadership roles—after all, since Trump said he knows more than they do—one would hope he would have chosen people who were smarter and more knowledgeable. But perhaps those people don't exist; we should know by now that nobody knows more than Donald. Take it from him.

And speaking of denizens of the deep, who is more qualified as a *bona fide* bottom dweller than Steve Bannon, lately from the home of the 'alt-right' *Breitbart News.* It's been reported that Trump seeks out lots of opinions, but tends to select the last one heard. As Trump's top political advisor, it will be Bannon's words that will be the last ones whispered in Donald's ear. Do not underestimate the solace and comfort that hate groups, the sick and paranoid, have found in Bannon's selection. Based on the significant increase in reported attacks on minorities since the election, our homegrown wannabe terrorists now feel part of the American mainstream—comfortable coming out to harass and bully and more. And now the man, whose publication the KKK and White Supremacist groups have adopted as their own, is mere steps from the Oval Office.

During this period of time, designed to prepare the new

President for his awesome responsibilities, Trump has given us a preview of how he will govern. He intervened in the Carrier decision to move jobs from their plant in Indianapolis to Mexico. It's reported Carrier caved when given the enticement of a $7 million sweetheart deal; but it was most likely their parent company's Pentagon contract, worth billions, that induced their sudden jolt of patriotism and empathy. Somehow, I seem to recall the concept of crony capitalism—'government intervening in the free market economy to choose winners and losers,' as a big no-no by Republicans. Suddenly these actions are deemed praiseworthy.

Remember when Trump trumpeted taxing manufacturing companies that left the States by imposing a 35 percent import tariff in order to sell those products here? Now all that is past tense. Instead, he and vice president-to-be Pence GAVE a subsidy to Carrier to remain—paid for by Indiana taxpayers! Some precedent; one can already see companies lining up to get their share. Well, if the country has to declare bankruptcy because of all the taxpayer giveaways, at least we have a leader well versed in the practice.

The lack of transparency and conflicts of interest in this administration remain massive problems, and they interact with each other. While saving 1,000 jobs is critical to those impacted, one can't help but wonder how many thousands of American workers would be employed and jobs created if Trump were to bring back HIS manufacturing jobs. Actually, to repeat, one can't help but wonder (and only wonder), since there appears to be no way to find out just how many people are employed by Trump in foreign countries manufacturing shirts, ties, eyeglasses, perfume, and other *tchotckes*.

All of Ivanka's clothing and jewelry are made overseas. Maybe I missed it, but I don't recall his suggesting a 35 percent import tariff on those products. He's the first president in recent history not to reveal his tax returns, so there's no way of knowing all the foreign countries in which he does business. Just imagine the outcry if this was Hillary or Obama!

One of the biggest legitimate concerns during the election was Hillary's apparent conflation between the State Department and the Clinton Foundation. That pales by comparison with Trump's estimated hundreds of business activities in dozens of countries—all of which could be impacted by decisions made by government—whose officials his administration will appoint. And naming his kids to manage his/their business interests is truly hiring the fox etc., etc. He has to completely divest himself and turn it all over to a legitimate blind trust, or every decision made by his administration will be questioned—and deserves to be.

Another concern remains his ongoing attacks on the press. Banning news organizations, calling out reporters by name, and encouraging the crowd to boo the 'lying press' are chilling reminders of the actions of totalitarian governments. It was so bad during the campaign that some reporters needed Secret Service protection to escort them out of the venues. Trump went right back to that theme on the first stop of his 'thank you' tour.

Trump hasn't had a press conference since he was elected—something he often, and rightly, chided Hillary for. A free and open press is as necessary to democracy as an informed electorate. There cannot be the latter without the former. Threats and demagoguery are an anathema in a free society, and it is appalling.

This opinion piece began with the words, 'It's finally over.' On reflection, it's actually just beginning. Let's hope this isn't the beginning—of the end.

11 JANUARY 2017

THE TROUBLE WITH DONALD
(SPOILER ALERT: HE'S SERIOUSLY NUTS!)

"There's a reason narcissists don't learn from mistakes and that's because they never get past the first step which is admitting that they made one."— JEFFREY KLUGER

What follows is not meant to be about politics—it's not about issues or political parties. This isn't even about the election, writ large. That's done and over; decision made. But it is about the character and mental stability of the person who will shortly become the President and leader of the free world—actually he could be the most important person on the planet—what he does, for better but especially for worse, could impact everyone in every country the world over.

Voters make decisions based on a wide variety of variables. What is generally assumed is that having won the nomination, the basic minimum standards—the prerequisites needed to be an effective leader—have been met. The difference with Trump was that he had no past history as a public servant to scrutinize. Still, given his reputation as a successful businessman, there was a natural assumption he was a relatively intact, intelligent, literate, curious, creative, honest, critical thinking, problem solving individual—the basic characteristics which, in varying degrees, heads of large organizations and successful politicians possess.

One would think.

But polls indicate none of these characteristics—whether present or absent—was as important to Trump voters as their desire for change. Disqualifiers for a typical politician running for any office, let alone the Presidency, were ignored or characterized differently. He mocked a person with a disabling condition, criticized a war hero because he had been captured, demeaned Gold Star parents, refused to release tax returns, manufactured all of his products outside the U.S. while condemning the same behavior in others, failed to pay federal income taxes for years apparently taking advantage of massive business losss (*The New York Times*, Feb 2015), and made demeaning statements about women and minorities. Readers can add their own examples, and there are many more to choose from. But, most every other Republican running in the primaries, and certainly Hillary, represented the same old, same old.

Change was demanded, and change is what we got. But, we also got something else; a seriously flawed human being. And, no matter the politics, this should not be ignored or characterized differently.

See if this description by the Mayo Clinic, together with criteria in the Diagnostic and Statistical Manual of Mental Disorders (DSM-5), sounds like anyone you know.

- Has an exaggerated sense of self-importance
- Expects to be recognized as superior to others

- Exaggerates achievements and talents
- Requires constant attention and admiration
- Has a sense of entitlement
- Expects special favors and unquestioning compliance
- Takes advantage of others to get what they want
- Has an inability or unwillingness to recognize the needs and feelings others
- Behaves in an arrogant or haughty manner
- Values themselves more than others
- Looks down and belittles others in order to feel superior
- Becomes angry or impatient when not receiving special treatment
- Insists on the best of everything, car, home, possessions
- Hypersensitive to criticism – perceived or real
- Difficulty taking responsibility for mistakes and apologizing
- Doesn't trust easily and has few, if any, close friends

These characteristics are symptoms of Narcissistic Personality Disorder, a severe mental illness. And, it describes Donald Trump. An aspect of the condition is that he believes he can do no wrong. If he does anything, that alone, *ipso facto*, makes it right. Slights and criticisms, real or imagined, must be addressed. He lies often and easily, even when the truth is readily available in print and video. His ego is fragile. He's extremely vulnerable and on guard constantly for any threat, which may explain his inability to sleep and compulsion to Tweet as an immediate response to any perceived slight or negative statement.

Supporters continue to say that Trump will become 'Presidential.' That day will not come. He is who he is. He's still fighting the election he won. It will always be about him. And, until something happens, and he gets himself in a situation of his own making and is impeached, or he resigns, or his term expires, the country and the world will be holding a collective breath.

One thing is sure. His self-interest, however he defines it, will come before all else. Here's hoping his closest advisors will be able to do for him what he seems unable to do for himself—to look beyond his own fragile ego and act for the greater good.

We need to ask ourselves how we got here. For one thing, most folks would agree that, in the end, we had two lousy choices. Many people voted against a candidate (Never Hillary; Never Trump), not for a candidate. Having omitted one of them, there was only one choice left. Others who couldn't tolerate either, the majority in fact, stayed home.

Political parties need to take a fresh look at the primary process. Wide open primaries, open to all candidates from all parties, that occur on the same day nationwide might be one way to involve more than base voters in the process.

The Republican and Democratic National Committees need to do precisely what a narcissist would never do—take a good long objective look at the current process, admit there are serious problems, and work cooperatively to develop solutions resulting in voters having a choice between two, or more, really great candidates. If only!

There is an old, purportedly Chinese, curse that seems to have been delivered in spades: *May you live in interesting times.* This might be one import we could have done without.

29 JANUARY 2017

TICK TOCK... TRUMP'S FIRST WEEK

"As democracy is perfected, the office of the President represents, more and more closely the inner soul of the people. On some great and glorious day, the plain folks of the land will reach their heart's desire at last and the White House will be occupied by a downright fool and a complete narcissistic moron."
— H. L. MENCKEN, JULY 26, 1920

His list of 'accomplishments' is long. Voters are now waking up to the person who will lead our country for the next yet-to-be-determined period of time. Ah, Donald, we thought we knew ye well. You are exceeding all our expectations.

To recap: **Jan 19, 2017.** Trump said he would cut funding for: the Dept. of Justice's Violence Against Women Programs, the National Endowment for the Arts, the National Endowment for the Humanities, the Corporation for Public Broadcasting, the Minority Business Development Agency, the Economic Development Administration, the International Trade Administration, the Manufacturing Extension Partnership, the Office of Community Oriented Policing Services, the Legal Services Corporation, the Civil Rights Division of the Department of Justice, the Environmental and Natural Resources Division of the Department of Justice, the Overseas Private Investment Corporation, the UN Intergovernmental Panel on Climate Change, the Office of Deliverability and Energy Reliability, the Office of Energy Efficiency and Renewable Energy, and the Office of Fossil Energy.

Jan 20, 2017. Trump increased without notice, interest on FHA loans to be effective immediately, ordered the federal Justice Department to postpone a hearing on a voting rights law in Texas found by lower courts to be purposely discriminatory, waived penalties for the health care mandate, ordered all regulatory powers of all federal agencies frozen, ordered the National Park Service to stop using social media after showing side by side photos of crowds at the 2017 and 2009 inaugurations.

Jan 21, 2017. Trump brought his staff to cheer his comments at the CIA during which he condemned the 'dishonest press' for reporting that he had, in fact, in a Tweet, described CIA tactics as reminiscent of the Nazis, ordered the press secretary to hold a no-questions-allowed press briefing accusing them of inaccurately reporting the size of the crowd at the inauguration and insisted, erroneously, that this inauguration had the largest audience in history, "period."

Jan 22, 2017, (Sunday). He rested. However, advisor Kellyann Conway defended the press secretary by calling his presentation regarding crowd size 'alternative facts.'

Jan 23, 2017. Trump reinstated the global gag order which defunds international organizations that mention abortion as a medical option. He announced, through Spicer, that the U.S. will not tolerate China's expansion onto islands in the South China Sea—essentially threatening war with China. Trump repeated the lie that 3-5 million people voted illegally thus costing him the popular vote. He instituted a federal hiring freeze, and then asked that the border patrol be increased three-fold—at a time when more Mexicans (and no doubt Americans) are leaving the States than those entering.

Jan 24, 2017. Trump again reiterated that there were 3-5 million illegal voters. He used examples of dead people still on the rolls, 'illegals' risking felony charges to vote, and those registered in more than one state, as examples. He asked for a congressional study, costing millions, to determine the extent of the problem. Turns out several family members and staff are registered in more than one state. He Tweeted a picture of a photo depicting his inauguration crowd that will hang in the White House Press Room. The photo is dated January 21, 2017 the day AFTER the inauguration and the day OF the Women's March.

He ordered the EPA to stop communicating with the public through social media or the press, and to stop publishing any papers or research. All scientific communication was to be vetted by the White House. Same admonition to USDA. He ordered the resumption of construction of the Dakota Access Pipeline and the Keystone Pipeline. Meanwhile, the North Dakota legislature considers a bill that would legalize hitting and killing protesters with cars if they are on the roadways.

Jan 25 – Jan 27, 2017. Trump again spoke in favor of torture, which is a war crime. He also stated he supports reopening 'black sites' for interrogation of prisoners. He said he is considering lifting sanctions on Russia, called the media the 'opposition party,' stated he will order new planes and ships for the military—few of which have been requested, is considering a twenty percent tariff on goods coming from Mexico to pay for the Wall—thus initiating the beginning of a trade war and increasing the costs of consumer goods from Mexico, announced new 'extreme vetting' procedures which will stop, as of January 27, 2017 all travel to the U.S. from specific countries with high Muslim populations (none of which participated in 9/11).

Not included were countries the 9/11 terrorists actually came from—and, incidentally, where Trump also has businesses, and threatened the removal of federal funds for sanctuary cities. He has not divested from his holdings, or put them in a blind trust, and continues to make money from foreign businesses. Staff stated he will never release his tax returns because voters don't care. Polls say the vast majority of voters do indeed care.

Mr. Trump has had a busy week. He is keeping his promises—well, there is that inconvenient fact that we, the taxpayers, one way or another, will get stuck paying for his wall—with costs estimated to be about $1 million dollars per mile.

Mr. Trump does not attend the Presidential Daily Briefings. Mr. Trump admits he's not much of a reader. Mr. Trump has no experience in government. So how does he determine what actions to take on all these highly complicated issues?

The answer lies primarily with Mr. Bannon, the former publisher of 'alt right' *Breitbart News,* who recently suggested "the media should keep their mouth shut."

This is a government, at least thus far, that appears to be

run by his advisors. Trump, on the other hand, appears much more concerned about appearances—crowd size, popular vote, and the election results.

In spite of the fact that he declared January 20, 2017 the day of inauguration, a "National Day of Patriotic Devotion" (to him, no doubt), he has yet to become 'presidential.' He appears to be a man absent of dignity and incapable of self-awareness. He has generated the most robust resistance of any president in history, as well as the lowest approval rating of any president one week into their term. In this, he is definitely the winner—hands down. And it's just the first week.

One week down; 207 weeks to go. Maybe. As he and his alter ego Bannon continue down this tyrannical road, where opponents are described as enemies, perhaps it will be a lot less.

WE HAVE MET THE ENEMY

"Critical thinking: the other national deficit."
—BUMPER STICKER

Those six words do as good a job as any in defining where we are as a nation today. We seem to have delegated logical thought to the loudest voices, to the most repetitive voices, to those voices promulgating fear and distrust, to the voices who find scapegoats in the defenseless and different.

We've become tribal—each moving to our own corner, talking only to each other, refusing to acknowledge and separate fact from fiction, haranguing instead of engaging in civil discourse. There is little effort to hear or consider the other side of an issue. Compromise is a dirty word; politicians are punished for engaging in it. We accept that with which we agree and reject any information to the contrary, even and maybe especially, if there's no doubt as to its truth. Logic, facts, and rational thought be damned!

This isn't a recent problem; it's been growing for long time. It's fed by religious fundamentalism and bigotry ('what

I believe is more valid than what you believe, because God speaks only to me and mine'), a distrust bordering on hatred of government ('it's the enemy and too big'), a passion for unfettered capitalism ('regulations prevent economic growth'), privatization of everything, thereby thwarting transparency and accountability ('private funding is always better than public funding because taxes can be reduced'), and money in politics ('pay to play', 'do what I say or you will be primaried in the next election'). Politicians must be accountable to big funders and lobbyists, instead of those uninformed voters.

But, it has reached the stage where the lack of compromise and tribalism is impacting the very fiber of this country. Just look at us. Because compromise is out of the question, nothing gets done. Problems fester and grow. The impact is destroying this country from within more quickly, and just as surely, as any outside enemy.

The outside enemy now is ISIS. It must be destroyed. Everyone agrees. That's a beginning, but also, it seems, an end. Here's an example of what intransigence has reaped: One way to curtail ISIS, everyone agrees, is to significantly impede or stop their sources of funding. There's a position in the Treasury Department designed to do just that.

This is the one person in the entire government, next to the Commander in Chief—who is, or would be, in the position to fight terrorism and the financial crimes ISIS depends on to fund its operations. That person is Adam Szubin. Check out his credentials. After a successful hearing, Senator McConnell said he is imminently qualified for the position, yet he refused to bring this permanent appointment to a vote for over 325 days. Why? Because some members of the banking committee said Mr. Szubin supported the Iran deal. In other words, he supported President Barack Obama. It was more important not to give the President a 'win' than to provide the mechanism to help defeat ISIS.

What are we doing? Where are we going?

Setting up circumstances that result in short term self-fulfilling prophesies have taken the place of critical thinking (and common sense) that could result in long term problem solving. Using the previous example, some politicians said that President Obama wasn't doing enough to stand up to ISIS, but then denied him the tools he needed to do that. If something happened, we knew whom to blame.

Similarly, state legislatures have made massive cuts to education funding and instituted frequent testing—not to determine what the students need to learn next, but how well the system and teachers are performing. Resources are cut to conform to reduced budgets. Scores decline. We know whom to blame.

We are past the point of dysfunction and heading to the downright dangerous. Politicians, aided and abetted by some media, deliberately inflame, scare, stoke fear, create lies and repeat them—all for political or financial gain. This country is being destroyed from within. We have become a nation of sheep... if we don't wake up, we are doomed to be led like them... and we know that did not end well for the sheep.

It was Pogo who said, "We have met the enemy and he is us."

20 MARCH 2017

FOR TRUMP VOTERS:
WHAT WILL IT TAKE?

"I thought it was funny when he announced he was running to be President. I was like, is this seriously who we have to vote for? Yes, I voted for him because I was sure he wouldn't win, and I kinda wanted to send a message."

— TRUMP VOTER AT A WISCONSIN FOCUS GROUP.

This isn't meant to be a rhetorical question. With all due respect, what does Trump have to do for his supporters to admit that his Presidency is a mistake?

This isn't easy. In fact, it's very difficult to look at a given set of actions or facts, compare them with our own set of values, expectations and priorities, and to admit we've made a mistake. We're human. But we're also adults and we're expected to take responsibility for our actions. By all objective measures, and because of its implications, even at this early stage in his Presidency, it's time to assess whether there are significant reasons to doubt whether Donald J. Trump has the prerequisite skills and abilities to be successful as President of the United States.

Republican consultant, Frank Luntz, conducted a series of focus groups prior to the election. He found that voters supported Trump for a variety of reasons that were mainstream, and that didn't reflect the views of the alternative xenophobic right as personified by Steve Bannon and Stephen Miller who want to stop immigration from non-European countries.

You voted for Trump because you couldn't, under any circumstances, vote for the Democratic alternative. You voted for Trump because you wanted change. You voted for Trump because he had proved himself to be a successful businessman. You voted for Trump because he says it like it is and speaks his mind. You voted for Trump because you believed the country was in crisis. You voted for Trump because he had proven himself to be a strong leader. You voted for Trump because he had the guts to say what he believed, even if it wasn't always politically correct. You voted for Trump because he portrayed strength. You voted for Trump because he said that he cared about everyday Americans—especially those who hadn't gotten a fair shake. You voted for Trump out of a combination of frustration and anger with the current state of affairs. You voted for Trump because he was going to drain the swamp of 'elites.' You voted for Trump because he promised to build the wall and Mexico was going to pay for it.

You believed in Trump so strongly that you would have voted for him even if he had run as an Independent. In many ways, you rejected the old standards of the Republican Party, and like Trump himself, you challenged the *status quo.* You are neither racist, nor xenophobic, nor stupid. You are a proud patriot and you love this country.

You didn't support Trump blindly. You were aware of, and uncomfortable with, his comments about Senator McCain, about the Gold Star family, about women, about people with disabilities, about over-generalized views concerning certain groups of people, about his lack of knowledge of world affairs, about his lack of previous public service, about his flip-flops, about his crudeness, about degrading individuals in the press and making them a target, about his belief in conspiracy theories.

You believed that he would choose people in his cabinet to make up for his lack of knowledge and experience. You believed that if he were elected, he would become 'presidential.' You believed his priorities were your priorities. You still believe all of that, but you are becoming increasingly uncomfortable with his impulsiveness and lack of judgment, with his lack of preparedness, with his choice of advisors and many cabinet officials who have no experience with, or commitment to, the agencies they were appointed to lead.

You are concerned about the many advisors and cabinet members who are billionaires, former employees of Goldman Sachs, and who represent Wall Street. "Trump being Trump" is becoming more of an excuse than a trademark. You're noticing that his and Melania's living arrangements and weekly travels are costing taxpayers a lot of money unnecessarily. He seems to be creating enemies out of friends, and vice versa. And you wonder what's going to happen next in terms of revelations about the Russian connections, his tweets, and his many unresolved conflicts of interest.

You are becoming more and more uncomfortable with

unelected and inexperienced family members engaged in developing public policy, and it's confounding that he seems to lack the ability or interest in telling the truth—even about little things. You wonder if he is telling the truth about the big things. He seems incapable of admitting he made a mistake. It appears he spends more time watching cable news than attending security briefings, and he puts more faith in the former than the latter. That's worrying.

But, you continue to hope that time on the job will make the difference. After all, he's doing what he said he'd do... getting rid of Obamacare and taking a hatchet to the budget. But the American Health Care Act (Trump's version of health care) hits older and poorer Americans the hardest, while giving huge tax cuts to the ultra-wealthy. And, the budget he proposed, while unlikely to pass as is, surprised you because it too hits the poorest and those in greatest need—those he promised to help the most.

He kept his word about increasing the military budget, which already surpasses the next six countries combined, and more money for Veterans Affairs. But, you're concerned about the impact if funding is cut or eliminated for the National Health Service, programs that promote medical research, Meals on Wheels that assists over 500,000 vets, and other programs that are relatively small in cost but huge in scope. And, U.S. taxpayers will be paying for the wall after all. You've noted that the cost of his seven weekend trips to Mar-a-Largo so far could pay in full some of the budget items that he proposed to cut. As you get ready to write your check to the IRS, you remember that he promised to release his tax returns after he was elected and the audit was complete, but now he's saying he'll never release them.

And, you remember that he wasn't going to take a salary, but now says he will collect it and return the money to the Treasury at the end of the year. It occurs to you that he has the advantage of using the money throughout the year, and then claiming a tax deduction at the end of it.

So, back to the original question. Just what will it take to face what is becoming more obvious with each passing day. What does Trump have to do before you say that you've had enough and pass that message on to your Congressman. It may be a single act—or it may be the continual drip, drip, drip of revelations about his character, his connections, and/or his policies.

It may help to know that what you're coping with, what you're experiencing, actually has a name. It's called 'cognitive dissonance.' It occurs when the beliefs you hold, and hold dearly, are in direct conflict with new information—with a new reality. Kind of like "I can't believe my lying eyes."

So, you have a choice of adhering to a non-existent reality or facing facts and making a change of viewpoint and heart. And, oh boy, that's difficult. But the mental stress and discomfort of cognitive dissonance is worse. It's exhausting to continually try to find reasons to justify behaviors and actions you would never tolerate in anyone else.

Here's the ultimate test: pretend Trump has a "(D)" after his name. Then think about how you would react to those same behaviors. Any of them. Even one of them.

But here's a comforting thought voiced by Charles Darwin: "Tis not the strongest of the species that survive, or the most intelligent, but the ones most responsive to change." Or, put another way, if you don't change direction, you will end up where you are heading. We all will.

And, it's only week eight.

06 APRIL 2017

A PROBLEM OF THEIR OWN MAKING

"I am deeply concerned that his (Trump's) choice for Supreme Court will be a rubber stamp for the President's radical agenda."
— SENATOR MAZIE HIRONO (D HAWAII)

By the time you read this, it's likely to be over except for the shouting—and wailing. We may have a new Supreme Court Justice, but it will come at a very high price. Surely there are lessons to be learned from this politically, and perhaps, permanently wrenching experience—one that further divides Congress and the country.

Let's see how we got to where we are. Issues to consider include how the 'super majority' rule came to be, what happens if the "nuclear option" is chosen by the Republicans to move the appointment of Judge Gorsuch forward, concerns about this particular nominee and, finally, how this whole divisive brouhaha concerning the appointment of Supreme Court justices could have been avoided in the first place.

The Constitution lists very few instances where a simple

majority vote is not sufficient for conducting business; confirming a Supreme Court Justice is not one of them. Examples of actions requiring more than a simple majority include voting on an impeachment trial, overriding a veto, ratifying a treaty, and proposing to amend the document itself. But, over time, the Senate changed the rules to give the minority party the power to block action—as long as it reached a super majority threshold.

The Senate filibuster is the voice of the minority in action and can stop most votes dead in its tracks—unless the majority decides to return back to a simple majority—the so-called nuclear option, which is limited to executive and judicial appointments. As applied to the nomination of Judge Gorsuch, a simple majority of 51 votes would be all that's required for confirmation. And, that would alter how future nominees for the Court might be considered as well.

If you think the filibuster is a bad thing when Democrats use it, you might be interested in knowing that this past Congress held up dozens of Obama's appointees and refused to consider many more; including, and especially, judges. The devil isn't just in the details; it's also in the eye of the beholder.

If Gorsuch is confirmed, it's because the Republican Senate chose to institute the nuclear option returning to the 51-vote simple majority. This may be good for Republicans as long as they hold the Senate, but the day will come, the shoe will be on the other foot and they will likely regret this decision. But Democrats, when filibustering, may force McConnell to proceed using the 51-vote criteria. What if the next Trump nominee is to the right of Attila the Hun? Democrats are sunk without the super majority and filibuster; the ideology of the

Court will shift dramatically and for a very long time to come.

So, why are Democrats casting their fate on this vote when it's the next Supreme Court vote that could cause that seismic shift? The answer is, at least partially, the nominee.

Confirmation hearings uncovered serious flaws with Neil Gorsuch's past rulings, as well as his performance in private conversations with Senators and publicly before the Judicial Committee. He refused to say how he would vote on certain issues, which isn't unique, stressing he would rely on the law and nothing else. But it's the 'nothing else' that's bothersome. His ruling allowing a trucking company to fire a driver for leaving his malfunctioning transport, in minus 14-degree weather, because he was literally freezing to death, made no sense then and no sense now. And, embarrassingly, the Supreme Court actually struck down a previous ruling of his while he was at his confirmation hearing. Gorsuch ruled that, under the Free Appropriate Public Education Act, the bare minimum of services for eligible special needs students met the letter of the law. The Justices disagreed.

Trump also said that any nominee of his for the highest court must meet his litmus test and, given the opportunity, rule to overturn Roe *v* Wade. That's a critical concern when considering government interference in personal decisions and women's health. And now, after the hearings, it's been discovered Gorsuch appeared to have plagiarized the work of others. Finally, many senators, after reviewing years of his rulings, have determined Gorsuch has a predilection to vote in favor of corporations and big business, and against the 'little guy.'

So, could all this have been avoided? Absolutely. Senate

Democrats view this Supreme Court seat as one stolen from the previous administration.

When President Obama, fulfilling his duty under the Constitution, nominated Judge Merrick Garland to fill Scalia's seat, the Republican Senate refused to do their duty under the Constitution to 'advise and consent.' McConnell said that because it was 'so close' to the end of Obama's term (11 months), the people should decide who the next nominee should be, as determined by the winner of the 2016 election. That's just ridiculous. A presidency doesn't end with almost a year to go, and voters don't determine Supreme Court justices. Not only did Senate leadership refuse to give this moderate nominee an up or down vote, they refused to even meet with him.

In no way could this be viewed as a rejection of Judge Garland; he was never given a chance. It was absolutely and only a rejection of President Obama. But Obama was not up for Supreme Court consideration. Not yet.

McConnell and the Senate leadership brought this on themselves. They should have gone through the process, brought Garland up for a vote, and if he lost, that would have been that. Constitutional responsibilities met and time to move on. And, even after Trump was elected, and during the transition phase, they still could have gone through the motions, voted Garland down if that was the decision, and moved on to Trump's nominee. But it wasn't enough to reject Garland, when McConnell also had the opportunity to slap Obama in the face.

So, yes; all this angst will follow this highly partisan judge to his new position and forever taint this 114th Congress in the process. If Neil Gorsuch survives, it means the nuclear option has been utilized and a precedent set.

Expect the favor to be returned.

30 APRIL 2017

THE FIRST ONE HUNDRED DAYS

"We now know that Trump's self-adoration is not a mere personality glitch. It is instead an engine of intimidation of a furiously dominate aspect of his personality."
—RICHARD COHEN, *WASHINGTON POST* COLUMNIST

April 29th marked the first 100 days of Donald Trump's Presidency. And while he now says this is an 'artificial milestone,' it's one he set for himself as promised in his Contract with the American Voter.

His list of 28 promises is long; we can recite some by heart—repeal and replace Obamacare, build the beautiful wall to be paid for by Mexico, institute the Muslim ban, declare China a currency manipulator, etc. The reality is there has been one major accomplishment and that's the nomination and confirmation of a Supreme Court Justice. For some, it's enough to assure the Court regained a 5-4 conservative majority. Objective achieved. But there is much more we've learned during the past 100 days, having nothing to do with policies or legislative goals. It's about the man. It's about Donald Trump—who he is at his core.

The President of the United States has always served as the exemplar of who we are as a nation. This person has been our avatar to the world, a representative of our country's values, our moral authority. Whether we voted for that person or not, that is who he is to the world. He is us. Let that sink in. To the world, he is us.

He and his supporters vowed that Trump the President would be different from Trump the Candidate, that he would become 'presidential.' What that conveys is really separate and apart from policy accomplishments.

The term conveys someone people look to as a leader, whose behavior symbolizes the best of who we are, who expresses the ideals and values on which this country is based, someone who serves as a role model for our kids, someone we can aspire to in terms of character and point to with pride. This milestone of 100 days is as good a time as any to assess whether Trump has become 'presidential.' And, while open-eyed supporters acknowledge he has not, they add, 'Give him time; give him a chance."

He has had his chance. He is who he is—or to quote him, "I am what I am" (grammatically that's incorrect even if Popeye said it first). He may be President, but he is not us.

Who is Donald Trump at his core? First, he's a liar—about big things and little things (promising to divest to prevent conflicts of interest, releasing his tax returns if elected, stating that 3-5 million people voted illegally, Tweeting that a former president wire tapped his phone, saying "I never heard of WikiLeaks" to "I love WikiLeaks," to ordering the

Justice Department to prepare criminal charges against WikiLeaks, lying about the size of his inauguration crowd and the rallies against his policies, his Electoral College votes, his promise to drain the swamp while adding Wall Street billionaires to his cabinet, his insistence that the millions of people protesting him are bought and paid for. And more. So much more. He may be President, but he is not us.

He will lie about anything. He will lie about what he has just said. He lies so much that we've come to expect it. He is a pathological liar—not someone who lies occasionally, or 'spins,' or stretches the truth, but someone who lies as a matter of habit. We're even told by his staff not to take what he says literally. How can anyone, friend or foe, believe anything he says? The answer is that his word is meaningless and he cannot be trusted. He may be President, but he is not us.

Second, he's obsessed with himself. We've learned there is no one like Donald Trump. Just ask him. Leading up to the election, and on Inauguration Day, he professed that only he could repair the damage, only he could fix the country, only he could stop the carnage. Demagogues talk like that. He speaks in superlatives. He sees himself as infallible, as 'the best,' and the rest of the world as something less. He never apologizes for anything. Like a child with poor self-esteem, he needs constant validation. He may be President, but he is not us.

He's obsessed with numbers, the past election and the latest poll results. Since he sees himself as infallible, any information to the contrary must be incorrect—'fake news.' Nothing, absolutely nothing, is more important than being a winner or maybe more precisely, not being seen as a loser.

Since he places so little value on truth, he is free to denigrate facts if they contradict his view of himself. The mainstream media and judiciary are all against him and not to be trusted. Instead, he puts his trust in conspiracy theorists—as long as they support him, that's all that matters. His life revolves around protecting his thin skin and affirming his fragile ego. He may be President, but he is not us.

There is a cruelty about his actions that defies who we are as a country. He seemed genuinely affected by the gassing of children in Syria, but refuses to allow any children, from Syria or elsewhere, to come here as refugees. The world is witnessing the largest refugee crisis since the Second World War, and Trump has placed a ban on all of them, 'until we figure this thing out.' And, every immigrant without papers, regardless of their contributions to their communities, the length of time they've been here, or the fact that some know no other country, are now susceptible to deportation and separation from their families. He has fanned the flames of hatred, distrust and bigotry. He may be President, but he is not us.

And there is this. His knowledge base is as thin as his skin. His lack of preparation is as astounding as it is embarrassing. He is consistently inconsistent. One day NATO is obsolete, the next not. One day China is a currency manipulator, the next not. He said that Frederick Douglass is doing an 'amazing job,' and praised dictators Erdogan and El-Sisi. His Tweets leave everyone off balance and wondering if he's thinking rationally when he goads North Korea. He may be President, but he is not us.

He thinks out loud, doesn't apply a filter or think about

the consequences of his statements, has difficulty staying on topic, and is easily distracted. He lacks the finesse and communication skills that a wide vocabulary would provide. He repeats himself, not to reframe or rephrase, but because he seems to lack other language options. No one believes he actually writes his Executive Orders; he offered that he often doesn't read them before signing. He has delegated governing to cabinet members and assigned family with no governing, public service or diplomatic experience to resolve problems in the most fragile of places. His conflicts of interest remain glaring. He may be President, but he is not us.

During this 100-day period, we are learning how fragile our Democratic Republic is, and how a few words or actions can put it all at risk. When nothing is predictable, when the definition of truth is no longer relevant, then the only rational responses are anxiety, fear, anger, and resistance. We look at the person who is supposed to represent the best of us and we see the opposite. He may be President, but he is definitely and emphatically not us.

Some people have compared this administration to watching a train wreck. But the problem is we are not mere spectators—not when we're on the train, traveling to unknown destinations at breakneck speed, and the conductor is a 10-year-old.

One hundred days have gone, but 1,360 remain, and not a single one of those days can be taken for granted.

10 MAY 2017

THE ONLY LOGICAL EXPLANATION
FOR FIRING JAMES COMEY

"The reason Congress created a ten-year term is so that the director is not feeling as if they're serving with political loyalty owed to any particular person."
—JAMES COMEY, FORMER FBI DIRECTOR

Some of us have been waking up with a bad case of whiplash following the stunning action by the White House, accompanied by a bunch of explanations that make no logical sense. Here's the tick tock of just the most immediate events.

Last week, FBI Director James Comey asked the Justice Department for additional funds and resources to support the Bureau's investigation into possible collusion between the Trump campaign and the Russian government. It can be inferred, based on that request, that Comey had every intention of moving forward and that the investigation into the relationship was going to continue.

A few days later, on May 8, Comey testified that the FBI was continuing to investigate whether there was a relationship between the Trump campaign and the Russian government during the 2016 election.

The next day, Donald Trump fired James Comey.

The justification used by the administration is ludicrous. It involves actions 10 months ago, and again, just prior to the election regarding the Clinton email investigation. These include the press conference last July when Comey announced the investigation closed, and no charges would be filed against Clinton. He did however, severely criticize her and her aides for mishandling information. Then, 11 days before the election, Comey announced the reopening of the case because of recently discovered Clinton emails on Anthony Weiner's computer. Trump effusively praised the latter action, and it may well have been the key variable that helped him win the election. It certainly didn't hurt.

Why would Trump punish an action he previously praised? And, if he was so bothered, why didn't he ask for Comey's resignation on taking office? And, why would he continue to heap praise on Comey even as late as last week? It makes no sense that Trump would fire the FBI Director for actions that, intentional or not, helped propel him into office. This sudden concern for following procedures is hardly consistent with the ethos of this President, who is somewhat ethically challenged in this area. So, what changed? What caused Trump to do the about-face that's triggering this whiplash?

The fact is that three people had been tasked, through their agencies, with investigating different aspects of the Trump campaign connections to Russia. They were Preet Bharara, U.S. Attorney for the Southern District of New York; Sally Yates; Acting Attorney General; and James Comey, FBI Director. All have been fired by Trump.

Here's the only logical explanation. Trump is so terrified

by what this investigation will uncover that he's willing to take the heat caused by this firing in order to appoint his own person to lead—and then shut down—the investigation. Also, White House staff reported Trump was furious that Comey did not support his allegation that Obama wiretapped Trump Tower.

Think about this. Apparently, judging from reports by administrative spokespersons, the time from formal request to actual firing took about 24 hours. Compare that to the 18 days the National Security Advisor, Michael Flynn, remained on the job after his boss was notified he was a national security risk. Sally Yates testified that Flynn lied, that there were additional underlying concerns about his behavior vis-à-vis Russia, and that he could be vulnerable to blackmail. Eighteen days. In the meantime, Flynn continued to remain privy to highly classified information and to sit in on top level meetings. Had the findings not leaked and become public, one wonders if he would still be there. Trump continues to defend him even now. Why?

Something stinks. The immediate solution to discovering its source is to appoint a special commission, or an independent special prosecutor, acceptable to both Democrats and Republicans. If Congress won't act, it will be up to 'we the people' to put pressure on our elected officials until they do.

By the way, the letter written by Trump to Comey is a classic example of "up yours." The second paragraph, where Trump mentions Comey's assurances to him that he's not under investigation, is so self-serving that it's obviousness is nausea inducing. And the last line, "I wish you the best of luck in your endeavors." is so banal, canned, and trite that I hope the next time it's used by anyone, it's directed to Trump, as he's escorted out of the White House.

27 MAY 2017

TRUMP'S BUDGET —
THE CON MAN COMETH

"Poverty is a state of mind."
—DR. BEN CARSON, SECRETARY OF HOUSING AND URBAN DEVELOPMENT

The federal budget is like a giant mirror. It reflects the values and priorities that serve as the nation's moral imperative. It encapsulates what the government wants to achieve through the allocation of revenue.

Unlike campaign promises or rhetoric, this is where the rubber meets the road; the budget designates exactly what programs, services and people will receive funding and support, and therefore, who and what will benefit; by omissions and cutbacks, who and what will not. It's Trump's roadmap for how to Make America Great Again through the allocation of resources. Put another way, the budget should be Trump's manifestation of campaign promises. But it is not.

This is Trump's budget, not the final version—that will be determined by Congress. So, if it's going to change, why bother discussing it now? The answer is that it's important to see how Trump's promises translate into what he hopes will be actions. This much is clear. It is a slap in the face (or a body slam if you prefer) to the poor and middle class Americans who believed his promises and put their faith in him with their votes.

It was the ultimate con.

Simply put, the people who helped put Trump over the top have been kicked to the bottom of an ever-growing heap of losers—Trump's favorite pejorative, as long as it doesn't apply to him. Here's Trump's view of how to Make America Great Again over the next decade.

- Slash Medicaid and the Children's Health Insurance Program by $850 billion affecting millions of poor families.
- Cut food stamps by $191 billion.
- Cut funding for the Temporary Assistance for Needy Families by $22 billion.
- Cut Social Security Disability benefits by nearly $70 billion. Many of these cuts will hit not just families, but also schools serving children with handicaping conditions.
- Cut student loans by $143 billion.
- By not addressing Social Security and Medicare retirement benefits, by eliminating the employee contribution cap and increasing contributions, funds could run dry and retirees living on fixed incomes could face steep cuts in benefits.
- Women's health will be impacted by not funding agencies offering legal abortion services, even though

federal dollars already cannot be used for abortions. Free or low-cost health screenings, and family planning services would no longer be available through these clinics.

- The Centers for Disease Control and Prevention will see their budget cut by 18 percent.
- The National Institutes of Health, the nation's premier medical research agency, will be cut by 18 percent.
- Scientific research funding to the American Association for the Advancement of Science will see their budget cut by 17 percent.
- Services from the VA will be cut to pay for choice in medical providers.
- Public education will be cut by $11 billion, eliminating such things as afterschool programs, art and physical education, foreign language instruction, ongoing teacher training—just a sampling of the 22 programs cut or eliminated.

Here's more: Cuts in the State Department budget affecting embassy security (well, who needs that?), food safety inspection, the FAA, mental health and drug rehabilitation, programs for rural areas—the impact will be felt throughout the economy and, sooner or later, will affect almost everyone.

Or maybe you have $50,000 a year to pay for your nursing home; add another $50,000 for your spouse. That's the current average cost nationwide, and it's rising. And, you'll need that nursing home because if you're under 65, you'll likely not be able to afford coverage for preexisting conditions. Had a mole removed lately? So sorry. That's a preexisting condition.

But, if you're among the fortunate one percent, your taxes will go down bigly, thanks to the elimination of the Estate Tax and the Affordable Care Act— Obamacare. The wealthy will receive huge tax cuts. The poor, the young, the old, and the sick will pay the bill. The con man cometh.

This budget will not pass as is; Congress will amend the most egregious cuts. But whatever the final result, voters will remember that Trump violated their trust. No one likes being conned.

The good news is that Congress will have the final say. Further good news is that some Republicans in leadership positions are distancing themselves from the budget and, as Trump's approval ratings sink and more information about the Russian connections roll in, from Trump himself. But since Republicans are in the majority, the end result is TBD. The good news is that 33 Senators and the entire House is up for reelection in 2018 and if Trump has forgotten his promises, voters will see to it that Congress does not.

One further comment on the impact of this budget; if Dr. Carson believes his comment that "Poverty is a state of mind," perhaps he'd be willing to test that assertion on the people he cares for the most. Just think of the money we'd save if all that was needed were classes in the power of positive thinking.

10 JUNE 2017

THE COMEY HEARING

"Lordy, I hope there are tapes."
—JAMES COMEY, IN RESPONSE TO DONALD TRUMP'S SUGGESTION THAT
HE HAD TAPES OF THEIR CONVERSATIONS.

Last week's hearing with the former FBI Director James Comey exposed three loose threads. The first was the character of Donald Trump, the second was the character of James Comey, and the third was the Russia connection. It's worth pulling on each to see what they reveal.

Trump's actions, as described under oath by Comey, and under the penalty of perjury, are consistent with what was already known about Trump and his character. Above all else is the fact, proven over and over again, that Trump lies. It's the single behavioral characteristic that defines him. He lies about the important and the inconsequential.

He lied about winning the most electoral votes since Ronald Reagan when G.W. Bush, Bill Clinton (both times), and Barack Obama (both times) won more. He claimed thousands of people were bussed across state lines from Massachusetts to vote in New Hampshire. The AG's from both states said there is no evidence to support this claim.

He told a group of U.S. sheriffs that the murder rate in the US was "the highest in 45-47 years." The rate is actually at an all-time low.

He lied about the size of crowds at his inauguration; about releasing his tax returns; about divesting from his businesses; about the thousands of Muslims dancing in the streets on 9/11; about the national homicide rate "horribly increasing during Obama's presidency."

He lied about three million votes being cast illegally. He said sanctuary cities "breed crime;" actually, they report less crime than other cities of similar size.

He claimed that the New York Times and the Washington Post were failing papers because they didn't support him. Subscriptions have increased since his election.

He said he "has received awards on the environment." He has not. He said he received a five-minute standing ovation at CIA headquarters; in fact, the attendees were never asked to sit down.

He said he would never demand a loyalty oath from anyone, when there's video of him doing exactly that.

And then, just this week, he said to his cabinet and key staff, " Never has there been a President, with few exceptions—the case of FDR, he had a major depression to handle—who has passed more legislation and who has done more things then what we've done..." Truman passed 55 bills within his first 100 days; Trump signed 48 in his 142 days in office. Many, such as designating buildings and appointing board members to the Smithsonian, have no major impact on Americans. He has yet to sign a major piece of legislation.

But, you get the point. The man lies as easily as he breathes. He is what he does; this is who he is. He's a liar.

Comey served Republican and Democratic administrations prior to this one, and has managed to offend and upset both. While people from both parties have questioned his judgment, few have questioned his honesty or integrity.

Over the years he served in leadership roles with the FBI. Comey testified before Congress numerous times under oath, and has never been accused of lying.

On this occasion, he spoke without notes, under oath, recounting his one-on-one conversations with Trump in person and on the phone. He asserted that Trump requested his loyalty and that he 'hoped' Comey would drop the investigation of Michael Flynn.

Comey took contemporary notes to document the two in person conversations because he was concerned that Trump might lie about them. And then, he offered a statement that, if anything, confirms his honesty. He stated he sent a copy of those notes to a friend who then, under his direction, sent them to *The New York Times*. He did this in response to Trump's tweet about the possibility of 'tapes,' and that he felt it was important to get a statement of events out to the public with the hope that a Special Counsel would be appointed. Surely, he must have known that Trump would focus on the leak rather than its content.

And, here's what is really telling. According to Comey, not once in any conversation, did Trump express concern or even interest into the hacking and interference in the 2016 election. It's important not to lose sight of the fact that all of this hubris has arisen as a result of Russia's attempt to interfere with the most important aspect of our Republic—the election of a President.

And, that brings us to the third thread. This will be the work of investigative bodies for the foreseeable future; to determine the extent and effect of Russian involvement in the election, their motives and procedures, and to determine what help, if any, was provided along the way. Efforts to prevent this from happening in the future must be an end goal.

This is the most critical of threads—it is the longest and the most likely to be intertwined with others. As this one is pulled, by all the investigations sure to result, the entire structure of the Trump Presidency may disintegrate.

This attack on the United States needs to be viewed with the same scrutiny as a military attack—and the results could be as dire.

14 JUNE 2017

A TIME TO REFLECT...
ON GUNS

"Elevate those guns a little lower."—ANDREW JACKSON

"Guns do kill, unlike cars, that's all they do."
—THE LATE MOLLY IVINS, COLUMNIST

Maybe every generation feels the country is at a tipping point and, to quote the 60's protest song, on *the eve of destruction*. But, this seems different. Today's America feels more sinister and meaner. Maybe it comes down to an erosion of trust. In the past, there were some basic assumptions—another word for trust: that our Democracy would remain the envy of the world, that our neighbors would be nice, that tomorrow was predictable, that our kids would have a better world than ours.

Now, the lack of trust in government, in institutions and in each other seems systemic. We don't assume basic goodness anymore. I remember when politicians were heroes. I remember when wanting to be a teacher was a noble goal. I remember when citizens had guns just to hunt. But, to quote another 60's song, *The times they are a-changin'.* Few people would say, "For the better."

What has changed? Here are two related propositions.

The first is that we have the worst government money can buy. A lot of money is required to run for office; people want to influence laws for their benefit. Thanks to Citizens United, the vaults are open, and cameras are off. 'We the people' has morphed into 'we the corporation.' People sense they're on their own; that no one has their back.

The second assertion results from the first. That the proliferation of guns in this country has resulted from promoting the lack of trust in each other, and the view that we can't rely on others to protect us from harm and, ever increasingly, from those 'who aren't like us'.

Depending on who 'us' is, we've become ever more afraid of each other. So, here comes the NRA. Their interpretation of the 2nd Amendment presumes every citizen, by default, is a member of the militia. Now we finally have confirmation that it's a dog eat dog world—and it's armed to the teeth. *But it doesn't make us safer.*

Here are some facts.

In 2007, *Reuters* reported there were 90 guns per 100 people. Now, according to the Congressional Research Office, the number is 112 guns for every 100 individuals. This should be the safest place on the planet! Just the opposite is the case. According to the *American Journal of Medicine,* the United States gun murder rate is 25 times higher than the other 22 high income countries—combined!

Researchers from the World Health Organization found

Americans were seven times more likely to be accidentally killed with a gun when compared to other high-income countries. This same study also showed that although we have less than half the population of those 22 countries combined, the U.S. accounts for 82 percent of all gun deaths.

Not surprisingly, since people are being shot at an ever increasing rate, the NRA ups the ante. States are adopting their 'open carry' legislation, a 'guns everywhere' policy, and suggesting that 'stand your ground' be the default position in the case of a shooting. Want to bet that implementation will depend on the race of the shooter and victim?

More guns equal less safety. To believe otherwise is delusional and dangerous. Even the NRA knows this; what other explanation could they have for not allowing guns, hidden or otherwise, at their national convention?

Let's hope future generations never sing the anthem, *the eve of* **self**-*destruction,* because it sure seems to be where we're headed.

23 JULY 2017

"IT'S MUELLER TIME"

"Perimeter defense may not matter if the enemy is inside the gates."
—ROBERT MUELLER

Yup, the tee shirt is on order. The countdown has begun; not to impeachment, but to Trump's resignation and the end of this national nightmare. And, the funny (as in weird) thing is that the fall of Donald J. Trump has been instigated by the man himself.

It was his action in firing James Comey that led to naming Robert Mueller as Special Counsel. And, it was his latest interview with the "failing" New York Times that led to the resignation of the spokesman for his legal team. Seems Trump neglected to tell him about the interview. Trump is either incredibly stupid, or he has a death wish. Actually, never mind the word 'or' in the previous sentence.

So, why is he going to resign instead of waiting for the inevitable impeachment trial? The answer is that such a trial could result in criminal charges. *The Washington Post* and

The New York Times deserve the highest accolades for their fearless work in uncovering the facts that will lead to Trump's resignation. It's abundantly clear it is not they who are the real 'enemy of the people.'

These newspapers report that Trump is trying to set up roadblocks to the investigation by trying to discredit members of the Mueller team. He's also checking on his ability to pardon family members, staff and even himself. If he, his staff, and family members were innocent, Trump would insist that the Mueller investigation, along with the committees in the House and Senate, continue unabated, with the full cooperation of the administration. People who are innocent don't ask about pardons.

What has put Trump's fears in overdrive is that Mueller is going back in time to establish past business dealings, patterns, and financial transactions. Purportedly included is the sale of property in Palm Beach to a Russian oligarch at a profit of millions of dollars, even though Trump had only owned the property for a short period of time. Money laundering is a reasonable explanation for such willingness to pay an exorbitant price for property neither owner ever lived in and was actually torn down a short time following the transaction.

Mueller's team is reportedly looking at financial records from foreign banks and, here's the ultimate threat— subpoenaing years of Trump's income tax returns. Then there's his sycophantic response to Putin that can only be explained by a need to ensure that whatever Putin has on him remains hidden. What other explanation can there be for his obsequious behavior?

Trump's ability to use the English language is limited, but he knows the meaning of the word 'loser.' If impeachment proceedings are initiated, he will be seen as the biggest loser on the planet. He cannot take that risk. He will resign, using the excuse of his health, his family, his business; and, as he does habitually, blame everyone else—the press, Congress, Hillary, and of course, Obama, for all his ills.

When this is all over, there needs to be some serious national introspection, and at least two outcomes. The first is that all this originated as the result of Russian interference in our elections. That is an act of cyber warfare that must be dealt with by applying even stronger sanctions, among other things.

The other is that those choosing to run for president must meet specific eligibility criteria—including release of all pertinent financial records including tax returns, a physical and mental health examination conducted by a qualified third party appointed by the Justice Department or other agency, and insistence that laws regarding nepotism and divestment of financial holdings be followed.

In the meantime, just Google "It's Mueller Time" to order your tee. It's likely to become a collector's item.

26 AUGUST 2017

WHAT WILL IT TAKE?
(PART II)

"The truth will set you free but first, it will make you miserable."
—JOHN A. GARFIELD

"To abandon facts is to abandon freedom."
—TIMOTHY SNYDER

Political pundits, professional politicians, the media and 75 percent of the voting public have been dead wrong about Donald Trump. With every gaffe spoken, every insult dished out, every ridiculous promise made, every lousy staff selection, every lie told, every threat made, they were sure it would be the end of Trump. And, had the assaults on civility and reason not come so often, perhaps that would have happened. But it's difficult to fully process and respond to today's events when the next day your attention is drawn to something else he did or said, that's even worse. Pause and repeat.

While the rest of us are mortified and angered, nothing he does seems to matter to his most avid supporters. They know his knowledge is as deep and thoughtful as the latest nugget gleaned from the brilliant thinkers on *Fox and Friends*. They know he's unable to learn anything requiring more concentration than that of a flea. They know he's made poor choices for advisors and staff who lack the expertise to make up for his deficiencies ("I only hire the best people" but has fired eight of them since inauguration), and they know he has exhibited an incredible lack of judgment in terms of decision making.

They know he lies; they know he preaches to others what he doesn't do himself in terms of hiring and buying American... hypocrisy doesn't bother them. They know he's making big bucks off the presidency; they know he's destroying America's reputation overseas. They know he has a special place in his heart for Putin, and they don't care why. They know he has emboldened domestic terrorists by his hateful rhetoric and unwillingness to call out behavior that's antithetical to everything this country stands for ("There are very fine people on both sides"). Nazis, and those who march with them, are not 'fine people.'

They know he spends more time watching the news and playing golf than he does governing—which, all things considered, is probably a good thing. They know he's made outrageous statements scapegoating members of the press—"Those people are responsible for your problems," they are "Enemies of the people," "Scum," and "They don't love this country."

It seems there isn't a day that goes by that he doesn't do or say something that is an embarrassment to the office and this nation. And his supporters don't care. Imagine that! But, if you're still a Trump supporter, you don't have to imagine; you already know that. You don't care. It simply doesn't matter. Blame it all on 'fake news.'

You don't care about these, or dozens of other actions, or statements that you would find intolerable had they been uttered or acted on by anyone else in that role. It doesn't matter that his actions are tearing the nation apart. His supporters don't care. Imagine that! But, if you're still a Trump supporter, you already know that. You don't care. It simply doesn't matter.

On August 22, 2017 General James Clapper, who has worked for every President from Kennedy to Obama, and is the former Director of the Defense Intelligence Agency, former National Security Director, and former Director of National Intelligence, said in reference to Trump's rally in Phoenix:

"I don't know when I've watched and listened to something like this from a President that I found more disturbing... Having some understanding of the levers of power that are available to a president if he chooses to exercise them, I find this downright scary and disturbing. I really question his ability, his fitness to be in this office. This behavior and divisiveness and the complete intellectual, moral and ethical void that the President of the United States exhibits... and how much longer does this country have to, to borrow a phase, endure this nightmare?" And "I worry about Trump's access to the nuclear codes."

That statement would keep most people awake at night... but probably not you. Instead, you will attempt to discredit Clapper, and thereby discredit his statement. That's what Trump does; he attacks the messenger to divert attention away from the message. But what may be beginning to keep you awake at night is cognitive dissidence. It's tough work to maintain that façade in the face of ever increasing and obvious facts.

Consider this. Based on all the things he's done and somehow gotten away with, it appears Trump was right about this one thing: *"I could stand in the middle of 5th Avenue and shoot someone and I wouldn't lose voters."* Think about that. He believes he could shoot a weapon in front of a crowd, wound or kill someone, and you would continue to support him. Is he right?

Before you answer, consider this. What does Trump's statement say about what he thinks of you, his most ardent supporters? He must believe you're not terribly bright—that you lack critical thinking skills and judgment, knowledge of right and wrong, and are devoid of any sense of morality or ethics. Given all that he's said and done over the past two years, until now, and lost little of his base, perhaps—in this one instance—he's finally right. So, the answer to the question, 'What will it take?' for supporters to finally say enough is enough, is still unknown. Even shooting someone isn't a deal breaker. And yet...

Trump's base of support *is* gradually eroding. Ever so slowly, people are beginning to see that his behavior is way outside the range of normal—that he's erratic and lacking consistency; a bully with no core beliefs. His attempts at being presidential fall apart the next day—he reads, haltingly, someone else's words on a teleprompter (sounding like someone reading a hostage statement). But, those words are often in direct conflict with his own, sans teleprompter.

Members of his own party are slowly beginning to

distance themselves. It's a beginning. And you. Those of you who support him even now... what will it take for you to say enough is enough? Seriously. What will it take?

14 SEPTEMBER 2017

SHELTER FROM THE STORM—
A QUESTION OF EMPATHY

"Democracy is based upon empathy and the recognition that some decisions are solely for the community's benefit without regard to one's own narrow self-interest."
—JOHN HICKENLOOPER, GOVERNOR OF COLORADO

Waiting for Hurricane Irma to come and go got me thinking—about what happens after the storm—about all the fallout from what is a deadly, never seen before event; the second once in a 500-year storm in a little over two weeks.

I predict that for a time, misery will love company. Regardless of political party, religion, race, education level, financial status or any other variable, the storm will, to some degree, impact everyone in Florida. Some in manufactured and mobile homes will make it through unscathed; others in mansions will not. Folks will pull together to help because we need each other to get through the aftermath and clean-up; at some point, they/we will be the beneficiary of empathy and concern from our fellow citizens, which will translate into positive action helping us all return to normalcy.

And then, when the winds calm, sunshine returns, and everything is back where it belongs, we will all retreat to our respective corners, having learned nothing about translating and generalizing the value of empathy and compassion into actions that actually make a difference in the lives of others every day—people we don't know and will never meet.

We come together when a massive disaster strikes impacting entire populations but what about all the individual disasters that are part of everyday life for many of our fellow citizens? Do you care? Can you—do you—bother to imagine what it's like to walk in someone else's shoes? That ability is one of the differences between many Trump supporters and most everyone else—please note that I did not say Republicans and everyone else.

People tend to vote for those who reflect their values; who they themselves are or aspire to be. It's probably an exercise in futility to expect adults to change their values or character, so it's worth identifying those elements that resist change. After all, why spend valuable time and effort trying to teach a fly to talk, or maybe, to teach Trump supporters to care for, and about, others they don't know and will never meet. They aren't interested in trying on their shoes, let alone walking a mile in them. Empathy is not their strong suit. Nor is it Trump's.

We like to think we're all part of a social compact we make

with one another as citizens of this already great country. And, regardless of what religion we practice (or don't), doing the 'right thing' can pretty much be summed up by 'do unto others,' and 'treat others the way you want to be treated.' The Golden Rule is a good working definition of empathy; it's putting yourself in someone else's shoes. But, those words fervently said on Sunday are not always appreciated, let alone practiced, on Monday.

For instance, would you be willing to pay 17 cents more for a Big Mac if it meant that workers there could feed their own families? Would you be willing to pay extra for goods if it meant Walmart employees didn't qualify for food stamps—the end result of which benefits the richest family in America? Would you be happy if DACA recipients were able to stay in the only country they've ever known and become citizens? Would you be willing to pay more for your health insurance so that others have it as a right?

For many of us, maybe most of us, the answer would be an emphatic 'Yes.' And, while we're at it, why would anyone support a tax cut they will never see, that was designed by and for multi-millionaires and billionaires, while millions of their fellow citizens suffer needlessly?

There have always been people in society whose concerns are basically for themselves, their family, and maybe, others like them. In order to justify their nonaction, they cite the welfare queen, the high school dropout, the addicted, the undocumented, the unmotivated; to prove those in need are unworthy and undeserving.

Trump and his administration have made this not just acceptable, but something to strive for, by systemically hacking away at social programs, civil rights, and regulations that benefit the citizenry, but cut into corporate profits. His lack of empathy acts as a two-way mirror—reflecting both on him and those who continue to support him.

Well, some of us are about to be on the receiving end, and in great need of, empathy and compassion—and action. People all over Florida, Texas, and beyond will have lost everything because of just lousy luck. Or, maybe they chose to live in a flood zone—or what has become a flood zone. Or, maybe they decided to take a risk, save their back and not put away the lawn ornaments that broke the windows, that flooded the house, that made it unlivable. Or, maybe they had the chutzpah to choose to live in Florida, knowing perfectly well that, sooner or later, they were bound to be hit by a hurricane. For whatever reason, would you, the taxpayer, deny these people help from FEMA if you had the power to do so?

A favorite response of Trump supporters to opinions like these is not to address the content, but to label the writing and the writer 'liberal'—or variations of the word, 'libtard,' comes to mind. Disgusting. Not the first syllable, but the last. They use 'liberal' as a verbal weapon, the ultimate insult.

Webster defines 'liberal' as "possessing or manifesting a free and generous heart; a broad and enlightened mind, free of narrowness, bigotry or bondage... any person who advocates liberty of thought, speech or action."

'A free and generous heart.' Empathy defined. Who would not want to claim that? Oh, right.

15 OCTOBER 2017

LOOKING FOR
PROFILES IN COURAGE

"It takes a great deal of bravery to stand up to your enemies, but a
great deal more to stand up to your friends."
—DUMBLEDORE, *HARRY POTTER*

"To announce that there must be no criticism of the President, or
that we are to stand by the President right or wrong, is not only
unpatriotic and servile, but is morally
treasonable to the American Public."
— THEODORE ROOSEVELT

The question has been asked before: What will it take for Trump supporters to declare that   enough is enough, that the President is putting our democracy at risk, and that he is no longer worthy of support?

Maybe it's helpful to retrace how we got here in the first place. A lot of voters were dissatisfied with the two major candidates during the last election. Faced with a vacuum of choice, enough Independents and swing voters decided to join the Republican base and try something different. They recognized Trump's character flaws, didn't much like what he said or how he said it, but thought he was a successful businessman who seemed to understand the frustrations of the working and middle class. Besides, it was taken as a matter of faith that he would become 'presidential' once in office. And, since the polls showed Hillary was going to win anyway, why not send a message?

Well, message received. His voters put their faith in Trump, hoping for the best. What the country got was so much less.

Trump has not modulated any of his noxious behaviors. He continues to govern by Tweet, is impulsive in statements and actions, places his need for praise above all else, belittles and bullies those who disagree with him, shows no empathy for others, appears to become more unstable with each passing day, has appointed inexperienced and unqualified people to important positions within the White House and as heads of Departments, stated that people chanting racial and anti-Semitic slogans and carrying Nazi banners were 'good people,' and hasn't expressed a concern about Russian interference in our election, or supported committees looking to prevent interference in the future. Additionally, he has antagonized our enemies and confused our friends.

Whatever his political policies may be, his personal characteristics have been a key factor preventing their implementation. His only big legislative success has been the confirmation of his Supreme Court nominee which, given the makeup of the Senate Judiciary Committee and the Senate, was a foregone conclusion.

Nine months into this presidency have seen dozens of

respected conservative Republican commentators, politicos, and pundits run the other way. Peggy Noonan, Charlie Sykes, Bill Kristal, David Brooks, Jennifer Rubin, Steve Schmidt, Joe Scarbourgh, Nicole Wallace and George Will, among many others, are voicing not just concern, but alarm at Trump's actions. And now, finally, a key Republican politician has demonstrated the courage to come forth and say that the emperor has no clothes.

Republican Bob Corker, Chair of the powerful Senate Foreign Relations Committee, a fiscal hawk and acknowledged conservative, has said aloud what all but a few of his colleagues are reportedly saying behind closed doors or off the record; the President is unfit for the office he occupies.

Consider what it has taken for Corker to call out the President's lies and actions. He endorsed and supported Trump. He campaigned for him and with him. At the urging of other Senators, Trump considered him for Secretary of State (but rejected him because he was 'too short'). Corker has never voted against any Trump supported legislation. But, he was the only Republican Senator to speak out about Trump's comments following Charlottesville. Corker said then that Trump lacked the stability and competence to be successful, but hoped that would change.

Clearly, Corker has become more alarmed over time, now saying that the national security team of Tillerson, Mattis and Kelly provide the adult supervision "that helps separate our country from chaos" and that every day is an effort to contain Trump. Behind closed doors, Senators and Representatives express concern that Trump is morally, psychologically and intellectually unfit for office. Corker stated that anyone concerned for the nation would have to be concerned about this Presidency—and added that Trump is moving us toward World War III. Think about that. The Republican Chair of the powerful Senate Foreign Relations Committee, who is privy to information requiring the highest security clearance, believes that the President himself is a danger to this country and agrees with the White House national security team, that Trump needs to be contained.

So, when will others say in public what they're saying off the record? Who will be the next profile in courage? It's important to note that not a single Republican Senator has contradicted Corker's view of Trump. When asked, they dodge, obfuscate, and deflect, but when will they do their job, show concern for this nation and join Corker in stating the obvious; that Trump himself is our biggest security risk and presents a clear and present danger.

Corker has shown courage in his pronouncements. It's time for others in the Senate and House to do the same. Before it's too late.

09 NOVEMBER 2017

UNCOVERING THE TRUTH
—IT'S NOT EASY

"Don't believe everything you read on the Internet."
—GEORGE WASHINGTON

"One thing I can promise you is this. I will always tell you the truth."
—DONALD J. TRUMP

FYI: One of the above statements was not made by that person. The other was. One is accurate, although the accreditation is not. The other is written as stated, (Charlotte N.C. Aug. 18, 2016), but has been documented to be inaccurate—thousands of times. One is fake news; the other is not.

We all hate being played for a chump but all of us have been snookered... one might even say 'trumped' (check out the *Urban Dictionary* definition) from time to time. We've passed along information assumed to be correct, but turned out to be fake. And, we've had plenty of company from

Democrats and Republicans alike.

What is not fake news is that Russia interfered in our last election. A major tactic was to place fake news stories on social media designed to influence voters. Be assured, if you are a Facebook user or have a Twitter or similar account, you too are probably complicit in the spread of lies—the not-so-nice, but accurate, synonym for 'fake news.' But, unless you were a willing accomplice, you didn't know it.

According to testimony before Congress, Facebook estimated that 126 million voters (that's half of the voting public) were exposed to Russian backed posts. Twitter executives estimated that 37,000 accounts were linked to Russia. We know how quickly posts and Tweets can go viral, but the number of shares and retweets may be more of an indication of gullibility than truth. No one is immune. *MSNBC* commentators admitted they got suckered into retweeting fake news, and Sean Hannity, as well as other *FOX* commentators, apologized on air and in Tweets for repeating fake news. How does this happen? Are we really so gullible? Actually, the answer is 'Yes.'

Confirmation bias is the tendency to interpret new information based on what we already believe, and to reject information that counters those beliefs. Thanks to confirmation bias, base support for both Hillary and Trump was unwavering; however a huge chunk of voters didn't like either choice and were up for grabs. But Russia liked Trump, and bots and posters were let loose.

Their goal was to post fake stories about both candidates, but mostly for the benefit of one. Then readers did the rest. Here's a typical example: Russia actually invented fake

Americans. Last year, Melvin Redick of Harrisburg, PA, a friendly looking American with a backward facing baseball cap and young daughter, posted a link to a new website on Facebook. "These guys show the hidden truth about Hillary Clinton, George Soros and other leaders of the US. Visit *DCLeaks* website. It's really interesting." Readers, looking to confirm what they already believed, or maybe just curious, took it from there by visiting the site and responding with likes and shares.

Mr. Redick doesn't exist, but his was one of the first signs of unprecedented foreign intervention in our elections. Whether the truth or fake news, we believe what we already believe. And, if our beliefs weren't well formed, fake news was there to guide us to their conclusion. And, oh, how they could target! Ever view posts that supported stopping immigration, ending affirmative action, reducing Medicaid, ending food stamps? Do we have news sites for you!

As unsettling as this is, it gets worse. The election is over, but fake news continues unabated. We remain willing accomplices. We retweet and share what we like to people who agree with us—eventually it reaches those uninformed, eager to lap up the latest conspiracy theory.

The First Amendment is being weaponized to launch distrust and drive us further apart. Fake news is circulated to sow mistrust of immigrants, gun owners, Democrats, Republicans, minorities, the rich ('they're taking it all'), the poor ('if only they'd work as hard as I do'), politicians, and the media ('they all lie'). And on it goes. The end result is the erosion of trust in our institutions and each other; a torn and divided America. From a Russian point of view, that's gold.

Mission accomplished.

The International Consortium of Investigative Journalists, and other sources, suggest tips for spotting and stopping fake news.

- Is the story too outrageous and crazy to be true?
- Are other reputable news organizations silent on the same story?
- Who wrote it? Is the author credible?
- Photos, quotation marks and videos are not necessarily proof!
- Go right to the source by using Factcheck.org.
- Use Snope's Field Guide to Fake News Sites
- Don't confuse satire with fact. i.e. "Trump is desperate for a legislative win to prove his final year in office isn't a total disaster." Or "New evidence Hillary killed Lincoln." (most satire isn't so obvious)
- Is the attention-grabbing headline a gross exaggeration of the story?
- Google is your friend. Use it.
- If unsure, pass it by.

Now that the impact of fake news is known, and that there are ways to combat it, we have an obligation to fight back; we won't always get it right, but we have a duty to try. Who we are as individuals is based on our values, on what we believe to be true, and that's based on information we receive and choose to use.

Our actions are based on what we presume we know. We better get it right. We need to get it right. We owe that to each other—regardless of who we voted for.

02 DECEMBER 2017

THE ASSAULT ON TRUTH

"If this is who we are or who we are becoming, I have wasted 40 years of my life. Until now it was not possible for me to conceive of an American President capable of such an outrageous assault on truth, a free press or the First Amendment."
— GENERAL MICHAEL HAYDEN

This statement by the former CIA and National Security Agency Director was in response to Trump's Tweet on Nov. 25, 2017: *"Fox News is MUCH more important in the United States than CNN, but outside the U.S., CNN International is still a major source of (Fake) news, and they represent our Nation to the WORLD very poorly. The outside world does not see the truth from them!"*

Actually, it is the President who represents our nation to the world. He hardly needs *FOX* or *CNN* to interpret who he is. They just need to train their cameras on him and let him talk— or Tweet. Odds are, what you'll get is a barely discernable statement, verbal or written, with lousy grammar, fourth-grade vocabulary, and syntax that would drive that fourth-grade teacher to drink. More importantly, odds are that it will contain exaggerations, inappropriate comments and/or lies.

PolitiFact rated a whopping "69 percent of Trump's statements as mostly false, false, or pants on fire." Five percent were rated as "absolutely true." Consider that! Would any of us maintain a friendship with someone who's truthful five percent of the time? Should any nation trust another whose leader is honest five percent of the time?

Trump is not our first language/learning impaired President, but others were sufficiently aware of their deficiencies to use staff to review and edit before making pronouncements. But self-awareness of deficiencies is one of Trump's deficiencies. He doesn't see any.

Nor is he the first President to lie, but Trump takes lying to a whole other level. The lies seem to arise from one overriding need—that of self-aggrandizement—the need to not just protect his fragile ego, but to assure himself and everyone else, that no one is better at anything than Donald J. Trump. He does that by manufacturing adoration, while belittling others who pose a threat.

Almost every speech he makes, regardless of theme, purpose, or location has to include statements denigrating Hillary Clinton or President Obama. Or both.

Michael Gerson, former Republican presidential advisor and speech writer, describes Trump as a "wrecking ball motivated by grievance."

Trump lies about information that's provable and readily available; he's a pathological liar who makes up an alternate reality. He states regularly that President Obama never achieved a three percent quarterly growth rate in his eight years. *Fortune* magazine finds that three percent, or more, growth occurred eight times during those years. Now he's even questioning whether the voice heard round the world on the Access Hollywood tape is his, although there's a video of him stating "I said it." Perhaps that video is fake too.

Gerson talks about Trump being untethered from reality and the source of a continual pattern of deceit coming from the White House. Each day brings a new degradation of the office. What once was unacceptable—even unimaginable—is just one more assault.

Four days ago, on November 29th, Trump retweeted three white supremacist videos which had been proven fake. That resulted in public rebukes from the Dutch government and British Prime Minister, and praise from former KKK Grand Dragon, David Duke. Let that sink in.

After a while, you run out of flabbergasts.

And, that's the real danger. There's never enough time to react and refute the latest outrageous Tweet or statement before the next one is delivered. It's impossible to keep up. And, so is the facile response of "no big deal, everyone lies, that's just what he does."

What would have once been considered abhorrent is now accepted as the norm. But this is not normal. This is not who we are.

Donald Trump has become an enemy of the people. He, via his puppeteer, Steve Bannon, is systematically destroying our institutions and our government. He is tearing apart our nation apart. He is fostering all the 'isms' by engaging in them himself—thus giving permission to all those who have a grievance to blame it on 'the other.' He is the consummate liar and con artist. Never in our history has the enemy within been any stronger and more dangerous than now.

Nothing is more important than honesty because everything else rests on it. It is our right as Americans to demand it. And that's the truth.

28 DECEMBER 2017

DONALD J. TRUMP: THE AVATAR OF AMERICAN CORRUPTION

"Corruption requires authority plus monopoly minus transparency."
—AUTHOR UNKNOWN

Corruption is dishonest, or unethical, conduct for personal benefit by someone entrusted with a position of authority. Simply put, it's using a position of public trust for private gain. And that's who Trump is—a corrupt and morally bankrupt salesman/politician and, unfortunately for the world, the most powerful person in it.

Consider that the country seen as "the shining city upon the hill," an example of democracy and decency for the world to emulate—where no one is intrinsically valued less than anyone else—has, at least temporarily, ceased to exist. Living in such a moment should make us reconsider who we are, what has gone wrong, and what has led us to this moment.

Mostly, it revolves around lies. It revolves around *quid pro quo*. It revolves around prejudiced denigrating of groups of people. It revolves around Trump using his position to enrich himself and his family. Corruption thrives in a political monopoly, with most Republicans in Congress closing their eyes and holding their noses, while Bannon's puppet signs off on their donor-driven agenda. Executive power has gone unchecked and corruption has thrived.

It would take volumes to provide examples occurring over the past year. So, how about we look at just the past few days.

Congress passed the "Tax Cuts and Jobs Act" that Trump defined as a "middle class tax bill." Vice President Pence gushed, "It's a middle-class miracle."

It isn't.

Average people are not prime beneficiaries. Businesses and the ultra-rich get the most when they need it the least. For the next eight years, those earning between $49,000 and $86,000 will receive a small tax cut. A very small, nonpermanent tax cut. Bottom line: the top one percent gets 83 percent of the tax cut—and theirs is permanent.

Trump said it repeals Obamacare. It doesn't.

The Bill ends fines for those not carrying health insurance. We make up the difference when 13 million people without insurance use the ER for non-emergencies. Meanwhile, even given constraints placed on it by Trump, this year almost nine million people enrolled in this 'dead' plan.

Trump said, "It's the largest tax cut in the history of the country."

It isn't. From 1918 to the present, it ranks eighth.

Trump said, "There's a great spirit for it, people want to see it." They don't.

Seems people have sussed out that the tax break isn't for

them. Polling varies, but between 41 percent to 55 percent oppose the Bill. One poll had that number at 70 percent.

His biggest whopper of all is that the tax plan "Will cost me a fortune, believe me!" We don't and it won't.

Just repealing the estate tax saves Trump and his family hundreds of millions of dollars. And, that doesn't count all the other goodies for fellow swamp dwellers—you know, those pesky hedge fund managers and real estate moguls, many of whom are donors to the party.

Trump campaigned on ending the carried interest loophole. He didn't.

No, Donald. We don't believe you. You are a liar.

One condition that allows corruption to thrive is lack of transparency. If Trump wants to gain back a modicum of trust, a good place to start would be to release his tax returns. The only justification for not releasing them is that the term 'liar' would again be fully proven. And, he chose not to have an end of the year news conference—again—a break from the past, and a finger in the eye of transparency. He has had one solo press conference since his election.

Now, let's look at *quid pro quo*.

It may be that the entire Russian "hoax" is a massive example that might go like: 'Want to be the most powerful man on the planet? I have information that can get you there. And, in exchange, there are those pesky sanctions... '

As to the passage of the tax bill, several lawmakers stated that a major factor leading to its support was threats from donors. Senator Lindsey Graham (R-SC) stated that, "Unless the tax bill is passed, financial contributions will stop."

Lobbyists wrote much of the bill—with specific inclusions

for themselves.

And then there's Nikki Haley, channeling Trump the Bully, stating that money to the UN and humanitarian efforts around the globe is going to be dependent on other countries kowtowing their agreement with whatever the USA bully says and does. And she had the *chutzpah* to call that 'respect.' That statement, approved by her boss, was worthy of a dictator.

Most nations have their share of corrupt politicians; those feathering their nest while pretending to do the public good. But there is a breaking point. Government breaks down and bad things happen when public trust is lost. Combine that with—thanks to passage of the tax bill—ever increasing income inequality, and it's a recipe for disaster.

Citizens are beginning to recognize that democracy cannot exist, let alone thrive, under these conditions.

AND THE WINNERS ARE...

"I'm the King of Palm Beach. Celebrities and rich people all come over to Mar-a-Lago. They all eat, they all love me, they kiss my ass. And then they leave and say, "Isn't he horrible." But I'm the King."

—DONALD TRUMP, *TRUMP NATION*, TIMOTHY O'BRIEN

By the time you read this, the President may have released the 'Trumpies'—his "Fake News" awards for 2017. To honor the time and effort he's taking for this highly relevant and important topic, it seems logical to review his tweets as an insight into the Presidential mind—as a reflection of what's worthy of his time, his judgment, and his comment.

As President and as an individual, Trump is unique. One of a kind. Nothing he says should shock or surprise, and yet he manages to exceed expectations.

Let's begin with what this isn't. Even though much of Trump's life and Tweets revolve around competing with and/ or putting down Obama and Clinton, this article isn't about them, and those Tweets are not included—with one exception. And, this isn't about the latest tell-all book, *Fire and Fury—Inside the Trump White House*. This is just about Trump; there's no need to rely on others to define him. His words alone suffice; he does this better than anyone else.

Fresh off his self-proclaimed success from signing the Tax and Jobs Act, fresh off of his golf-infused vacation, fresh off all-time highs on the stock market, Trump engaged in a series of 16 tweets in a single day that deflected from those highs and focused again on his own shortcomings and insecurities. No perceived slight must go unpunished, even if he hurts himself in the process.

It would be easy to laugh off his tweets as meaningless early morning ramblings, but we cannot. The Department of Justice, in response to a question posed by a U.S. District Judge, Amit Mehta, confirmed that "The government is treating the President's statements, whether by Tweet, speech, or interview, as official statements of the President of the United States." Since Tweets are likely to be the most ubiquitous (and perhaps only) content in Trump's Presidential Library (now that's an oxymoron if there ever was one), let's look at some of the winners since he became President.

Obama had my wires tapped. Although clumsily stated, there was no evidence at the time or since to support that claim.

If something happens, blame him. Trump was referring to the judge who put a hold on his first iteration of the travel ban. Almost sounds like he's saying a terrorist attack would serve that judge right.

Muslim migrant beats up Dutch boy on crutches! Trump retweeted a video by an ultra-nationalist political group that had been kicked off Twitter. The suspect was born and raised in the Netherlands, not a Muslim, and the video had previously been debunked. No claim as to who sent it to him.

Enemy of the American People. Trump's stunning statement about the press—minus *FOX News* and conspiracy theorists, of course.

They want everything done for them. Trump's description of Puerto Ricans following the devastation caused by hurricanes Irma and Maria. The U.S. response to this tragedy continues to be appalling.

Fire or suspend! Never one to miss an opportunity, Trump agitated against players taking a knee as a peaceful protest against racism and police brutality.

Trump body slamming the CNN logo—very classy.

Do the right thing. Trump's endorsement Tweet encouraging Alabamans to vote for an accused child molester for Senate, a former judge who had been kicked off the bench—twice.

She's a lightweight... begging for campaign contributions— would do anything for them. Trump's attack on Senator Kirsten Gillibrand for calling him out for self-confessed sexual assaults and allegations by others.

Since taking office I have been very strict on Commercial Aviation—zero deaths in 2017, the best and safest year on record! There hasn't been a fatality on a commercial U.S. carrier since 2009. The sun rose this morning— and is no one giving him credit?!

I too have a Nuclear Button, but it is a much bigger & more powerful one than his, (Kim Jong Un's) and my Button works! Really? As an aside, his statement seems highly... over-inflated. Bet that button is teeny tiny and non-functional. But I digress.

Of course, choosing from around 2,000 Tweets just since the inauguration is an impossible task. It's unfortunate that Tweets about Clinton and Obama couldn't be included, but there's only so much one can take.

A Facebook post takes Trump's competitiveness to its logical conclusion: 'this nightmare could be over with tomorrow if someone would tell the President that Obama can hold his breath for 10 minutes."

Perhaps the best summary of him by him is this recent Tweet:*"Actually... my two greatest assets have been mental stability and being, like, really smart." "As far as being elected President... I think that would qualify as not smart but genius... and a very stable genius at that."* OMG!

A Mexican proverb states, "Tell me what you brag about and I'll tell you what you lack." Psychologists call this defense mechanism a 'reaction formation.' I refer you back to his 'bigger than yours' button.

As a nod to Trump's statement about shithole countries (a perfectly permissible term since it was used in public by the President of the United States), please note the number of times he has said, "I am not a racist." That's exactly who he is.

Back to Tweets, as Sarah Huckabee Sanders repeatedly says, "The Tweets speak for themselves." Indeed.

Ah, for the days of 'covfefe.' That's as close to genius as Trump will ever get.

27 JANUARY 2018

WHY A BOOMING STOCK MARKET AND A GROWING ECONOMY ISN'T ENOUGH

"It's the economy, stupid."—JAMES CARVILLE

"Anyone who believes that exponential growth can go on forever is either a madman or an economist."
—KENNETH E. BOULDING

We accept some statements as truisms... until they aren't. Carville's proclamation has been the mantra of every presidential campaign since Clinton's first win. The assumption has been that if Americans are seeing more money in their pockets, an improving economy and a soaring stock market, that these markers would serve as indicators of a successful presidency. Campaigns are based around these 'kitchen table' issues. Whether these measures are a continuation of the Obama administration, or purely the result of the self declared 'genius' Dealmaker in Chief, it's clear they are being achieved.

Unemployment is the lowest in 17 years. The stock

market is reaching toward heavenly heights.

Corporate profits are at record highs. It has yet to be determined whether voters will see the pittance added to their paychecks from the Tax Cut and Jobs Act as a life-changer, but it's clear the economy generally is booming—well, minus the increase in homelessness and poverty—but those things don't count.

It's simplistic to think that the causes of these changes won't have long-term effects. Gutting regulations impacts consumers, the environment, health, safety, education, and much more. But it seems many voters are willing to trade possible negative consequences in the future for a strong economy now.

So, Trump should be one of the most popular presidents in the history of the Republic. Instead he is the most disliked and reviled.

Trump's approval numbers are continuing to stagnate at the lowest approval rating of any first term modern presidency. Depending on the poll, between 35 to 39 percent approve of his job performance, while 57 percent disapprove. His numbers have remained static since he was elected.

ABC News has been tracking public attitudes towards Trump since he rode down the escalator and they've observed what we already know—that he's a polarizing figure—he's loved or hated with little in between. When a random nationwide sample was asked to describe him using one word, the most common response was "incompetent" followed by "arrogant," "idiot," "unqualified," "racist," "liar," and "narcissistic." Some responses were unprintable. Only two of the top ten were positive and these were "great," and "strong." A recent poll of registered voters conducted by Suffolk University-*USA*

Today showed that 64 percent of those polled viewed Trump as setting the country on the wrong track.

Guess a booming economy isn't everything. But here's another truism to consider: "What goes up, must come down." And that brings us to the second quotation at the beginning of the article. Does anyone believe that a 1000-point rise in the Dow in less than two weeks is sustainable? What happens when the consequences of rollbacks in consumer protection, the environment, financial services, health and safety, and education hit home? What happens to the stock market when disaster strikes because a regulation was eliminated? What happens when children are denied the special education services needed to be successful? What happens when a pipeline bursts, and water becomes toxic?

Trump is taking full credit for the record markets; will he take responsibility for the inevitable consequences, not to mention the 'correction' or crash?

It's clear that when it comes to this President, the status of the economy is not a factor increasing his approval ratings. Why? What's missing? What means more to voters than a booming economy?

The answer is that it all has to do with character. Lincoln Park Strategies and Group Solver Inc. conducted a study about what voters want in a president; included were Republicans, Democrats and Independents. Regardless of party affiliation, all three groups valued the same top characteristics: honesty, leadership, intelligence, trustworthiness, and integrity. They valued them in somewhat different order, but they were seen by all three groups as critical. And it's these character traits that this President lacks, as shown in the *ABC News* Poll discussed earlier.

Thomas Carlyle said that "The greatest of faults is to be conscious of none." Here, at last, Trump finally excels.

So, it appears that a rising economy isn't as important to voters as being a *mensch*—a good and decent person of intelligence and character, whose word you trust, and who demonstrates the values you hope to see in your kids and grandkids.

While one can disagree on issues, there has never been a president in recent history who lacked so much in terms of character. It's as if, for Trump, none of these things matter or even exist. But what is so incongruous is that they also don't seem to matter to his supporters. The same actions that would never be tolerated in anyone else, Trump supporters either ignore or excuse. And that's a conundrum.

Here's a truism: There are still some things money cannot buy. Turns out they're the most important things. It's striking that as much money as Trump has, he cannot buy what is really, ultimately, the most important of assets: Respect.

11 FEBRUARY 2018

NOW IT'S OUR TURN

"There was never a democracy yet that did not commit suicide."
—JOHN ADAMS

When asked what kind of government the Founders had created, Benjamin Franklin's response was *"A Republic, if you can keep it."*

We're a nation divided. It seems that never, in our lifetime, has it been this bad. We can't even agree on a common set of facts and truths.

Everything we trust has been thrown open for debate. The integrity of institutions, the press, the judiciary, Congress as a co-equal branch, the Presidency, security and intelligence services, the electoral process—all the institutional touchstones in our lives—are being questioned. For some Americans, not only are institutions untrustworthy, they are malevolent, purposely seeking to destroy America from within.

We've become less trusting, not just of institutions, but

of each other. Even events like football games now have to meet a political standard. Or the next episode of a reality TV show. But, this isn't a game. This is real. We are us, and we don't like us very much. We've lost our common sense of what it means to be American.

We have choices: We can curl up in a corner and ignore political events around us; we can fuel the flames by allowing others to make our minds up for us; or we can acknowledge the danger and join others in working to fight it. If we seek to identify one common truth, one common problem that everyone, regardless of party or ideology can acknowledge, maybe we can choose to work together to resolve it.

Russian interference in the last election should be that common problem; it's a huge threat to our democracy. This we know: The essence of democracy is the vote. And while every election is determined by the people who show up, it never occurred to most of us that a foreign country could actively affect information voters use to make decisions.

We now understand that you don't have to physically change votes in order to change outcomes; just change the information provided and let 'share' and 'retweet' take it from there. And, we can agree this interference is destructive to the democratic process. We can also agree that Russia and other foreign entities will, unless stopped, continue their attacks.

Imagine this. Imagine Russia managed to get hundreds of thousands of Americans to innocently collaborate with them against one of our most trusted institutions. How could it be that patriotic Americans would choose to further Russian aims in opposition to our own?

According to sources as diverse as *Newsweek, Business*

Insider, ABC News, Rolling Stone, Politifact and *Snopes*—among many others—"#release the memo" originated as a Russian bot. FYI, this had to do with supposed abuses of the FISA court. Within days of posting, the tweet went viral. Americans colluded with Russians, albeit unintentionally, by retweeting the hashtag, ignoring warnings from the FBI.

What's being done to prevent attacks on our democracy in the future? Attorney General Sessions, when asked that question before a Congressional Committee in November, said he was unsure what his own Justice department was doing and agreed that was not an acceptable response. Congress passed bipartisan legislation (with only five nays out of 535) requiring the implementation of Russian sanctions. The President has yet to sign, saying that the threat of sanctions is enough.

It's not.

The Senate Foreign Relations Committee authored a 200-page report containing 10 broad recommendations, broken down into 41 discrete acts, the government could take to push back against Russian interference. It calls for the creation of a 'high-level interagency fusion cell' bringing together the CIA, FBI, and Pentagon to monitor and thwart future attacks. But, it takes the President to make this a priority.

If Russia can hack elections to the benefit of one party, the next time the other party could be the target. And, if Russia can successfully penetrate the electoral system in several states, as just confirmed by Homeland Security, they are also capable of attacking infrastructure—power grids, air traffic control, etc.

Social media must also be held accountable. Bots, then

and now, are responsible for some of the most egregious posts. Facebook and Twitter have all the technology needed to identify fake news and bot posts. They can do this now. So far, they have not.

But, it's really up to each of us. We need to vow not to share unverified posts—no matter how fervently we may hope the content is true.

Democracy is not a spectator sport; it requires more than voting every two years. And, even here, we are grossly deficient. If 'Did Not Vote' had been a candidate in 2016, it would have won in a landslide! In fact, in terms of numbers of votes cast, Trump would have come in third.

Benjamin Franklin must still be turning over in his grave.

America is in peril, and we have an obligation to future generations to fight to assure that this great nation, as we have known it, is here for them. For this generation, it's our turn.

22 FEBRUARY 2018

ONLY IN AMERICA:
STRAIGHT FACTS ABOUT GUNS

"To let these victims' lives be taken without any change is an act of treason to our great country. What we must do now is to enact change because that's what we do to things that don't work. We change them."—LORENZO PRADO, PARKLAND SURVIVOR

It used to be that the phase 'Only in America' was used in a positive and affirming way to set us apart from the rest of the world. What usually followed were statements encompassing the American dream—that anyone, with hard work and determination, can live a full and meaningful life and achieve their goals. Now you'd be wise to add the phase, 'Assuming you're lucky enough not to get shot.'

Fact: In America, it's 10 times more likely you'll be killed by firearms than in any other developed country. *(The American Journal of Medicine)*

Fact: The shooting in Parkland marked the seventh intentional school shooting since the start of this year. There were 11 additional instances when firearms were discharged on school property. *(New York Times, Washington Examiner)*

Fact: Of the 6,573 total shooting incidents in the US between 1 Jan 2018 and 14 Feb 2018, 1,827 people have died—330 were officer involved incidents and 445 involved either home invasion or self-defense. That leaves 5,798 incidents with no obvious legal justification. These statistics are just for the past month and a half. *(www.gunviolencearchive.org.)*

Fact: Since 1968, there have been 1,516,863 (that's million) gun related deaths on U.S. soil. Since the founding of the Republic, there have been 1,396,733 war deaths beginning with the Revolutionary War and ending 14 Feb 2018. **More Americans have died by guns here at home than in all the wars and conflicts combined.** *(Centers for Disease Control and Prevention, Congressional Research Service with numbers updated by Politifact)*

Fact: There are now more guns than people in the U.S. with about 120 guns per 100 residents, and that number is growing *(Graduate Institute of International and Developmental Studies)*. The U.S. has by far the highest number of privately owned guns in the world. Americans make up about 4.43 percent of the world's population and own about 42 percent of all the world's privately held firearms. *(Pew Research Center)*

Fact: Countries with strong gun control laws have fewer guns and fewer gun deaths per capita. Even suicides go down when there is reduced access to guns. *(The American Journal of Medicine)*. Guns do not make people safer. More guns mean more gun deaths.

Fact: Gun violence cannot be blamed on mental illness. Other countries have rates of mental illness comparable to ours. While up to 60 percent of mass shooters have psychological symptoms, factors such as alcohol and drug abuse, poverty, a history of violence and access to guns are much better predictors. *(United Nations Office on Drugs and Crime, Small Arms Survey via The Guardian)*

Fact: A review of 130 studies in ten countries found that new legal restrictions on owning and purchasing guns are followed by a drop in gun violence. *(Epidemiological Reviews, 2016)*

Fact: In Florida, more regulations are required to buy certain nasal decongestants than an AR-15. Yes, you actually have to register to purchase Sudafed and are limited to one package per purchase.

Fact: Want to get married in Florida? Hope it's not a shotgun wedding since you'll have to wait a mandatory three days before your marriage license takes effect. Or, you can choose to partake in premarital counseling. But there's no cooling off period for purchasing a gun, or any training required, prior to or after purchase.

Fact: If you want to buy more than a 25-pound bag of fertilizer, you'll have to register and be screened against a known terrorist watch list. But, anyone on the terrorist no-fly list can legally purchase a gun.

Fact: The National Rifle Association is more powerful than any elected official. The money they contribute to politicians, and the promise to fund an opponent of any Republican member of Congress who doesn't go along with their agenda, helps assure allegiance. Politicians are bought and paid for. The NRA has contributed $3.3 million to Sen. Rubio and $21 million, either directly or indirectly, to Trump.

The Constitution grants the right to own guns, but with all rights, come responsibilities. Kids in kindergarten understand that concept.

So now what? This time feels different thanks to the brave and articulate kids at Marjory Stoneman Douglas High School; they decided to proclaim to the world that they are more valuable than the right to own the product that mows them down. They refuse to accept that 'it's too soon to talk.' They see 'thoughts and prayers' as worthless pablum if action doesn't accompany them.

Americans may have reached a tipping point with the NRA and the politicians it supports, who care more about not upsetting their benefactor than preserving the lives of their constituents. The Second Amendment should be well regulated—not abridged—by applying reasonable constraints on a product whose purpose is to kill.

Thorough background checks on all gun sales, wherever they take place, should be mandatory, and licenses required to purchase guns. Assault-like military guns should be banned. A voluntary buyback system could be established for the millions already in existence. And, laws need to be made at a national level so they apply equally everywhere. Finally, restore the draconian cuts Trump made in the 2018 budget for mental health and school safety, and expand both.

"Only in America" should be a phase that exemplifies our positive exceptionalism. We are a magnificent country unique in so many ways. But, government must meet its first obligation— to protect lives. It will take a massive commitment to change a system that has morphed into an uncontrolled monster.

It's past time we take back the future and make it safe for us and generations to come. The place to start is with our elected representatives—and the ballot box.

10 MARCH 2018

ENOUGH IS ENOUGH

"This administration is running like a fine-tuned machine."
—DONALD J. TRUMP

"For some, self-delusion may be the only way to survive."
—AUTHOR UNKNOWN

The November 2018 election will center around two related issues: gun reform and correcting the biggest failure in ethics and leadership this country has known. Republicans in Congress, with few courageous exceptions, have refused to consider country before party, and people before donors. They have cast their fate with a corrupt administration and a President who is unstable and dangerous. And, we have a Republican-led Congress more beholden to the gun lobby than saving the lives of their constituents.

Consider Mr. Trump. His first responsibility is the safety

and security of this country. We were attacked by Russia when they intervened in the 2016 election. Electoral systems in seven states were hacked. Trump has done nothing to punish Russia or stop further intervention. Dan Coats, Trump's Director of National Intelligence, stated, "Frankly, the United States is under attack," adding Russia continues to "degrade our democratic values and weaken our alliances." But Trump has yet to make any statement condemning their actions.

The heads of the National Security Agency's Cyber Security Program and the FBI stated they've received no directive from the Trump administration to take any steps to stop this. The $120 million earmarked for the State Department in 2016 to combat Russian intervention has not been spent, or even allocated—not one penny. One is left to conclude Trump wants Russian interference to continue.

The basic question remains: What do the Russians have on Donald Trump?

Meanwhile, Putin threatens an arms race by announcing the development and testing of strategic nuclear capable weapons immune to U.S. defenses and, at least in the graphic, aimed at Florida. How does the President react? He doesn't. Instead, his next Tweet is about Alec Baldwin's impersonation of him on *Saturday Night Live*. His administration is imploding around him, several of his former staff have been criminally indicted—Kushner may be next—and those who haven't already resigned are fleeing in droves.

The basic question remains: What do the Russians have on Donald Trump?

Now consider gun reform. The killings three weeks ago awakened the nation. The *status quo* will not stand. Polls overwhelmingly support gun reform. *Quinnipiac* polling is clear; two-thirds of all voters support stricter gun laws— the highest in their history of polling—with 97 percent in favor of universal background checks. What's different now is that there is no difference between those who own guns and those who don't; 97 percent of owners also support universal background checks, and 67 percent of voters support an assault-style weapons ban— the highest number ever polled.

No one wants to take away the right to hunt, shoot for sport, or self-protection. People do want the National Instant Criminal Background Check System (NICS) beefed up so that it applies wherever guns are sold and all relevant data— including contacts with police and adjudications by mental health agencies—are provided. Assault-style rifles, the weapon of choice for mass shootings, are designed to kill; just ask any trauma doctor who has viewed the results. There is nothing that justifies their existence in a civil society.

Training and arming school personnel is the worst possible response to improving safety in schools. If enacted, it will result in disaster. As an aside, Trump's suggestion that he might go running, unarmed, into a classroom to save children is as far from reality as his claim that "I'll be too busy to play golf once I'm in the White House." Running into a classroom? President Bone Spurs would head in the opposite direction.

Trump is not on the ballot in November 2018 but be assured voters will be working to curtail his power, to rein in his excesses, and to follow up on the results of the Mueller investigation. The Republican-controlled House will not instigate impeachment proceedings, but if findings warrant, a Democratic controlled House will. And, sensible gun reform will be one of the first items on the agenda when Democrats win back the House, and maybe, Senate.

Enough is enough. The nepotism, the corruption, using public service for personal financial gain, the lack of transparency at every level, the appointment of unqualified people in the White House and to head government agencies, the graft and misuse of taxpayer dollars, allowing access to top secret information by staff who haven't passed security clearances, the constant and continual lies about the great and inconsequential, the dumbing down of the presidency, thoughtless pronouncements that have to be taken back the next day, cozying up to enemies while punishing allies, and the total disregard for the most basic component of our government—our security—it's all mind blowing.

Let's face it; the current President of the United States couldn't pass a basic background check, let alone obtain top secret clearance. And, now we have a porn star suing the President! What a class act.

The President may be self-delusional, but voters are not. He hasn't yet shot anyone on 5th Avenue, but he has done serious damage to our country, our government, its citizens, and our friends around the world.

In November, voters will turn out in record numbers, as they have in special elections, and by their participation and votes, confirm that finally and without doubt, enough is enough.

17 MARCH 2018

BACKGROUND CHECK
— TRUMP WOULD HAVE FAILED

*"What's in a person's heart and soul will not likely be changed by
the ability to command a helicopter to land on the South Lawn."*
—ROBERT DALLEK

*"In a President, character is everything... you can't buy courage
and decency, you can't rent a strong moral sense."*
—PEGGY NOONAN

S pring is here, the yard's a mess, and your daughter just announced she's getting married. She added her fondest wish is for you, her parents, to host the ceremony—in your back garden.

Being doting parents, you agree enthusiastically. The next few days are spent trying to find the right landscaper to construct a wedding-worthy back yard.

As luck would have it, you hear about a landscaper who, your neighbor says, promises he's the best in the area. Actually, it wasn't your neighbor who said he was the best, it was the landscaper himself. True, the neighbor didn't hire him; still the guy sounds very competent.

Recognizing the importance of your decision, you set out to do your own background check and get referrals from those who previously used the company—which promises to MYGGA (Make Your Garden Great Again). Nice slogan; exactly what you're looking for.

So, you contact Seniors Against Crime to inquire about MYGGA, and you discover the owner, Mr. Grump, has a multitude of complaints filed against him. Clients report he doesn't keep his word—saying he'll be at your home on a given day but doesn't show up. Mr. Grump says the owner(s) must have misunderstood. Well, that's possible. Then there's the problem with installations. He promised to provide specific plants, but installed others instead. Grump said the promised plants weren't available, and these were better choices anyway. And, because they were better, they cost a bit more. Actually, quite a bit more. Well, you get what you pay for, right?

Meanwhile, Grump is calling frequently to tell you how great his company is, and provides you with recommendations from homeowners A and B, all the way through the alphabet. But, when asked for names and phone numbers, you get trumped; Mr. Grump says he'll provide them but never does. He does provide photos of gardens he says his company installed, and they look wonderful. You again ask for contact information, but Grump says it's privileged; homeowners don't want to be pestered with calls. Perfectly understandable.

The basic background check reveals that while Grump hasn't been arrested and has passed all of his drug tests, it appears some local codes may have been violated. And, there were/are multiple law suits filed by growers who weren't paid for plants, and disgruntled homeowners who said they didn't get what they paid for. All were settled out of court—which must mean Grump was right. Right?

You also discover Grump has questionable hiring practices. It appears his labor force was not adequately trained on how to use heavy equipment, read planting guides, or informed they had to clean up the mess they made. Well, perhaps that, too, is understandable since key members of staff have the same last name as the owner—Grumps all over the place. Nice that he's taking care of family. You like his values. Grump texts you promising the BEST AND MOST BEAUTIFUL GARDEN IN THE NEIGHBORHOOD! BELIEVE ME! And, with that, you sign the contract.

Epilogue: The bride and groom eloped, to the great disappointment of all involved. The foundation of your house is severely damaged, resulting from a collision with a backhoe. The garden is in such disarray that complaints have been filed with the Deed Compliance Office; neighbors and the HOA are suing you. MYGGA is no longer in business, but you understand Grump has opened a new enterprise; it's a course about how to identify scam artists. The cost to enroll is several thousand dollars. You eagerly sign up.

Lessons learned: Because you did your homework, you wouldn't have hired Grump in the first place. Surely, a potential POTUS deserves as much formal scrutiny as your landscaper. Think about this—Presidential candidates aren't even subject to a basic background check; that's left up to opposition research. So, here's a suggestion—all candidates running in the primaries for POTUS, regardless of party, must meet all the requirements for Top Secret clearance. If key cabinet and other officials are subject to these clearances, a potential president should be as well. That process would begin as soon as a candidacy is announced.

When this nightmare of a presidency ends, perhaps Congress can propose a special committee of legal and governmental experts, to include former presidents and vice presidents, (with the exception of the current occupants), to develop a list of prerequisite attributes needed to be a successful president. Voters could use their best judgment, having that list of universally accepted attributes, to help make their decision.

For the length of this country's existence, we've been incredibly lucky. Universally accepted norms of behavior and performance have been taken for granted, and when the occupant of the White House failed, actions were taken to remediate the problem. The difference now is one of severity; Trump has done catastrophic damage to the foundations of our country, and its institutions, that will take years—and perhaps generations—to repair. Much of this failure is due to his lack of character and a paucity of ethics.

What is abundantly clear is that Trump could not obtain Top Secret clearance. That alone should be a disqualifier. Further, a list of universally accepted attributes available prior to the primaries would, to continue the gardening metaphor, help to further weed out the Grumps. From there, judgments could be based on the policies and promises of individual candidates.

In the end, voting will always be a leap of faith. At least a list of basic essentials, combined with Top Secret clearance, can assure that proven character and ethics will serve as the people's safety net and that candidates like Grump/Trump will never again make the final list.

25 MARCH 2018

THE SECOND AMENDMENT
—DISSECTED: THEN AND NOW

"A well-regulated Militia, being necessary to the security of a free State, the right of the people to keep and bear Arms, shall not be infringed."

— SECOND AMENDMENT TO THE UNITED STATES CONSTITUTION

These 26 words have generated intense discussion and arguments over the decades, but with little resolution in terms of a national understanding. The Supreme Court addressed this amendment seven times, yet it continues to be an issue fraught with misunderstanding, and one that has defied accepted resolution.

Let's start with an understanding of often ignored terms at the beginning and end of the amendment, as defined by Merriam-Webster:

'Well-regulated' means that something (in this case, a militia) operates properly through a set of rules (i.e. regulations) and laws.

'Militia' is a military force raised by the State from the

civilian population to supplement the regular army in an emergency. Notice the word is 'supplement,' not 'substitute" or 'supplant.' Defending yourself *from* the militia is not even implied.

'Infringed' means to curtail or act to limit. 'Ah Hah!' says the purest. Clearly the Amendment means that the right is limitless. Not so. Limits have always been placed on gun ownership. The one we're probably most familiar with banned certain firearms, including machine guns, back in the 1930's. In *District of Columbia v. Heller,* SCOTUS ruled that the Second Amendment "should not be understood as conferring a right to keep and carry any weapon whatsoever in any manner and for whatever purpose" and is consistent with banning "dangerous and unusual weapons such as M-16 rifles" and other firearms most useful in military service.

So, the right to own guns is not unlimited and never was. Efforts to set reasonable limits, i.e. *to regulate*, are clearly stated in the amendment as a reasonable condition. In Boston, back in the day, it was illegal to keep guns at home because they were so poorly made they often exploded. In 1824, the University of Virginia banned guns on campus—two members of the Board of Regents who made that decision were James Madison, the author of the Second Amendment, and Thomas Jefferson, who wrote the Declaration of Independence.

Times change—along with knowledge, cultural norms, accepted practice, technology—and laws. That is, after all, the point of legislation; to make laws appropriate to time and place and *for the public good.* Which brings us to today.

It brings us *precisely* to today when millions of people worldwide, rallied for sensible gun reform. Following each horrific event in the past, there has been that outcry, but nothing changed at the federal level. Trump is pretending ignorance. Well, 'pretending' is may be overdoing it. But, this time it's different. It's beyond embarrassing when fifteen-year-old kids make more sense than members of Congress. It's heart grabbing when teenagers have to beg adults to protect them. The demand for gun reform is not going to disappear; we are not going back to the *status quo*. Ever. It will be a key issue in the 2018 election. This is a movement.

Here are the regulations around which there appear to be a consensus:

1. Ban future sales of assault style weapons. They can't even be used for hunting if the hunter wants anything left that resembles a trophy—or food. They belong on the battlefield. Institute a buy-back program with the Department of Defense picking up the tab and the gun.

2. Implement and broaden comprehensive background checks. That means no sale anywhere, by anyone, to anyone is complete until the background check is complete. Share data bases between agencies and states so that individuals with violent police records, or mental health problems that have led to violence in the past, are prevented from purchasing a gun.

3. Prosecute adults for child neglect and endangerment if they do not store weapons and ammunition safely.

4. Laws must be passed at the federal level to assure equal application nationwide.

No more excuses; no more blaming video games,

single parenting, mental health problems or poverty. Every developed country does so much better than we do in preventing gun violence. It's not that they have fewer mental health problems per capita, or fewer violent video games, less 'moral decay,' or that they are less prone to crime. It's simple. They have stronger gun laws. They've made it much harder for the wrong people to get a gun. The only variable that sets us apart is our easy access to them.

The kids from Marjory Stoneman Douglas are living up magnificently to their school's namesake. Ms. Douglas said, *"Be a nuisance when it counts. Do your part to inform and stimulate the public to join your action. Be depressed, discouraged and disappointed at failure and the disheartening effects of ignorance, greed, corruption and bad politics— but never give up."* She might have added, 'and call BS when you see it.'

We owe it to these kids, and our grandchildren, and our country to do the same; to never give up until we have sane and sensible gun laws. To quote the movement's mantra, "Enough!"

30 MARCH 2018

THE KIDS FROM PARKLAND

"What we must do now is enact change, because that is what we do to things that fail: We change them."

— FLORENCE YARED, PARKLAND SHOOTING SURVIVOR

Most of us are old enough to have lived through a few of those historic "times that try men's (and women's) souls." It's when we look in the rearview mirror, after time has passed, that we realize life will never be quite the same again. 1968 was such a year. America's response to the ongoing horror of Viet Nam, the assassinations of Martin Luther King and Bobby Kennedy, the stunning events at the Chicago Democratic Convention, the display by athletes in Mexico City protesting discrimination—all were events that contributed to a sea change in America.

Life was never quite the same, because America was never quite the same.

Here and now, in 2018, we are experiencing a similar shock to the system. We have a President who has upended every norm of civility and discarded values most of us take for granted. He has changed that proud 'shining city on a hill' to a nation that is disintegrating from without, and imploding from within. He has let loose the politics of fear by promoting division through prejudice, bigotry, and hatred of the 'other.' He's made it OK to denigrate the brown, the black, the Jew, the disabled, the poor, the immigrant, because he has done it himself. Even some white supremacists carrying swastikas are 'good people.' All that is bad enough; what's worse is that his supporters don't care. And some are imitating him.

The multiple curses of greed, division, incompetence, and government by auction to the highest bidder came home to roost. And with it, the sense that things would get worse. And they did.

On Valentines Day, 17 kids and staff were gunned down at Marjory Stoneman Douglas High School in Parkland, FL; it was the most traumatic and devastating event the survivors will likely experience in their lifetime, and one most of us can't imagine. It's impossible to predict how we might behave under similar circumstances, but curling up in a ball comes to mind. Not these kids. They turned their grief and anger into action and did what few would have thought possible; they put the NRA on notice. They changed the national discussion around guns. They put the blame where it belonged—on guns, and on the organization that believes the right to own a gun outweighs the right of innocent kids to live.

So, why conflate the actions and behavior of the President with events following Parkland?

Trump is a bully. It's his instinctive response to anyone he doesn't like. He uses his power to intimidate, to ridicule those he views as weaker. He makes fun of them, he encourages others to hurt or harm. His favorite go-to is a nickname; Liddle Marco, Lyin' Ted, Crooked Hillary, Pocahontas Warren—it goes on. He trivializes what others view as important. And, some of the people who support him also seem to feel comfortable publically trivializing the survivors' response to the killings, and even bullying the survivors themselves.

Some of the leaders who organized rallies to stop gun violence have themselves received death threats. A picture of a student photographed tearing up a gun range target was photoshopped to make it appear she was tearing up the Constitution.

Almost simultaneously with their first appearance following the killings, rumors were floated that the kids were 'crisis actors' being paid by George Soros, or being coached by Hollywood left wingers. And, just days ago, FOX's Laura Ingraham taunted David Hogg, a survivor and student leader, as a 'whiner' because some of his college applications were rejected. She apologized only after advertisers began dumping her. A Maine candidate for office, Leslie Gibson, said of survivor Emma Gonzalez, "There is nothing about this skinhead lesbian that impresses me and there is nothing that she has to say unless you're a frothing at the mouth moonbat." Iowa Congressman Steve King tried to exploit her Cuban heritage and mocked her lack of Spanish language skills.

These kids aren't much younger than many of those advocating change in 1776: James Monroe and the Marquis de Lafayette were both 18. Alexander Hamilton was 21.

If you look and listen to the kids from Parkland you will see future leaders. They do not suffer fools lightly, and they will jump into the vacuum of morality that has been created by this presidency and by organizations devoid of decency—like the NRA.

Maryland Congressman, Jamie Raskin, speaking to the crowd in Washington at the March for Our Lives rally, said, *"America's high school students are leading a revolution against political complacency and collusion with the NRA. And I want you to know that you are not only acting in solidarity with the students from Parkland, but you are acting in the finest tradition of American's young people who have always stood up to change America when nobody else would do it."*

Mark your 2018 calendar. Track events. This is the year when the next sea change begins. These kids will see to it.

07 APRIL 2018

TEACHERS SAY "NO MORE."

"In a completely rational society, the best of us would be teachers and the rest of us would have to settle for something less."
—LEE IACOCCA

"They're behaving like teenagers demanding a new car."
—OKLAHOMA GOVERNOR MARY FALLON'S REACTION TO TEACHERS STRIKING FOR IMPROVED FUNDING FOR SCHOOLS, IMPROVED PAY FOR SUPPORT STAFF, AND SUFFICIENT FUNDING TO RETURN TO A FIVE-DAY SCHOOL WEEK.

All over the country, public school teachers are agitating and striking for better pay and improved funding for schools. They're demonstrating that quality education is worth fighting for.

Teaching: there are few professions requiring so much preparation (most teachers now have Masters Degrees) and ongoing effort—both during and after the normal workday—and are of such critical importance to our children and the long-term health of the nation.

Public education has been viewed as the most important civic institution in our country, yet teaching is one of the lowest paid professions. While starting salaries for teachers and other professions may be similar, when experience is factored in, teaching quickly falls to the bottom of the list.

What we're seeing today is the result of the crisis brought on by the movement to privatize public education. It's the perfect example of a self-fulfilling prophesy.

If you want a predetermined outcome—the failure of public education—you act to assure that outcome. You drastically reduce funding at the federal, state and local levels which increases class size and decreases student achievement. You keep salaries low to discourage the best and brightest from entering the field. Your reduced funding impacts a district's ability to hire critical ancillary staff like counselors, school psychologists, classroom aides, and nurses. Your lack of funding forces the elimination of enrichment classes like art, music, physical education, technology, and technical classes.

You have no funds to purchase updated textbooks and curriculum materials; some are falling apart with age and use. You leave it up to teachers to purchase classroom supplies because funds are so tight that even basics like paper are sometimes rationed. You can't afford to purchase current technology for either students or teaching staff. Some buildings are forced to remain in serious disrepair putting students and staff at risk. You use pension funds as the state piggy bank.

You see to it that educational decisions are made by politicians, not educators, so you work to keep school board members as elected officials. You see to it that teachers and administrators are excluded as much as possible from the decision-making process. You demonize unions and their members. Finally, after all this damage is done, you emphasize standardized testing as the only measure of success. Ta Dah! Prophesy confirmed.

And, just to assure a final death blow, appoint and confirm a totally unqualified Secretary of Education who has never taken a course in the subject, whose children never attended public schools, and whose expressed goal is to privatize the "failing" public school system.

Ah, but the news is there's an alternative. It comes under the rubric of 'school choice.' Vouchers are traded in for students; when students move from public to private schools, they get to take their funding with them. If the student isn't successful and is returned to public school, that funding rarely follows the student back. Charter schools get to pick their students; public schools serve everyone who walks in or wheels through the classroom door.

There are some companies on the U.S. stock exchange that own for-profit charter schools that aren't required to hire certified staff, use state required curriculum, or the same standardized testing required by public schools. Yet they are publicly funded, while being privately run. Such a deal.

Failing charters—and there are many—often go out of business in one location only to pop up in another. For instance, based on 2017 Florida data, privately run charter schools were three times more likely to fail than traditional public schools. This isn't an argument against all charter schools; there are many outstanding ones, just as there are many outstanding public schools. But, in the latter case, their success is often in spite of politicians, not because of them.

Self-fulfilling prophesies work both ways. If federal, state and local government valued quality public education, that's where the resources would go. Public schools would be able to hire the best and brightest and pay them accordingly.

James W. Frick, educator and administrator, said "Don't tell me what your priorities are. Show me where you spend your money and I'll tell you what you value."

If politicians won't fight for the best public education possible, then teachers, administrators, and parents will. It's about time we all say, 'Enough is enough.' It's about time we value our most important asset, our children, and commit to the long-term goal of an educated, inquisitive citizenry, capable of critical and independent thinking, who know the value of lifelong learning, and know how to learn to learn.

Whatever problems exist in the world, they will not be solved without the benefit of quality education. It's worth the price because without it, the cost to all of us will be immeasurable.

14 APRIL 2018

WELL, WHAT DO YOU KNOW—
IT REALLY IS ALL IN THE MIND.

Conservative: Someone who holds traditional values and is cautious about change or innovation.—MERRIAM-WEBSTER

Liberal: Someone open to new actions or opinion; values civil rights, individual freedom and thought.—MERRIAM-WEBSTER

Ever think conservatives and liberals talk past each other and don't really communicate? You'd be right; they look at a set of facts and arrive at very different impressions, reactions and conclusions. Turns out we really do see the world differently, and that serves as the backdrop for how we get, interpret, integrate and use information.

There have been numerous studies, summarized neatly by *Scientific American, Time, The Atlantic Magazine,* and even *Business Insider* among others, that verify these differences and their impact.

When it comes to individual views, we're all on a continuum depending on particular issues and their importance to us. So, keep in mind what follows are generalizations, but they help provide a reference point when it comes to how we see the world, and how the world sees us.

Here are the key differences researchers found on specific variables:

Fear: Conservatives tend to feel more threatened, anxious and afraid than liberals. Comments or events that generate fear will get attention from conservatives. Researchers found that the reaction to fear and anxiety is the biggest psychological differentiator between conservatives and liberals.

Adaptability to change: Conservatives are more resistant to new ideas and approaches; they tend to value the status quo. Order and predictability are assets. Liberals are more comfortable coping with change and adapting to it and, depending on the issue, actually welcoming it.

Problem solving: Conservatives tend to rely on past practice and a step by step method to solving problems. Trying new approaches doesn't come naturally or easily; liberals are more open to even dramatic change if it solves a problem. They also are more comfortable with the trial and error approach to learning.

View of the world: Conservatives tend to see things in black or white, all or nothing. They value order and are uncomfortable with nuance and ambiguity. Liberals rarely see things in strict categories and are comfortable making exceptions to a rule. They tend to have larger social circles and are more interested in big issues, whether they are directly impacted by them or not. Conservatives tend to focus on interests closer to home, unless community or world issues affect them, or their families directly. For conservatives, 'others' as defined by a different culture, race, ethnicity, religion, belief, and sometimes even gender, are often seen as a threat. Liberals generally do not see differences as a concern and tend to welcome diversity in their personal environment. Liberals have a 'live and let live' philosophy, while conservatives value everyone adhering to the same set of rules—generally theirs. An example might be the teaching of religion in public schools. Many conservatives would be happy with that as long as it was their religion. Liberals would likely object to any religion being taught in public schools, but if it was, then they would want all religions taught and without preference.

By any measure, these are big differences. And they have a big impact. So, let's look at Trump's behavior and how he strategically appeals to the natural inclinations of his conservative base.

It began at the beginning. Instead of an uplifting announcement declaring his candidacy, Trump primed the fear and anxiety reflex by introducing the issue that would be the hallmark of his campaign and the go-to of his administration. "Mexico isn't sending their best. They're bringing drugs. They're bringing crime. They're rapists."

But, it's not enough to gin up fear; now it has to be alleviated. "Elect me. I'll build a big beautiful wall. Only I can solve the problem." Christians being executed, gangs operating with impunity, bad people with bad intentions flooding our airports; it goes on. But, here's the solution: "Only I can keep you safe."

The other area deserving attention is a very different view of the world, writ large. As an example, here's a comment made as a reaction to current teacher protests: "We must teach our children that their teachers and professors lie and cannot be trusted." Another writer added, "Everyone lies and can't be trusted." These statements are extreme examples of an 'us against them' mentality—the need to believe the worst of everyone that isn't 'us.' There's also a tendency to take selected examples and generalize to everyone in that religion, culture, race or gender. It keeps life simple, but it also promotes fear, anger and hate. Trump preys on these fears and a world view that drives people apart. That's not a mistake. It's purposeful.

Almost a century ago, H.L. Mencken wrote, *"The whole aim of practical politics is to keep the populace alarmed (and hence clamorous to be led to safety) by menacing it with an endless series of hobgoblins, all of them imaginary."*

Perhaps Mr. Trump can read after all. He certainly has this practice down pat.

Here's another difference between the two views; while conservatives are generally pessimistic about the future, liberals tend to be more optimistic. That view comes in especially handy these days.

I wonder if there's ever been a study that measures the 'happiness variable' between conservatives and liberals. I have a feeling which group would score higher.

It's also been my personal experience that liberals prefer wine to other legal stimulants, so here's to liberals, and the conviction that things will get better, that this too shall pass, and lessons will be learned. But, in the meantime, pass the Cabernet! *L'chaim.* Peace out.

MAKING A CASE FOR A THIRD PARTY
—OR—

*"As a child, my family's menu consisted of two choices:
take it or leave it."*
—BUDDY HACKETT

Take it or leave it. Most people would say that's no choice
at all. We wouldn't shop in a store for ice cream if we
only had a choice of two flavors, neither being especially
tempting—so it's amazing that Americans aren't screaming
bloody murder that we're stuck with just two viable choices
for the most important elected position on the planet.

But, what people are doing, in increasing numbers, is
what most of us would do at the ice cream store; they're leaving
it. They're walking away. The number of people making the
choice not to vote in presidential elections is going up. In
2016, it reached a 20-year high. Why? An *ABC-Washington
Post* poll found that Clinton and Trump were the most disliked

presidential candidates in more than 30 years. That goes a long way to explaining why people chose not to participate.

A reality TV host with zero public service experience, questionable intelligence and morals, plus the verbal skills of a fourth-grader vs. a candidate with decades of experience, but a track record that left voters questioning her judgment, truth-telling and trustworthiness, didn't give voters much to get excited about.

Both candidates entered the race with so much baggage and so many negatives, that too many who did vote chose the candidate they disliked the least—the lesser of two evils. In this great nation, we should be affirmatively choosing a president based on their positions on national issues. When it comes to character, that should be a given. In 2016, it was not.

In the world's bastion of democracy, more people stayed home than voted. If 'don't give a damn' had a name, s/he would have won in a landslide.

This might explain the significant rise of Independent, or Non-Party Affiliated (NPA) voters. They tend to be more moderate in their views, and are the fastest growing political group across the country.

These voters may be more open to working together, to compromising, to prioritizing country-before-party (because they don't have one), than those who automatically vote along party lines. The fact that they refuse to identify officially with either party, as well as their numbers, make this the group to be reckoned with.

This is the group that determines who wins elections—if they show up. But this is the group that was conspicuously missing in action in 2016. And, from their viewpoint, who could blame them, given the choices.

Larry Sabato, Professor at the University of Virginia, confirmed that "Because of the structure of the contemporary party system, every president is polarizing." Captain Obvious couldn't have said it better. But, if we're ever to return to a political culture where the other person isn't the devil incarnate, one thing has to happen. Both parties need to remake themselves to reflect the best of who their voters are, as well as their professed principles. If that doesn't happen, more of us will become NPA's who look elsewhere, as moderates from both parties come together to support a viable third party candidate.

In the past, both parties have relied on 'norms,' standard past practices, behaviors and expectations we've taken for granted. For instance, some modicum of past successful public service and the release of several years of income tax returns, for starters. A past, free of corruption, would also be nice. These should be requirements. But, so too should the ability to gain top secret clearance. If this clearance is required for high level cabinet and other key officials, then it should be so for all presidential candidates. An announcement to run for president from anyone should immediately trigger this process—regardless of any previous offices held. That alone will discourage some from entering the race, especially if the results were to be made public.

If both parties are to remain relevant into the future, they need to stop putting their fist on the scale, or adjusting their platform based on the whims of a candidate or their supporters. I'll leave it up to Republicans to comment on their problems—the fact that the party allowed Trump to participate under their banner is itself mind-numbing. Reagan and Buckley must be turning over in their graves. As far as Democrats are concerned, the existence of super delegates and having them make a selection before the first primary vote is cast, use of non-democratic primary caucuses, and the clear lack of neutrality at the state and DNC level, all did a disservice to the term 'democratic.'

Leadership in both parties needs to take a long hard look in the mirror. After picking up the shattered glass, each would benefit from setting up a high-level commission to address the changes that need to be made, to institute those changes for the good of the Republic, and to ensure the current two-party system remains both viable and relevant.

Who we are as a country, and as individuals, ultimately comes down to the choices we make. But, we have to have decent options to begin with. If what has been our favorite ice cream shop no longer offers quality products, we will find one that does.

Or, we'll build our own.

09 MAY 2018

TRUTH MATTERS;
BUT NOT TO DONALD

"No legacy is as rich as honesty."—WILLIAM SHAKESPEARE

"His physical health and stamina are extraordinary."
—DONALD J. TRUMP ON DONALD J. TRUMP, DECEMBER 2015

The United States isn't. It's a divided nation and it's wreaking havoc on the body politic, friendships, and family relationships.

This division isn't between Republicans and Democrats, or liberals and conservatives. It's between Trump supporters and everyone else. This is one of those rare times in American politics where party and ideology are completely subservient to personality.

Even the most basic values can't be taken for granted with this President. Take, for example, truth. Yes, it still matters; it's so important it's a felony to lie under oath. Without truth there is no trust.

And yet 35 to 38 percent of the electorate choose to brush

aside this truth—that the President is a chronic pathological liar. Pathological lying, according to the *Psychology Dictionary*, is a "continued, compulsive propensity to tell lies out of proportion to any obvious benefit, other than an internal need to be seen in a positive light." In Donald's case, he lies to boost himself and denigrate anyone he views as a competitor, or who disagrees with him.

Above all else, he must be seen as a winner. And for him, it's a zero sum game. His competitors must be losers while he must be seen as the best.

He had to have the biggest crowds (they weren't; not at his inauguration or at a recent rally in Arizona where he claimed 15,000 attended a venue that, according to the Phoenix fire department, held 4,200). He had to attend the best school (it isn't) and graduate at the top of his class (he didn't). He has to know the best words (only when compared to a third grader). He had to win with the biggest landslide since the 80's (he didn't). Voter fraud cost him the popular vote (nope). The tax cut had to be the biggest in U.S. history (it wasn't). The new tax law would cost him a fortune (he'll make a bundle).

According to fact checkers, his State of the Union speech to Congress and the American people contained 55 lies.

That his lies are easily documented, using video, independent sources, and his own words, doesn't matter. His life is based on feeding his ego, and if that requires lying, so be it. A pundit put it this way: "Trump is the guy who visits you in the hospital to tell you what a bad day he's having." Whether the matter is important or inconsequential, it must always be about him.

His lying is so blatant, his demand for attention so constant, that it's impossible for his supporters to ignore. And they don't. Instead, they rationalize and make a conscious decision to suspend judgment. When pollsters ask how they feel about his lying, the response back is they don't care. While they wish he wouldn't Tweet, talk, bloviate or 'exaggerate' so much, they say 'It doesn't matter because he's getting things done.'

But lying does matter. These same people wouldn't tolerate it from their spouse, kids, business associates, friends, or politicians from the other party. True, while no policy consequences result from lying about things like crowd size, policies that are built on lies are highly impactful and damaging.

Trump's campaign was built on the lie that immigrants are dangerous; they're murderers and rapists, and "present a significant threat to national security and public safety." He would have been more truthful had he said 'watch out for those native-born Americans since, according to the conservative Cato Institute, they have much higher crime rates per capita than immigrants, legal or not. Money, billions of dollars worth, would be better spent solving Flint's water problem and helping Puerto Rico recover from Irma, rather than building the wall.

Since the election, there has been a 20 percent increase in hate crimes against immigrants nationwide. In some locales the incidence is much higher. If that's not an intended consequence, it's certainly a predictable one.

Trump stated that our southwest border was "wide open," allowing illegals to flow freely into the country. That's a lie. The Department of Homeland Security stated that illegal immigration was lower in 2016 than at the end of the recession and had been steadily declining before Trump was elected. So, what's the purpose? It's to frighten; to give voters a boogieman—someone to blame for their problems which, as Trump has said, only he can solve.

Lies have consequences. No one is perfect but when the President of the United States purposely lies, repeats the lies, never apologizes or admits he's wrong, and calls out news organizations and journalists presenting different documented information as 'fake news' and 'enemies of the people,' then we're in trouble.

And so is he. Aside from the fact he cannot win reelection with 35 to 38 percent of the vote (assuming he lasts that long), the remaining percentage believe Trump is dishonest and lies routinely (poll by *USA Today*). People don't trust liars and won't vote for them. He has his base, but that's all he has.

Sooner or later, Trump's pathological lying will be his undoing.

The bad news is that we have a President of the United States who's completely indifferent to the truth.

The good news is that the majority of Americans are not.

19 MAY 2018

FIRE, READY, AIM
"THE MARCH OF FOLLY"

"... I see no reason why anyone should suppose that in the future the same motifs already heard will not be sounding still... put to use by madmen to nonsense and disaster."
— JOSEPH CAMPBELL

Throughout his campaign, Trump railed against the Iran nuclear deal. But, when asked to describe its contents, all he could come up with were one-liners about how bad it was. It's likely he still doesn't know what's in it. But, that didn't stop him from decrying it as "the worst deal the U.S. has signed up to." And, like most pronouncements of this administration, the only sure thing is if Obama had anything to do with it, Trump's knee-jerk response is to be against it. For Trump, the sequence of 'ready, aim, fire' begins with FIRE! Start with what you want to do and work backward until you find a justification.

The problem is he can't.

Members of his own administration, including Secretary

of Defense James Mattis and General Joseph Dunford Jr., Chair of the Joint Chiefs of Staff, supported staying in the deal. Both Mattis and Dunford testified before Congress that the nuclear accord has made the U.S. safer; Mattis praised the inspection regime remarking how 'robust' the verification procedures were. The International Atomic Energy Commission, tasked with monitoring Iranian compliance with the agreement, confirmed ten times that Iran has remained in compliance with the accord.

Since Trump can't state that Iran hasn't complied with the agreement, his argument for stepping away is that Iran is disobeying the "spirit of the law." But there is no distinct relationship between Iran's other actions vis-à-vis the agreement dealing with nuclear weapons.

Trump argues that Iran continues to threaten the stability and security of the Middle East. It's true that Iran's support of organizations like Hezbollah makes it a bad actor and they are maintaining their cache of ballistic missiles. But that has nothing to do with the agreement regarding nuclear weapons. That's like telling your kid if she completes her homework for a month, she'll no longer be grounded. She meets your requirement, but then you add that she didn't take out the trash every day, so she's still grounded. That was neither the essence nor spirit of the agreement. No one likes bait and switch.

Some pundits, Trump included, rant about the U.S. giving Iran billions. But what they neglect to say is that it was Iranian money, frozen in U.S. banks since the time of the revolution. Not a penny came from U.S. taxpayers. That was the honey pot, combined with debilitating sanctions, that helped bring Iran to the table.

There was nothing to prevent the U.S. and the other signatories from further negotiations on other aspects of Iran's behavior, while keeping the nuclear agreement intact. Instead, out of pique, jealously and hatred of Obama, Trump gave up authority to make the good better. He has no Plan B. So, now Iran has their money and Netanyahu has what he and the Saudis want, which is increased tension between the Sunnis and Shiites. What they seek is regime change, and hope we'll fight a proxy war with Iran on their behalf.

Only time will fully disclose the results of Trump's actions, but this much we know. The U.S. will reinstate economic sanctions, and American companies will be impacted. Boeing's $20 billion airplane deal is at risk, and they are not alone. Trump's action further isolates the U.S. from its European allies, and places in danger relationships with countries trading with Iran. If they continue these obligations, Trump's action may affect their trade with the U.S. When asked, John Bolton, National Security Advisor, did not rule out sanctioning them if they continue trade with Iran. Think about that. By maintaining their commitment to a multi-national agreement, our European allies could be sanctioned by us if they trade with Iran.

This clearly has huge negative financial consequences for our closest allies. And, if you think you won't be affected, think again, and again and again—every time it costs you more to fill up your gas tank. And, then there's the increased threat of war.

There are super hawks in this administration who are repeating the same errors that destabilized the Middle East by our invasion of Iraq. Both Bolton and Pompeo are eager for regime change in Iran. *The American Conservative* reported that Pompeo stated the U.S. should consider bombing Iran to wipe out their nuclear capabilities, saying "It would take under 2,000 sorties." He's likely to have Bolton's strong support for pushing such an attack.

So, what happened to the "ready, aim" part of the order? Be assured, Neo-Cons in Congress are working on just that. This time the target may be Iran itself. It's Trump's actions, not Iran's, that are further destabilizing the Middle East.

Historian Barbara Tuchman, in her book *The March of Folly*, titles her first chapter "Pursuit of Policy Contrary to Self-Interest." Her book documents the many 'shoot yourself in the foot' mistakes that have brought down governments and countries, and yet we keep repeating them, even when reasonable alternatives are available.

Iran is in compliance with the agreement. We are not. By stepping away, we are less safe. And, like lemmings, we are marching toward folly heading down the path that will extend the longest war in our history even further.

If we listened and learned, maybe history wouldn't have to repeat itself. Trump won't. Congress should. And, so should we.

THIS IS NOT NORMAL.
HE IS NOT NORMAL.

"Whatever is going to happen is really here now—if only one could see it."—H.G. WELLS

"You don't have to be effective to be destructive."
—BRIAN KLASS, *THE DESPOT'S APPRENTICE*

Trump has it down to a science. He may not be intelligent, but he isn't dumb. His decisions, Tweets, actions and comments are so fantastical, such a departure from the norm, and so frequent that it's literally stunning.

He uses one delusional Tweet to take attention away from another, more damning one. He leaves little time to react—and why bother, because the next thing he says, does or Tweets will be more outrageous than what came before.

But to ignore is to approve. To ignore is to forget. To ignore is to make the dysfunctional and abhorrent normal— and this Presidency is anything but. What follows are a few of the lowlights, which as of this writing, is only day 493.

- naming the free press as the "enemy of the people"
- setting domestic and international policy in 140 characters or less
- paying off a porn star to keep quiet about an extramarital affair; more accusers are in line
- hiring unqualified family members for high positions in the White House
- appointing people with no experience or background to head cabinet agencies
- denigrating Gold Star families
- appointing a foreign agent to a highly sensitive White House position
- not providing income tax returns as promised
- inadequate vetting for positions requiring top secret clearance
- providing access to highly sensitive information to staff without top secret clearance
- tolerating officials who use taxpayer money to fund lavish lifestyles and/or purchases
- continuing to financially profit from Trump holdings, foreign and domestic
- tolerating corruption at the Cabinet level
- lowering the level of discourse and decency
- approving removal of infants and children from immigrant families seeking asylum
- monetizing the Presidency by, as an example, doubling Mar-a-Lago membership fees shortly after being elected

- modeling lack of respect for others with differing opinions, religions, ethnicities
- calling self-identified Nazis 'very fine people'
- calling the FBI Nazis
- lying so often only 13 percent of electorate consider him honest and trustworthy
- disregarding cyberattacks on the vote—an act of war by a hostile foreign power
- mocking someone with disabilities
- bullying anyone who exercises free speech if he disagrees with the content
- calling African nations and Haiti "shithole countries"
- signing Executive Orders decimating clear air, water regulations, consumer protections
- increasing the National Debt to $21 trillion due to tax cuts mostly benefiting the top 1 percent
- on track to sign more Executive Orders than any president in the last 50 years
- denigrating American prisoners of war
- ordering a military parade that will cost taxpayers $30 million
- eliminating Cybersecurity Coordinator at a time when cybersecurity is under threat
- threatening to take away credentials of media outlets that run negative coverage
- 5 guilty pleas and 17 indictments re: Russian tampering of election to Trump's benefit
- first time ever hosting solo secret meeting in Oval Office with top Russian officials
- sharing highly classified information with Russian

officials about secret Israeli operation
- hiring staff member with record of spousal abuse
- admitting firing the FBI Director in order to curtail Russian investigation
- hiring staff who admitted to upwards of 40 previously undisclosed foreign contacts
- using his office and government agencies for personal vendettas against perceived enemies
- stating that everyone from Haiti is HIV Positive
- depriving needed resources to Puerto Rico to help recovery from the hurricane
- asking Dept of Homeland Security to track news sources including bloggers, journalists
- directly intervening in FBI's investigation of Russian influence into election
- verbally supporting autocrats Putin, Erdogan, Duterte, Xi Jinping and more
- communicating using insecure cell phones
- demanding Justice Department reveal intelligence sources
- calling for the imprisonment of the leader of the opposing party
- referring to U.S. government intelligence agencies as Nazis
- "I do it (attack the press) to discredit and demean you all so that when you write negative stories about me, no one will believe you." (Trump to L. Stahl)
- dictated his own medical report
- oversaw 58 dismissals or resignations (so far) from the Executive Office; a record

- poor vetting resulting in 26 withdrawals from consideration for government positions
- said NFL players who don't stand for the flag "maybe don't belong in this country"
- threatening people who are involved in a criminal investigation of him
- seeking immunity for Michael Flynn who pled guilty to lying re: contact with Russian officials
- encouraged police not to "be too nice to thugs;" slamming "laws to protect criminals"
- currently averaging nine misstatements/lies per day

This list is a fraction of Trump's attacks on institutions, people, and the Constitution. These are not normal. Not one.

See if this quote by Timothy Snyder from his book, *On Tyranny*, rings any bells:

"Fascists despised the small truths of daily existence, loved slogans that resonated like a new religion, and preferred creative myths to history or journalism. They used new media...to create a drumbeat of propaganda that aroused feelings before people had the time to ascertain facts. And now, as then, many confused faith in a hugely flawed leader with the truth...."

The dots are there for connecting. This is what autocrats and aspiring despots do.

Michael Gerson, George W. Bush's speech writer and a conservative journalist, writes that Trump's pattern of deceit has a numbing effect. You just want it to stop. It's so tempting to tune out and turn off. That's what he wants. But by doing so, everything, every decent thing of value, is placed at risk.

Keep your own list. Add to this one. If there was ever a time to give a damn, this is it.

04 JUNE 2018

"WITCH HUNT"—A PRIMER

*"The lubricants of a democratic system are faith, trust and belief.
Vladimir Putin is attacking that... he has no greater ally in this
effort than the President of the United States"*
—STEVE SCHMIDT, REPUBLICAN STRATEGIST, APRIL 5, 2018

On October 28, 2016 the FBI Director sent a letter to Congress releasing damning information about Clinton's emails days before the Presidential election. Although the FBI has a general rule not to make news near the time of an election, James Comey said he was complying with an assurance he made to Congress—if new information arose, he promised to inform them. Lousy timing for Clinton, but a gift from the gods for Trump.

Turned out there was nothing new; the emails discovered were replicas. But by the time that announcement was made—'nothing to see here, folks'—the election was two days away, early voting had begun in earnest, and thanks to James Comey, Clinton's campaign was seriously wounded. Two days later,

Trump praised Comey for releasing the letter to Congress.

But, here's what voters didn't know. Since July of that year, the FBI had also been investigating Russian involvement in the 2016 election. The Bureau, however, did not share this information with Congress or the public. Voters were completely unaware of any investigation or the extent of Russian involvement in the Trump campaign.

Two months after the inauguration, on March 20, 2017, the FBI finally announced it was investigating whether members of the Trump campaign colluded with Russia to influence the election. On May 9th Trump fired Comey—the person who may have been partially responsible for Trump's election. The stated reason was that Comey mishandled the probe into Clinton's private email server. To quote John McEnroe, "You cannot be serious!"

Here's what's for sure. The release of information about one investigation but not the other, and the clear documentation of interference by the Russians, made public long after the fact—made it more likely that Trump would gain votes and Clinton would lose.

The extent that either of these events made the winning difference for Trump, and the lethal difference for Clinton, we'll never know. But, it strains credulity to assume neither impacted the outcome. If Comey was out to get Trump, as Trump later asserted, he sure had a funny way of showing it.

Actually, Trump had every reason to send Comey—whom Trump should have considered his BFF—chocolates and roses. But instead, he fired him. Why?

Even the most ardent Trump supporter cannot believe that Trump was upset about Comey reopening the Clinton investigation. While the FBI couldn't have been pleased about Comey's actions so close to the election, only Trump had the authority to fire him.

The only logical explanation was that Trump wanted to put a stop to the Russian investigation. One day after the firing, on May 10, Trump told two Russian diplomats, "I just fired the head of the FBI... I faced great pressure because of Russia. That's taken off." And, he admitted during an interview with Lester Holt one day later on May 11th, that "the Russian thing" was on his mind when he fired Comey.

The definition of obstruction of justice is "impeding those who seek justice in a court." Just a guess, but firing the head investigator for the purpose of stopping an investigation might meet that requirement.

One week later, on May 18th, Trump claimed he was a victim of a "witch hunt," a term he now uses continually to discredit the Russian investigation.

There are two issues at stake. One is trying to determine exactly what Russia did to intervene in the election, and presumably, to develop strategies to prevent future attacks. The second is to determine the extent Trump campaign operatives were involved in assisting with Russian interference.

Here's something else we know for sure. Repeating something ad nauseam does not make it true. This is not a witch hunt. It's a real investigation with real results. Thus far, and this is only what's known, four campaign staff have pled guilty or made plea deals to charges ranging from lying to the FBI, to conspiracy, money laundering, tax and bank fraud. Thirteen Russian nationals and three Russian companies, were indicted on conspiracy charges related to Russian propaganda efforts designed to interfere in the 2016 election. Two others have also been indicted, bringing the total to 19 individuals. So far.

Given the secrecy of the Mueller investigation, there's much more that has not been revealed. And, speaking of that, 'witch hunt' is a euphemism for things that don't exist. Interference in our election by Russia exists. What also exists is significant evidence— indictments and plea deals involving key members of the Trump campaign and governing team— that suggests Russia had help and support in accomplishing their objective.

No matter how the Mueller investigation ends, Russia is achieving their goals; Donald Trump was elected President, and with that has come the steady attacks on American institutions and values.

Russia has shown that you don't need a conventional war to destroy a country. All you need is a power hungry, vengeful narcissist without a conscience, desperate for attention and sycophants to do his bidding. Steve Schmidt describes Trump as Russia's 'useful idiot'—"When Trump attacks the intelligence community and Justice Department, when he attacks and undermines institutions, he is doing Putin's bidding, his work for him."

Witch hunt? He wishes.

09 JUNE 2018

Q: WHO ARE WE?

A: A NATION OF IMMIGRANTS.

"When human lives are endangered, when human dignity is in jeopardy, national borders and sensitivities become irrelevant."
— ELIE WIESEL

It isn't often we ask that question because most of us take it for granted. We're Americans. We're unique in a multitude of ways. But the foundation of our uniqueness is our history; the fact that, but for the luck of the draw, and the daring of our parents, grandparents and great grandparents, we wouldn't be here at all. Our original sin of slavery brought many others, forcibly, in chains. With the exception of Native Americans, we all came from somewhere else.

Our nation and our government were formed differently than most. We began with a set of ideals and principles first. The Cato Institute, in the preface to their publication of the Declaration of Independence and the Constitution, makes the point that the founders outlined their moral vision in the Declaration, and it was this that served as the basis for the Constitution.

Morals and principles are standards. There is "a higher law of right and wrong from which to derive human law." It's not political will, but a higher moral reasoning which is the foundation of our political system. If there's anything that makes America exceptional, it's that basic moral foundation that set us free from British rule and put us on a path that is—or was—the envy of the world. That's why we're here now; that magnetic pull for a better life.

This isn't to say we haven't made mistakes along the way. We have. Lots of them. It occurs most often when one or more of the three branches of government doesn't carry out their responsibilities as outlined in the Constitution. We are now in the midst of making another massive mistake.

The policy of taking children away from their parents at the border—many of whom legally present as asylum seekers—must stop. Congress must do their duty: Stop Trump and stop the terror that's being conducted in our name—yours and mine.

There is no legal justification for it. More importantly, there is no moral justification for it.

And just to be clear, this is not an Obama law or a Democrat law, and anyone who makes that statement is lying. This is a policy enacted by Attorney General Sessions at the behest of Trump.

To see young children distraught at being torn from their parents is not who we are.

To see children being held in cages and holding pens, like animals, is not who we are.

To see children sobbing in fear, and adults being told

they cannot comfort them, is not who we are.

To conflate legal asylum seekers with misdemeanor criminal behavior is not who we are.

To see crying, traumatized kids used as leverage for a border wall is not who we are.

What is happening at the border is reprehensible. It conjures up vivid reminders of internment camps for Japanese Americans. It's a reminder of what took place in Nazi Germany. This must not be allowed to continue.

Our 'leaders,' and those who support these awful actions, need to review our founding documents to understand why so many Americans of all political persuasions find this behavior so gut-wrenching. This, emphatically, is not who we are, and it must stop. It is simply a matter of that higher law of right and wrong. And this is wrong.

Holocaust survivor Elie Wiesel said, *"That is why I swore never to be silent whenever wherever human beings endure suffering and humiliation. We must take sides. Neutrality helps the oppressor, never the victim. Silence encourages the tormenter, never the tormented. Sometimes we must interfere. When human lives are endangered, when human dignity is in jeopardy, national borders and sensitivities become irrelevant."*

We are Americans. That's who we are, and that means we won't stand by and remain silent in the face of injustice and demagoguery.

HOW TO REDUCE THE INFLUENCE
OF MONEY IN POLITICS

"It is money, money, money! Not ideas, not principles, but money that reigns supreme in American Politics."
— ROBERT BYRD

"The United States Congress is incapable of passing laws without permission from corporate lobbies and other special interests."
— AL GORE

These quotes from opposite ends of the political spectrum illustrate the influence of money in American politics.

We are a nation divided. While this didn't begin with the election of Trump, the division has metastasized from a gap into a canyon. When this is over, we need to find ways to come back together. Solving big problems, on which most of us agree, could be a place to start.

Members of both parties and all persuasions agree that 'We have the best (or worst) government money can buy.' A 2016 survey (*Ipsos*) found that 72 percent of those polled, representing most every demographic, wanted the parties to work together to reduce the influence of money in politics. A *New York Times/CBS* poll in 2015 reported that 84 percent of respondents said the influence of money was creating major problems in governance.

It's a problem when, regardless of party, money determines how your Representative or Senator votes on any given issue. It's a problem when, regardless of party, individual members spend half their time raising money for the next election. It's a problem when, regardless of party, laws passed by Congress help contributors and big money interests, often to the detriment of their own constituents.

When it comes to money, both parties are equally vulnerable, and individuals in both parties have proven to be equally corruptible. As corruption becomes more the norm and as voters are ignored in favor of big money interests, they lose faith in the system, convinced that politicians are just out to serve themselves. Disenchanted citizens don't vote. And more and more are becoming disenchanted. During the last presidential election, *more people stayed home than voted for either candidate.* (Survey Monkey, *fivethirtyeight.com*)

Participation is vital to a democratic republic, otherwise we become an oligarchy—a government by and for the rich. Some say we're already there. It's time to consider actions to reduce the influence of money in politics. Here are some ideas:

Term limits for Congress might be a good place to start. Twelve years is enough; that's six terms in the House and two in the Senate with no moving back and forth between the two. With overlap, members in both Houses can provide/receive mentoring and guidance. While we're at it, instead of longevity being the basis for naming committee chairs and ranking members, allow members of each committee to vote their choice. Perhaps talent and ideas can replace entrenched experience, which often leads to more of the same old, same old.

A lifetime ban on lobbying will help members focus on their current job, not the obvious one down the road. Now, 50 percent of Senators and 42 percent of Congressmen move into lobbying jobs after leaving Congress (techdirt.com). Ever wonder what they did to receive those offers? People we elect need to represent us, not big money corporations and industries.

Easy access to lists of contributors and amounts donated would strengthen transparency so voters don't have to dig up information themselves. Make it a requirement that every six months every member of Congress must disclose every donation over $1000. Providing this information, using a combination of social media or email to all their constituents, should be a requirement. Thanks to Citizens United, the bank is open for corporations, but candidates could choose to refuse all money from PACs and corporations. That's one positive way of getting voters' attention and could generate a race to the top.

Shorten the election calendar and you reduce the amount of money needed to campaign. In 2012, it cost about $20 million to run for a Senate race and around $3 million to run for the House. The vast majority is spent on advertising. Some spent a lot more, some a lot less, depending on the size of the district and other factors, but regardless, it's too much. Two months of campaigning is plenty of time to annoy the public with robo calls, TV ads, and other messaging initiatives. Primaries, if held on the same day nationwide, could be limited to one month of campaigning. Once a beginning date is set, anyone who jumps the gun would be hit with a hefty fine—which would go directly to their opponent.

Expand public financing by requiring an automatic contribution of, say, $5.00 from every income tax filer; the taxpayer could deduct that amount for the current year. It's a painless way of increasing public funding and decreasing the need to rely on outside interests that could, and regularly do, demand a quid for their quo.

Establish a blue ribbon commission of statesmen/women to review our election process with the aim of reducing the influence of money in politics, and increasing voter participation. This would include recommendations to Congress to legislate any changes to the current system.

Money in politics has become an evil accessory that has overtaken everything else in the political process; it's harming the system and alienating voters.

Government must be seen to be responsive to the people and not big money interests if we are to survive as a democratic republic.

28 JUNE 2018

A HOUSE DIVIDED—
TRUMP'S FONDEST WISH

"The people can always be brought to the bidding of their leaders. All you have to do is to tell them they are in danger and to make them afraid."—HERMANN GOERING

"There is nothing which I dread so much as a division of the republic into two great parties... in opposition to each other. This is to be dreaded as the greatest political evil under our Constitution."
—JOHN ADAMS

The country is torn in pieces. Trump has taken grievances, some real, most manufactured, and purposely nurtured them, prodded them, and fed them so they fester and grow. He's not interested in solving problems—just the opposite. He needs them to survive. He needs chaos. He needs division.

In 2014, Pew Research Center conducted a series of surveys that revealed the differences between Republicans and Democrats were growing—in fact, divisions then were greater than at any time since the Civil War. Before the election of Trump, according to Pew, polarization had reached a dangerous extreme. Compromise became a dirty word— an insult to throw in the face of the person who had the *chutzpah* to try to solve a problem by moving toward the center.

Fast forward to 2018. If the divisions were dangerous in 2014, they are cataclysmic now. There were so many indicators of upcoming disaster along Trump's way to the Presidency; all of them were based on stoking the fires of inequality and 'otherness,' while promoting fear. Rapists and criminals crossing the border to kill, maim, rape, take our jobs; nothing is like it was, he was going to make America great again when everyone knew their place, when everyone had a place, when a job was the job from day one until retirement.

At the Republican convention, Trump said that the nation was in crisis; that attacks on police and terrorism were a threat to our way of life, that the country was a domestic disaster, and an international humiliation. America was beset by poverty and violence at home, and war and destruction abroad. Your country is falling apart. Be afraid. Be very afraid. Look again at the quote by Goering.

Trump then provided the next step in the propaganda equation. Fear+Anger = the Savior coming to the rescue. He said, "I am your voice." "I alone can fix it." Those are the words of a despot.

His idea of fixing things was to identify the enemies; Democrats who promoted high taxes causing multibillionaires to outsource your job. And, those foreign workers who are taking jobs that your kids could have. And, those ungrateful blacks and browns, who have the nerve to rebel against police brutality. And, the lack of patriotism as judged by the refusal to stand for the pledge and anthem in peaceful protest. And, allies who are taking too much from us, and enemies who are really our friends in masterful disguise—it all has to be countered with an 'America First' mentality.

Hypocrisy is of no consequence. The fact that the Trump family continues to have their products manufactured overseas is incidental. The fact that only one of 144 job openings on Trump properties went to a U.S. worker (*Vox*, Feb. 13, 2018) is of no consequence. The fact that videos demonstrate, without a doubt, that some police officers in some cities have brutally attacked citizens posing no danger, all are meaningless exceptions and/or fake news. All the institutions that have been the bulwark designed to hold society together are 'disasters.'

The unwritten norms we took for granted about how we treat each other, care for each other, about how we're always stretching to make a more perfect union—all thrown away like yesterday's garbage.

It's clear that Trump thrives on division and mistrust—more than that—on fear. But the day of reckoning will come, and then what? When this is over, the real test begins.

Steve Schmidt, former Republican strategist, called it the ultimate experiment—whether the country can survive a president this incompetent. What happens after he leaves office will determine whether we do.

Now is the time to consider steps that could help put the pieces back together; the self-examination inherent in the 'truth and reconciliation concept' could be the glue needed to regain trust and respect for each other. Without that, this great experiment of Representative Democracy will fail.

We have to accept that we all are striving for that more

perfect union, while acknowledging there's more than one way to get there. But whatever route we take, racism, discrimination, and xenophobia must never ever again be acceptable.

So, here are a couple of ideas. How about both the Republican and Democratic nominees for president choose their vice presidential candidate from the other party. Yes, this is radical, but it almost happened when John McCain wanted to choose Joe Lieberman as his VP. Every voter would be putting their trust in someone from the other party, no matter who they voted for. Of necessity, the Executive Branch would be modeling civility and cooperation, and would be responsible to everyone—not just those from the president's party.

Another idea is to change the seating arrangement in both houses so that Republicans and Democrats sit next to each other; there would no longer be 'their side of the aisle.' It would confirm, at least visually, that we really are all in this together. Who knows—they may actually start talking to one another.

This is the time to think outside the box. When all this ends, it isn't going to be pretty. Divisions could become deeper—and permanent. If that happens, we will not survive.

Lincoln said that a house divided against itself cannot stand. Trump's goal is to divide.

When this ends, we have to find ways for this democratic republic to survive him, and to come together, united around the principles that made this country great to begin with.

03 JULY 2018

SCOTT PRUITT:

SWAMP CREATURE EXTRAORDINAIRE

"I want the entire Washington establishment to hear the words I am about to say. When we win... we are going to Washington and we are going to drain the swamp."
—DONALD J. TRUMP, OCTOBER 2016

H e's gone. But he should not be forgotten.
Ever since his first foray into personal nest building at taxpayer's expense, it was just a matter of time. But, who knew it would take so long, with so much damage being done and tolerated along the way. And, trusting his boss would not fire him, Scott Pruitt continued to exceed himself in ways that are still being fully investigated. So now that he's gone, read this as a eulogy to a swamp creature extraordinaire. That he lasted as long as he did is a testament to his boss; how to use a real stinker to your best advantage, even though the object of your affection is screwing the taxpayer.

Pruitt's appointment by Trump to head the Environmental Protection Agency must have been out to break the record for graft and scams. Let us count the ways:

Had a soundproof phone booth built to use in his office. There is a SCIF (Sensitive Compartmented Information Facility) in the building, but apparently that was a few steps and an elevator ride too far. Cost to you: $44,000.

Paid $1,500 in taxpayer money for 12 fountain pens and another $1,500 for journals. Amazon offers personalized pens (not Montblancs mind you, but still perfectly functional) for under $50/doz. Same for journals. Might be a good way for staff to keep track of his graft. Cost to you: $3,000.

Insisted on flying first class, arguing that it was easier for his over-the-top 24-hour security detail to guard him. There was the additional advantage of being away from those rowdy, unkempt, economy coach travelers who, by the way, pay his salary. Cost to you for flights: $105,000 (first year only). Cost to you for the unprecedented security detail: $3 million, thus far.

Attempted to lease a private jet for his travels which would have cost you $100,000 per month, had advisors not objected and blown the whistle.

Spent his first six months in DC in a condo owned by a lobbyist and his wife, while paying just $50 per night. Can you say *quid pro quo?* Yes. At about this same time, the EPA approved a pipeline expansion for an energy company connected to the lobbyist's firm.

Against White House admonition, he gave massive raises to two of his staffers, yet denied knowing anything about it. Turned out he gave his personal stamp of approval, as documented by internal emails. One got a raise of almost $56,000—just short of the median household income in America. She (yes, it's a 'she') must be very, very good.

Hired a good buddy to monitor environmental cleanup at Superfund sites. Unfortunately, that pal had just been banned from the banking industry for life and was looking for a job. Also, unfortunately, he had zero relevant experience to do the job at the EPA.

Staff whistle blowers stopped him from purchasing two bullet proof desks for his office. Had that gone through, the cost to you would have been $70,000. When aides expressed concerns about his spending, he demoted or reassigned them.

Used a full motorcade with sirens blaring to go to a French restaurant in DC. The escargot must have been *magnifique*. Cost to you: a lot.

Used his staff to run personal errands such as finding him a specific lotion sold by The Ritz (which features "sweet notes of ylang ylang, jasmine and uplifting bergamot"), searching for a used (?) mattress from a Trump hotel, and hunting down specific luncheon items to match his elegant culinary tastes. Cost to you: untold $1000's in wasted staff time.

Installed biometric locks on his doors and ordered a bug sweep. Cost to you: $9,000.

Attempted to get his wife a restaurant franchise by working through relatives of his employees.

Purchased 'tactical pants.' Reason unknown. Would be fun to guess. Cost to you: $1500. Sounds like a perfect lead-in for a "Wait, Wait Don't Tell Me" episode of the NPR radio show.

Allowed a foreign agent, and longtime friend, to plan

a trip to Morocco at government expense for a purpose unrelated to the EPA. Cost to you: $100,000

There are also alleged actions still being investigated which include making travel decisions based on his interest in visiting certain countries or cities, then asking staff to provide something for him to do while there to justify taxpayer funding. He also allegedly directed staff to find reasons for him to return to Oklahoma, at taxpayer expense, on long weekends to supposedly lay the groundwork to run for office. Seriously. And there are allegations of scrubbing his appointment schedule, apparently to hide his activities or lack thereof.

So, the question is, why did he last so long? Because, unlike Tom Price who was fired over excessive use of (just) first class flights, Trump liked Pruitt. "He's doing a great job. "He's being viciously attacked."

Pruitt was/is the subject of more than a dozen ongoing ethics investigations, but ethics and wasting taxpayer dollars are apparently not a huge concern to his boss, who sells his own access for $200,000 annually (annual membership dues at Mar-a-Lago doubled after Trump was elected). And he did as requested—getting rid of those pesky clean air and water regulations and environmental protections, enacted by the you-know-who administration. There were even rumors that Pruitt was maneuvering to take Jeff Session's place as Attorney General, should Trump decide to metaphorically pull that trigger.

Scott Pruitt appears to be the least politically aware politician ever. He either didn't learn from his mistakes, or he didn't care. There are no other explanations.

One of the many mantras of Trump's campaign rallies was the unison robotic response of DRAIN THE SWAMP! The fact that Scott Pruitt stayed in his job as long as he did, in spite of egregious misuse of power, speaks volumes about the person who continued to support him—until he had no choice.

So, I guess their synchronized swimming program, taking place in that swampy cesspool they share with so many others, may have to be cancelled. Oops—perhaps not. Based on early information, Pruitt's replacement has been practicing all the moves and is ready to jump in; he plans on adding coal ash to the existing muck.

17 JULY 2018

TRUMP AND PUTIN... WTF?

"It's always a great honor to be so nicely complimented by a man so highly respected within his own country and beyond."
—DONALD TRUMP ON VLADIMIR PUTIN

"I can't say I've been specifically directed by the President"
—ADM. MICHAEL ROGERS, OUTGOING HEAD OF THE US CYBER COMMAND
AND THE NATIONAL SECURITY AGENCY, IN REFERENCE TO STOPPING
RUSSIAN DIRECTED HACKING AIMED
AT THE 2018 U.S. MIDTERM ELECTIONS.

It's hard to believe what has just occurred. Sometimes it feels like we're living in an alternative universe.

The President of the United States has chosen to ignore and denigrate the findings of our national intelligence agencies regarding Russian meddling in the 2016 election, and to support Putin's disclaimer instead. Think about that.

The nation's top intelligence officer, Director of National Intelligence Dan Coats, likened the past and continuing

Russian cyber attacks to the terror threats preceding the 9/11 attacks. Think about that.

"The warning lights are blinking red again. Today, the digital infrastructure that serves this country is literally under attack," warned Coats. Digital infrastructure includes so much more than influencing votes—it's "everything in our personal and professional lives" including cloud services, software networking that manages electric grids, you name it. That's digital infrastructure. Our country will be paralyzed if it's attacked. Think about that.

It is beyond stunning that Trump would side with Putin against his own government; against the people heading agencies he himself appointed. His job is not to represent himself. His job is to represent the United States. Think about that.

The definition of treason is "the betrayal of one's own country by consciously or purposely acting to aid its enemies." Think about that.

Way back when Trump was running for President, he said he could shoot someone on 5th Avenue and he wouldn't lose any votes. That action would, obviously, have a negative impact on the person shot, but what he did today negatively impacts this country and every citizen in it.

The President of the United States is a clear and present danger to our democratic republic.

Think about that.

25 JULY 2018

TRUMP'S TAX CUT

—PROMISES REVISTED

"It's a tax bill for the middle class; it's a tax bill for jobs, it's going to bring a lot of companies in; and it's a tax bill for business, which is going to create the jobs."
—DONALD TRUMP, OCT. 31, 2017

"Boy, am I good at solving debt problems. Nobody can solve it like me. Nobody even knows how to address the problem, but I do. $20 trillion dollars worth of debt. It's going to be very destructive unless somebody very, very good, and very very smart knows what he's doing. I understand debt, I think, maybe better than anybody."
—DONALD TRUMP, KISSIMMEE, FLORIDA, OCT. 11, 2016

It's been a bit more than six months since Congress passed the Trump tax cut. He and the GOP promised it would be a boon to America's working class, would bring back jobs from overseas and create more jobs in companies already here.

Time for a quick look-see. According to Americans for

Tax Fairness, 4.3 percent of *Fortune 500* companies gave a one-time bonus, or wage increase, tied to their business tax cuts. That's about 21 companies out of 500. But these same businesses spent 37 times as much on stock buybacks. Further, "analysis shows that 433 corporations out of the *Fortune 500* have announced no plans at all to share their tax cuts with employees."

Funny, too, how Republicans have been able to brush off the estimated $1.5 trillion in reduced revenue coming into the Treasury during the next 10 years as a result of those cuts (*CNBC*, John Harwood, White House Office of Management and Budget). The problem is that about 15 million Americans will be retiring during that time and going on Social Security and Medicare. Less money coming in, more going out, and you don't need to be an economist to see the problem. And you don't have to be a fortune teller to figure what's coming next—what conservatives have wanted to do for decades. This is the perfect excuse to 'revamp' (i.e. cut and or privatize) these programs. Just watch to see what's in Trump's next budget. And weep.

According to the nonpartisan Congressional Budget Office (CBO), lowered revenue from the tax cuts, which have gone primarily to the rich, along with increased spending, which has gone primarily to the military, is pushing the country toward an unprecedented level of debt which risks another financial crisis. The national debt is at its highest level since World War II, and the CBO expects the debt will rise sharply over the next 30 years.

The Treasury Department announced that the government is on track to borrow nearly $1 trillion this fiscal year—the first full year Trump has been in charge of the budget, and it's the largest amount in six years. CBO blamed it on the new tax law. By the way, that's an 84 percent jump from the previous year, when you-know-who was in charge (*The Washington Post*, Feb. 9, 2018).

Currently the national debt, 78 percent of the GDP, is expected to rise to 100 percent by 2030 and, get this, 152 percent in just 30 years.

So, aside from a massive debt increase and budget deficit, let's see what else we're getting with this tax cut. There are differences of opinion—all relatively small and none of them favoring the middle class.

Bloomberg News estimates that 60 percent of the tax cut savings will go to corporate buybacks with 15 percent going to workers. Morgan Stanley projects that 13 percent will go to workers, but Just Capital believes only six percent will make it back to workers. Whatever estimates you choose to believe, this is not a middle class tax cut.

The stock market is being artificially buoyed by these buybacks. And, some companies are in danger of committing hara-kiri in their eagerness to line the pockets of officers and board members. General Electric did exactly that.

According David Haggith, writing for *GoldSeek.com*, GE is worth less now than before the buybacks. Instead, the stock that had been on the Dow for the longest period of time (110 years), has been kicked off because of poor performance.

What else they could have done with their windfall? How about investment in R&D instead of buybacks. Wonder how many employees will lose their jobs? Actually, thus far, 12,000.

While Trump touted these one-off bonuses, it turns

out many were a down payment for bad news. The day after AT&T announced their $1,000 bonuses, they laid off many of the same people who received them. Lowes bonuses were promptly followed by store closures and lay-offs. Walmart announced they were raising some employees pay to $11 an hour. They also announced, almost simultaneously, the closure of 63 Sam's Club stores nationwide with thousands losing jobs.

As far as the middle and working class benefiting from Trump's gift to the rich, *Moody's Investor Services* predicted "The U.S. tax bill... will have limited effect... the tax cut for the wealthy will not trickle down..." It has never happened before; there's no reason to expect it will happen now.

Remember when Trump said the tax cut would result in a $4,000 pay raise for a typical family (*Fox Business*, Oct 16, 2017)? And when Speaker Paul Ryan raised the ante by saying, "at least $4,000" (see his official website www.paulryan. house.gov)? As *USA Today* suggests in an opinion piece, that was a trickle-down lie (Apr. 10, 2018). In fact, according to the PayScale Index, wages for U.S. workers actually fell by 1.4 percent in the last quarter, compared to 2017.

Trump also said the tax cut for businesses and corporations would bring back jobs to America. Neither he nor his family members have done that, nor have they announced any plans to do so. Why is that? Seriously, why is that?

Some companies did announce they'd be returning, but that was before Trump started his tariff war. Now, companies like the iconic Harley-Davidson are moving production for its EU sales overseas because of the increased cost of importing materials. Those are jobs lost here.

Fortune (June 29, 2018) reports that GM voiced concerns to the Commerce Department that auto prices could rise by thousands, leading to reduced sales, a smaller work force and lower wages. Ford is also warning of increased costs to consumers which could lead to layoffs. BMW just announced they're moving production of SUV's out of South Carolina to China, and Tesla, too, will be building a new plant there as a direct result of tariffs. Hyundai plants in the South warn about a possible loss of 20,000 U.S. jobs. *Agfax* reports that American farmers are going to be most directly and immediately hurt, to the tune of billions of dollars. The U.S. Dept of Agriculture is predicting farm business income will fall 7.3 percent this year—and this is just the beginning.

Whatever meager additions there are to workers' paychecks will be more than eaten up by cost increases of just about everything as a result of Trump's tariff war.

Here's that question again: What will it take for Trump's base to rebel? It will happen when his base is directly impacted by his decisions. Clearly character and morality, virtue and truthfulness, empathy and compassion, honesty and decency, intelligence and integrity are beside the point. But a hit to the pocketbook, or 401K, or Social Security, or Medicare, or insurance for your kids and grandkids with preexisting conditions—all as a direct result of his actions?

That just might do it.

29 JULY 2018

ONE MONTH INTO THE WAR:

NEWS FROM THE FRONT LINES

"Resistance' to Launch Civil War on July 4th!"
—ALEX JONES, *INFOWARS* FOUNDER (JULY 1, 2018)

What follows is real news... not 'fake news' promulgated by *CNN, MSNBC, ABC, CBS, Bloomberg News, HGTV, PBS, BBC, The Food Network,* and others of their lying ilk.

While some of you may be hiding your head in the sand refusing to acknowledge what's in plain sight, it's important you know we've been at war since July 4th of this year. Somehow, fake news has held back reporting attacks on The Red Hats* by Democrats, aka The Resistance, aka The Elites. The mainstream media's lack of transparency clearly proves they are in the pocket of these deplorables.

Alex Jones of *Infowars,* a good bud of the Red Hat Leader and fellow conspirator, made it clear that Civil War

2.0 would start on July 4, and the fact that none of you have any knowledge of this is proof positive that fake news is not reporting the really important stuff that's happening all around us. WE MUST OPEN OUR EYES to the disasters these Elites are causing to our challenged (in so many ways) Leader and his minions of supporters—that's minions, not millions.

So, as a public service, we determined to report from the front lines in order to edify and inform. Well, actually we can't do that. We tried, but The Red Hats are so busy defending our MAGA country against Elites, that all they could manage were repetitive responses via a bot—Sarah somethingorother, which always ends with, "I refer you to his outside counsel." We hoped to get a report in writing from the Great Leader, but it seems anything beyond 280 characters is a challenge. We had no problem accessing the Elites though; they have this 'thing' about transparency.

Dateline: Outside Mar-a-Lago: "I can see The Red Hats taking refuge in the dining room!! We Elites are carrying our usual artillery—copies of the forbidden Constitution and steaming carafes of Starbucks Grande Skinny Cinnamon Dolce Latte. It seems even the bedbugs and cockroaches have flown the coop in fear—oh, wait. Our Intelligence people report The Red Hats have retreated to the kitchen and are feasting on Chick-fil-A and Papa John's. Our Elite Army is doing exceptionally well since apparently The Red Hats have no Intelligence."

Dateline: Bedminster Golf Club: "OMG! After his golf cart was attacked, the Leader of the Red Hats has taken cover in a bunker between the eight and ninth holes. We are elated to have the support of Jeff Bezos who volunteered to deliver 100,000

MAGA engraved golf balls personally—via drone. It's being reported by the *National Inquirer* (NOT fake news) that several balls missed their mark and instead hit VP Pence who was, as usual, following the Leader. Mother reports his head nodding continues unabated, and he continues to keep the faith.

Dateline: The White House: "The Leader's official media platform, named after a bunny eater (who infects everyone within hearing with the eventual diagnosis of 'brain dead'), just released a 'memo from the field' written by the Red Hat Leader. Problem is, no one on our side understands it. He keeps repeating the same words like 'fantastic' and 'no collusion' and 'you'll have to ask my outside consil (sic).' Sentence structure and a limited vocabulary make communication difficult. The Leader does seem to have decent receptive language skills in Russian—as noted by his ability to follow instructions. Expressively, he keeps uttering 'covfefe.'

Dateline: Update, the White House: Bret Stephens, conservative writer for *The New York Times,* reporting on recent battles, said that the Red Hat Leader is like an uninvited guest who pees on your oriental carpet, breaks an antique urn, kicks your dog, makes a pass at your wife, and then sends you a bill for his inconvenience. The G-7, NATO, and the British Prime Minister can all relate.

Dateline: Battlefield near Capital Hill: "The Red Hats appear to have deserted the area. The streets are as empty as the day their Leader was inaugurated. One lingering soul was heard to whine their war cry, 'Womp, Womp,' as he ran towards the nearest Dollar Store for cover."

Dateline: Rallying the troops in the field: "The Elites report back that the Red Hat Leader has lost it. Spies inserted with the white-robe-clad, cross-carrying troops have reported he is now mumbling 'Pocahontas' on a regular basis and measuring acquaintances' cheekbones to determine enemy status. Sad."

Dateline: Library of Congress: "The Elites report they've found the perfect location for R&R following their recent successes. Libraries. How perfect is that; the one place you'd never find a Red Hat. One other point: The Elites have been communicating using grammatically correct sentences. Red Hats simply cannot break the code."

Note found on the battlefield, signed 'An Anonymous Elite': "I've escaped my captors! But the trauma! The torture! It was unbearable! I was forced, forced mind you, to watch episodes of Duck Dynasty repeatedly with Ted Nugent's one hit wonder (my captor couldn't recall the name either), playing incessantly in the background. The final straw was the threat that I would be surrounded by TV screens all showing Hannity 24/7! They promised, if I confessed my Elite status, I could avoid this torture. I'm a coward; the threat was more than I could bear. When my guard left to refill his bowl of Cheetos, I made my escape. Find me! I need treatment!"

This phase of the war is expected to end 6 November 2018. In the meantime, General Mueller will provide status reports to the American people using former Red Hatters who have reportedly seen the error of their ways. As for Alex Jones, tune in. His next big delusion is just around the corner. BOO!

*Please note: *The term "Red Hat" and its variations is not to be confused with women who gather to dine, kibitz and do good deeds while wearing fabulous red hats.*

05 AUGUST 2018

TELL ME AGAIN

—WHO ARE THE 'TAKERS?'

"You should be happy I'm a Republican. We can't all be on welfare."
—BUMPER STICKER

It's been an assumption (by Republicans) that governments run by Republicans enact economic policies that create a more efficient, effective and stronger economy for everyone. But is that true? First, it's helpful to list some key elements of a typical Republican economic platform.

According to *republicanviews.org/republican-views-on-the-economy*, Republicans favor limiting regulations, lowering taxes for corporations and the wealthy with the expectation that benefits will 'trickle down,' balancing budgets, targeting spending to items such as defense and security, securing as much private funding as possible for infrastructure, and privatizing areas that typically have been provided through public funding such as education, prisons systems, health services and retirement plans.

They support 'right to work' and abolishing unions, or at least, reducing their impact. They believe taxes that 'redistribute wealth' or fund 'unnecessary' programs should be eliminated. Basically, the smaller the government, the better. Grover Norquist, the poster child for small government, has said, "I don't want to abolish government. I simply want to reduce it to the size where I can drag it into the bathroom and drown it in the bathtub."

Investopedia.com (July 28, 2018) also discusses key differences between the parties approach to the economy. While Democrats support the profit motive as an important vehicle for full employment, they also support regulations to assure businesses and corporations don't take advantage of workers. Protections that support clean air and water, assistance to workers during economic downturns (even if it means running budget deficits), and government intervention when necessary to help influence the economy are part of their approach. They support viable Social Security and Medicare as earned benefits, and are against privatizing services when the goal is to make money rather than serve the public. Support for a living wage, and labor unions that advocate for their members, are important components of the Democrat's economic approach and philosophy.

So, what actually works? The States are a great place to look; they're often described as a laboratory or testing ground for ideas and policies. One way to determine the success of both Democratic and Republican economic strategies is to look at the performance of blue and red states in terms of poverty level, median income and unemployment. The 2018 rankings are based on these metrics as compiled and analyzed by *RoadSnacks* (roadsnacks.net). It should be noted that other sources (*thestreet.com, politicsthatwork.com, 247wallst. com/special-report*) have reported either identical or similar inclusions and rankings.

The poorest state is Mississippi followed by New Mexico, Alabama, Louisiana, South Carolina, Kentucky, Georgia, North Carolina, West Virginia, and Arkansas.

Now, let's look at who runs the government in these states to see if there's a pattern. Ta-dah! There is. Seven of the 10 lowest performing states have both a Republican governor and legislature (both houses) and that's been consistent over time. In other words, Republicans have had a free rein in terms of implementing their economic policy. The remaining three states have a Democrat governor, but the legislature is Republican, thus acting as a constraint on Democratic economic legislation.

So which states perform best economically? The richest is Maryland followed by Alaska, New Jersey, Massachusetts, Hawaii, Connecticut, New Hampshire, Virginia, California and Washington State. Again, the rankings and inclusion may vary somewhat depending on the metrics used, but these states appear consistently.

And yes, there's a pattern, but it's the opposite of the one cited for the poorest states. Six states have both a Democratic governor and legislature. Only one, Alaska, has both a Republican governor and legislature. The other three have Republican governors (all moderate), but the legislature is Democratic.

Politicsthatwork.com confirm blue states consistently

have significantly higher per person median household income, and lower poverty levels than red states. Blue states have a consistently higher standard of living; people even live longer in blue states.

Here's another statistic provided by *hungerfreeamerica. org*. They ranked states with the highest percentage of the population receiving SNAP (food stamps). With one exception, Oregon, every state is run by Republicans, and all but two voted for Trump.

An article in *The Atlantic* (updated March, 2017), cited a study by *WalletHub* that depicted the most "dependent states" as measured by federal tax dollars sent in, vs. federal money returned to each of the 50 states. The most dependent states are Mississippi, New Mexico, Alabama, and Louisiana. South Carolina receives $7.87 back for every dollar paid in federal tax. Regardless of the metrics used, note the consistency among the various studies.

The fact is, based on hard data and not assumptions, it's Democrats whose economic policies result in higher standards of living, less unemployment, less dependency on the federal government, lower poverty rates, and higher median incomes.

So, tell me again, who are the 'takers?' Grover Norquist was prophetic about one thing when discussing the presidency: "We don't need someone who can think. We need someone with enough digits who can hold a pen." That's exactly what he got. Unfortunately, so did the rest of the country. The results are programs, like the recent tax cut, that help the rich get richer to the detriment of everyone else.

Seems whoever is responsible for penning the bumper sticker citation at the beginning of this essay should substitute the word 'Democrat' for Republican. And, in our own self-interest, we voters should do the same.

22 AUGUST 2018

HOW TO PREVENT ANOTHER TRUMP —LESSONS LEARNED

*"He has the character of a con man and a demagogue...even if 30%
or 50% or 70% of his policies are defensible or even correct,
it's not worth it."*
—BILL KRISTOL, EDITOR OF THE CONSERVATIVE "WEEKLY STANDARD"
ON TRUMP'S "DEGRADATION OF PUBLIC LIFE AND DISCOURSE."

*"We are watching the denigration of the Office in real time. It's
horrific. He's a full-fledged bigot. He's a charlatan and a schemer."*
—DOUGLAS BRINKLEY, PRESIDENTIAL HISTORIAN
ON THE TRUMP PRESIDENCY.

Every successful organization goes through periodic evaluations. Our country does this every two years—that's essentially what voting is about. But, the lessons of this Presidency should serve as an impetus to review more than just the players and policies; so much has failed, devastatingly failed, that it's time to review the process itself.

Over the life of this country, we've come to rely on norms; some were established early on; most have come about over time. There's never been a reason to formalize them—until Trump. There are no written rules or guidelines for the expectations and assumptions we've come to take for granted. But these omissions have become commissions, resulting in daily disasters emanating from the White House.

The time has come to look at the process, and formalize in law and regulation, what needs to be made right.

The ideas that follow are nothing new or revelatory; for the most part they are the norms this President has broken, or are logical extensions based on areas of need that Trump's behavior has highlighted. You no doubt could add to the list.

In some cases, it makes sense they would come in force when candidates announce their intent to run. Others would kick in after the primaries, but before each party's nominating convention.

Here are some to consider:

Require all candidates meet the standards for Top Secret security clearance. The process would be triggered when a candidate announces his/her intent to run.

Public service at some level should be a prerequisite. Candidates should have experience answering to a constituency—be it voters, stockholders, citizen groups or beneficiaries.

Candidates should be required to undergo complete physical and mental health evaluations by reputable professionals approved by an outside panel. Results would be made public once a nominee is chosen, but before the nominating conventions.

Prior to the primaries, candidates would be required

to release and make public tax returns for at least the previous 10 years. Once elected, and while in office, returns should be made public annually.

To eliminate conflicts of interests following the primaries, the presumptive nominees would be required to sign an agreement that if they win, they'll relinquish all assets to a disinterested blind trust, not family members. This agreement would be monitored annually, or more frequently, at the request of Congress.

Family members would be excluded from consideration for any position, at any level, in any administration, paid or unpaid with the obvious exception of the First Gentleman or First Lady.

Vice presidential nominees would have to meet the same standards.

If these or similar requirements were to go into effect, a side benefit could well be an increase in the quality of candidates.

What must not happen is that we become inured to the changes Trump has imposed on his Presidency and, by default, the country. He cannot be allowed to set precedent. We cannot accept, as normal Presidential behavior, Trump's continual lying about everything great and small, his racist and xenophobic comments and policies, his denigration of anyone he doesn't like, his corruption and the tolerance of corruption in his administration, his petty vindictiveness, his daily attack on the Constitution— and that's just a start.

This Presidency is a nightmare. And it's one of our own making.

The norms listed above are meant to be examples. Make your own list of norms that need to be formalized. Send it to your Senators and Representatives and others who are in positions to make them reality.

Henry Ford said, "The only mistake is one from which we learn nothing." The past 18 months have yielded a lot of mistakes, all caused by the biggest mistake of all. Procedures and policies need to be in place to prevent that from happening again.

We have an obligation to ourselves and future generations that anyone as flawed as Trump is never again allowed access to one of the most important and consequential positions on the planet.

29 AUGUST 2018

IN SUPPORT OF
A PRESIDENTIAL ELECTION COMMISSION

"It's always darkest before it becomes pitch black."
—SENATOR JOHN MCCAIN

*"...we'll get through these challenging times. We will come
through them stronger than before."*
— SENATOR JOHN MCCAIN

September 11, 2001 was a shock unlike any experienced by
this country. Just seeing that date, even now, conjures up
the stuff of nightmares. It turned out there were warnings
and flashing red lights ignored by people who could have
made a difference. Lessons learned were detailed by the 9/11
Commission; our security and defense changed as a result of
their work. We came through that time stronger than before.

Our country is in trouble again, but this time the trouble
comes from within. Red lights are flashing.

If the past 19 months have shown anything, it's that
the current political process isn't functioning at anything

approaching optimum. It hasn't been working well for a long time. Trump just made the apparent, manifestly obvious.

There's a lot that needs to be addressed. We have a President who has contorted the administrative branch into a self-serving home for corruption. We have a Congress, that is thus far, unwilling to say enough is enough. We have an election system that an eleven-year-old hacked in 10 minutes. More people stay home than bother to vote. Our elected representatives average 30 hours a week raising money for their next election; that doesn't leave much time to work for us. Electioneering never stops and billions are spent. Many of our institutions are headed by hacks as payback for political support; the fact they have no experience or knowledge to do the job seems beside the point.

And finally, like the sword of Damocles hanging over all of our politics and government, is the root of all evil. Money feeds the system; it buys votes and politicians; lobbyists are unelected lawmakers. The system is feeding on itself and there is a level of corruption, that left unchecked, will leave us with a government by and for the rich—an oligarchy—lethal to a democratic republic.

We've been like the proverbial frog happily swimming in water that's ever so slowly getting warmer. It's hard to discern the difference a few degrees make over a long period of time, until we realize how close we are to disaster. As if to prove how perilous the situation is, we've actually chosen to elect a demagogue and wannabe despot as President of the United States. We chose a petty man of no honor or virtue, whose goal is to divide and conquer for his own ends. He does not serve this county. He serves himself.

We've reached a nadir in recent American politics. Trump didn't cause this. But he is the result.

The cause is a lack of attention to slow moving changes that, like dominos, start with a simple move but affect everything along the way.

It starts with money. Citizen's United acted as steroids for an already existing problem. Laws are passed only with the support of big money—to benefit big money. We need to find other ways to finance elections other than the legal bribery system now in place.

It's both stunning and logical that the candidate with the most money wins elections 91percent of the time. Different procedures could reduce the need for outsized money; for instance, by reducing the campaign season to weeks instead of months or years, the amount needed would also be significantly reduced.

There needs to be guardrails on the office of President to help assure that basic norms are formalized; like requiring the release of income tax returns and the same security clearance as any other high office. Requisites need to be set for cabinet level positions in terms of knowledge and experience, so they are no longer doled out as rewards for loyalty.

Democracy thrives when people participate. To that end, the election process needs to address ways to increase the percentage of people who vote. Given the vulnerability of states to hacking and their increasingly inventive ways to repress voting, new procedures already in use need to be studied that reduce these vulnerabilities while increasing turnout —for instance, moving to a stamp free, vote-by-mail system. Higher voter turnout rates also make it harder for outside influences to affect the outcome. Some countries actually require citizens to vote.

A way to address these needs and others is for Congress to establish a Presidential Election Commission. Like the 9/11 Commission, it needs to be independent and nonpartisan—its mission: to identify existing problems and produce recommendations.

The country is in serious danger; voters are giving up and disengaging. They see corruption and manipulation everywhere. When Senator Lindsey Graham (R-NC) said that the tax bill had to pass or donations would stop, that's a problem. It's a problem because he's right. And, it's a problem because when the tax law did pass, the next day the GOP Reelection Committee received a big donation from the Kochs, though minuscule compared to their tax savings. It wouldn't be much different if Democrats were in charge.

These are massive problems, but they are solvable. They have to be.

The dark humor quote by the late John McCain, "It's always the darkest before it becomes pitch black," only applies if we don't respond to a clearly identified need. It's time to shed some light and solve the problems. He also wrote so eloquently in his farewell statement, "We always believe in the promise and greatness of America... we never hide from history, we make history."

Here's a chance to do just that, and to "come through this, stronger than before."

THE ELEPHANT IN THE ROOM

"We have a small man, a vile man, a mean man, a corrupt man, a dishonest man running a criminal regime."
—STEVE SCHMIDT, FORMER REPUBLICAN STRATEGIST
DESCRIBES DONALD TRUMP.

The elephant in the room is no longer the Republican Party. Not anymore. The GOP is MIA. When offered the choice of principle and decency or power, with few noteworthy exceptions, the party leaders and the Republican Congress chose power. With any other President of either party, you didn't have to choose. But not with Trump; principle and decency have, from day one, not been options. Now perhaps, we have to add sanity.

This is no longer the party of Reagan and Lincoln. This is a party full of Trump sycophants led intellectually (using that term loosely) by the likes of the white supremacist twins Steve Bannon, from afar, and Stephen Miller, whispering in his ear. It's a party that tolerates corruption and accepts pettiness and banality as the price to pay for having their puppet in the White House, as erratic and impulsive as he may be.

Apparently, the cost for selling the party's soul amounts to tax cuts for those who don't need it, deregulation that damages the environment and screws the consumer, and judges who will validate those decisions and whatever else may be coming.

For some Republicans, the cost is too great. Those in office are released when they decide they can no longer win back home and refuse to goose step to Trump's tune. Decent people like Jeff Flake and Bob Corker, and a few others, may live to fight another day because they chose not to give up their principles for power. That will be remembered. Then there are the unelected leaders who no longer support a party that used to be theirs—one of principle cloaked in decency.

These people are legends; strategists, journalists, leaders with unquestioned Republican and conservative street cred, and they're either timing themselves out or actually leaving the party: Steve Schmidt, Joe Watkins, David Brooks, George Will, Nicole Wallace, Jennifer Rubin, Bret Stephens, Susan Del Percio, Bill Kristal, Charlie Sykes, Rick Tyler, Elise Jordon, Max Boot, David Frum, David Jolly. And more. All have deep roots and commitments to Republican and conservative values.

Some, like George Will, are so concerned about where Trump is taking this nation that he's advising Republicans and conservatives to vote for Democrats in the midterms. Think about that. He's asking Democrats to do what Republicans in

Congress will not—to do their job—to provide oversight of a Presidency run amok. George Will is not a traitor to the cause or his party. He's a patriot. He's putting the country first.

Joe Scarborough put it succinctly. "The Republican party he (Trump) leads, no longer deserves to survive." For Former Speaker John Boehner, it's already a *fait accompli.* He said, "This is the President's party, but it is no longer the Republican Party."

This nation needs a healthy two-party system where ideas and policies are debated among people who love this country above all else. When we can be assured that those people already possess the prerequisite character that encompasses empathy, decency, honor and trustworthiness, we can also be assured that proposed solutions to problems will be offered in good faith for the benefit of the country. But you can't get there until those prerequisites are in place—and they never will be with Trump.

The elephant in the room is no longer the Republican Party. It's Trump. He's taking up all the air and space, crowding out the decent and thoughtful, breaking everything he comes in contact with, creating crisis after crisis. Loyalty to him, not the Constitution, is all that is his measure of worth. Most of all, his Presidency is breaking faith with the American people. And, worst of all, he doesn't care.

We're so much better than this. Or, we used to be.

This will not last forever. At some point, we will need to come together in reconciliation if a viable two-party system is to survive. In the meantime, it's heartening to see those Republicans, who care deeply for the standards professed by their party, come out and come together to say 'Enough.'

If we are very, very lucky, perhaps Trump, as he glimpses his future—one that surely holds impeachment or the application of the 25th Amendment—will also decide to say 'Enough'— or in his case, 'Uncle.'

13 SEPTEMBER 2018

TRUMP'S UNDERMINING OF THE PRESS

"Our liberty depends on freedom of the press."
— THOMAS JEFFERSON

"The press should just keep its mouth shut."
—STEVE BANNON

The past nineteen months have seen the erosion of trust in American institutions in ways only our worst enemies could have wished. The intelligence community, the FBI, the Judiciary, the Justice Department, the State Department— Trump seems to think these institutions are his to command and that loyalty to him, not the Constitution, is the standard for their existence. He publicly questions their findings; insults and denigrates them on the world stage. What more could Russia want?

Trump has attacked American institutions generally, but none more than the media because, unlike the others, the press is an ever present source of information. Its job, across a variety of platforms, is to report events as they happen, here and across the globe. At its best, it's an independent arbiter of the truth. Obviously, this includes reporting news from the administration—and increasingly, the press has become the target of Trump's wrath.

A free press, the essence of democracy is now, according to Trump, "The enemy of the people." They are "scum," "disgusting," "liars," "the most dishonest humans," "vicious," "fools," "horrible," "America's biggest enemy."

Think of that—not Russia, not North Korea, not Iran, not even ISIS, but according to Trump, the American press is "America's biggest enemy."

Leslie Stahl, in a discussion with Trump prior to a *60 Minutes* interview, asked him why he demeans and vilifies the press so much. In a rare moment of truth, Trump replied, "I do it to discredit you all so that when you write negative things about me, no one will believe you."

On this, he has done a magnificent job. The term, 'fake news' is now ubiquitous. If he doesn't like a particular article, or reporter, or network, or book, or forum, or platform—it's 'fake news.' Articles critical of him or his policies are relegated to the trash heap of 'fake news.'

He may be as dumb as a dodo, but when it comes to manipulating an eager and fearful public, looking for both validation and scapegoats, he's a genius.

The first time he insults and slanders a person or publication, it's shocking. But that shock rapidly fades; like any good demagogue, repeat, rinse, and repeat. Repetition is the key. If you hear it all the time, it becomes expected. He can start a sentence and his followers finish it. The lie becomes truth while what is accurately reported becomes 'fake news.' Trump is Orwell's reality on steroids.

The prestigious *Columbia Journalism Review* cautions that these attacks on the press are really an attack on facts. Citing NYU professor Jay Rosen on the impact of media bashing, "If we can't agree on what the facts are, if there are no facts because they're in endless dispute, there is no accountability." Trump actually said, "Don't believe what you're reading or seeing." He has managed to delegitimize truth and, in the process, any accountability for his actions because there's no widely accepted version of what they are. How fortunate for him.

Here's a dose of truth. In terms of the popular vote, Trump came in third with "I'm sitting this one out" winning, Clinton second and Trump last. And his support is waning. Bigly.

Here's another dose of truth. Words have consequences. When the President of the United States says the press is "America's greatest enemy," what is a Trump 'patriot' to do when confronted with a reporter? The legal defense practically writes itself.

It's prophetic that the Founders were able to predict so far into the future. Thomas Jefferson said,

"No experiment can be more interesting than that we are now trying, and which we trust will end in establishing the fact, that man may be governed by reason and truth. Our first object should be to leave open to him all the avenues to truth. The most effectual hitherto found, is the freedom of the press. It is, therefore, the first shut up by those who fear the investigation of their actions."

As if to prove Jefferson's caution, Steve Bannon summed up this administration's view when he told *The New York Times* that the press should just "Keep its mouth shut."

Should that happen, this great experiment, "that man may be governed by reason and truth," comes to an end.

There will be heroes after all this is over. Counted high among them will be the publishers, reporters, commentators, networks, journalists and others covering all the platforms who have refused to keep their collective mouths shut; and who, amid threats, insults, and intimidation, have persevered in their efforts to tell the truth.

WHAT WILL IT TAKE?
(PART III)

"One of the saddest lessons of history is this: If we've been bamboozled long enough, we tend to reject any evidence of the bamboozle. We're no longer interested in finding the truth. The bamboozler has captured us. It's simply too painful to acknowledge, even to ourselves, that we've been taken."

— CARL SAGAN

"The people have often made mistakes, but given time and the facts, they will make the corrections."

—HARRY S. TRUMAN

Trump's one comment that will likely serve as the exemplar of his Presidency is this: *"I can stand in the middle of 5th Avenue and shoot somebody and wouldn't lose any voters, ok? It's, like, incredible."* Yup, it's incredible all right. He believes his voters are willing to overlook a crime because they happen to like the criminal. What an insult to their intelligence and judgment—not to mention sense of decency.

So, what happens when not one, but 2,975 people die on his watch? When Trump visited Puerto Rico following the devastation caused by Hurricane Maria, tossing rolls of paper towels at survivors, he bragged that officials should be "very proud" that hundreds didn't die from Marie as in "a real catastrophe like Katrina." And, he rated his administration's response to the disaster a 10—on a scale from 1 to 10—with "only" 64 deaths.

Independent researchers from George Washington University beg to differ. Their report determined that almost 3,000 people died, mostly in the aftermath of the hurricane. Blame for these deaths rests on the lack of power, safe drinking water, and access to health care and medical resources. But those are just categories. Providing the details makes these deaths more understandable in terms of the real life, long-term, impact of Maria.

People died from not getting dialysis or other maintenance medical treatment, from running out of medication, from heat strokes and dehydration, from heart attacks due to mental and physical stress, from disease and infections because of lack of sanitation.

These deaths were a result of not days, but weeks and months of negligence by this government.

To put this in context, these numbers make Hurricane Maria America's worst natural disaster in over a century, and comes close to the number of people killed in the terrorist attacks of 9/11.

Yet even with that knowledge, Trump had the *chutzpah* to call his administration's response to Hurricane Maria an "unsung success." Perhaps that's because dead people can't sing, and those who lost loved ones somehow aren't in the mood.

And, then he Tweeted, not in empathy—but to divert blame—saying those numbers are lies made up by Democrats. Not a single 'I'm so sorry for these tragic losses.' Or 'We need to learn lessons about getting resources to locales like Puerto Rico and the US Virgin Islands so that help is delivered after, not just before and during the event. And I'm going to set up an independent Commission to see that happens.' But nada. Zip. Zilch.

The fact that Puerto Rico is an island 'surrounded by water' is no excuse; the United States can get resources and help to remote war-torn areas of the world at the drop of a hat. But we can't get resources to Puerto Rico 1,500 miles away? Because it's an island? Surrounded by water?

There's only one word that adequately describes why people died—it's a painful word that shows a lack of care, concern, even interest—that word is 'neglect.' And that's a crime. It actually is a crime. Child Protective Services removes children from homes if there's evidence of neglect, but what happens when an entire people are neglected by their own government? Are there really no consequences?

One can't help but wonder if more help would have come sooner and stayed longer if Puerto Rico had Electoral College votes to award, or if these same American citizens had lived in Alabama or Mississippi, or if a Trump Tower had been located in San Juan. The bottom line is that the vast majority of these deaths weren't caused by the hurricane itself, but by neglect following the hurricane. Many, maybe most, of these deaths, were preventable. And this administration is culpable.

And, now the Trump administration has made a decision that is completely irrational. They transferred $10 million from FEMA, and another $29 million from The Coast Guard, to ICE for immigrant detention beds, deportation, and removal, right in the middle of hurricane season. Those funds weren't taken from administrative costs or other non-essential line items, but from Response and Recovery, and Mission Support.

It has to be difficult to accomplish two horrendous things simultaneously, but never doubt this administration's ability to rise to the occasion. Taking money from FEMA at a time when national disasters are most likely to occur, to fund the other national disaster designed to stop (illegally) refugee immigration while continuing to separate parents and children, has got to be the double whammy of all time.

This much is clear. The President is the head of this administration. He is the ultimate authority and carries the ultimate responsibility for what happens on his watch. This Congress will not hold him accountable. Will the voters?

If one hypothetical death on 5th Avenue isn't enough for Trump voters to jump ship, are 2,975 real human souls enough? If not, what will it take? Seriously. What will it take?

THE KAVANAUGH HEARING

"This week was a stress test for the American order. This is a triumph of common sense."
—HISTORIAN JON MEACHAM REFERRING TO SEN. FLAKE'S CALLING FOR
FURTHER INVESTIGATION OF BRETT KAVANAUGH

For the first time in a long time, perhaps the dam of oppositional politics has sprung a leak and maybe, just maybe, it is on the way to finally being broken. For the first time in a long time, while the entire country watched, we've seen a range of filtered and unfiltered behaviors covering the spectrum of human response. And, at the end, a remarkable Congressional profile in courage that came about as a result of respect, friendship, and the power of two women holding open an elevator door.

The Judiciary Committee's Hearing on Donald Trump's nomination of Brett Kavanaugh for the Supreme Court had been the scene of the same tribal politics that's been driving us further and further apart. We watched as Dr. Christine Blasey Ford and Judge Brett Kavanaugh presented, not just their story, but themselves. By the end of the day, we knew these people—seen to some extent through our own prism perhaps, but seen nonetheless.

We heard behaviors recounted that made us gasp in horror. We saw behaviors from Senators we thought we knew but, under stress and anger, a whole new side erupted into foaming accusations that could only push colleagues further away. We saw behaviors that were confrontational, petulant, entitled and self-serving; mean and partisan in the extreme.

Anyone with an ounce of reasonable objectivity was left wanting more information. As Senator Flake said, regardless of which side you came down on, some doubt would always remain. Repeatedly, the need for further investigation was expressed. Even if Kavanaugh were to be confirmed, there would always be a question about his role in the alleged assault and the credible accusations of at least two other women which would never be investigated. Time and again, Kavanaugh and the Republicans on the Committee chose not to ask for an FBI investigation that could, on the positive side, confirm his testimony and clear his name.

The one Republican on the Committee who was most likely to vote against confirmation was Senator Jeff Flake from Arizona. Then he announced he would vote to confirm.

But something intervened; something remarkable happened. Two women, Ana Maria Archila and Maria Gallagher, confronted Flake as he got on an elevator. They held the door open. They told him they had been sexually assaulted. They demanded that he look at them as they yelled their anger at having been ignored when they came forward and that this must not happen now. They intervened in his life. They made him attend to their pain.

Senator Flake returned to the hearing as each member summed up their arguments for or against confirmation. The camera stayed on Flake as his good friend, Senator Chris Coons (D–DE), gave his summary. He ended by repeating yet again the need for further investigation by the FBI. And then Flake stood and asked Senators Klobuchar and Coons to join him in conference away from the rest of the Committee.

We watched as four people who at least tried to change the trajectory of history: the two women who stopped that elevator with reminders that pleas for help and acknowledgement of assault must not be ignored, a Democratic Senator presenting logical non–partisan arguments, and one Republican Senator who said it was time to pause and investigate further before moving on the nomination. Senator Coons and the two women were the motivators but it was Senator Flake whose actions could have been responsible for assuring a lifetime appointment would not be given to someone who, depending on the information provided by the FBI, could be found to be ethically and judicially unqualified.

Senator Flake was a profile in courage that day. His colleague, the late Senator John McCain, would have been proud.

One person, any one person, can change history. In the long run, that may be the longest lasting and most important lesson of all. Unfortunately, unable to convince any of his

Republican colleagues to investigate further, Flake voted with the majority to confirm Kavanaugh, thereby changing the makeup of the Court for perhaps decades to come.

For conservatives—mission accomplished. For justice—to be determined.

13 OCTOBER 2018

THE POLITICS OF DIVISION

"The ideal subject of totalitarian rule is not the convinced Nazi or the dedicated Communist, but people for whom the distinction between fact and fiction, true or false, no longer exist."
—HANNAH ARENDT, *THE ORIGINS OF TOTALITARIANISM*

Who would have thought 38 percent of voters would choose to support someone who engages in bullying tactics as a default reaction, who thinks of his own needs and ego first—and last, who belittles and mocks anyone who disagrees with him—whether a private citizen or head of state—who demonizes large swaths of people and nations, who marginalizes fellow citizens, who lies as easily as he breathes, who thrives on disharmony and manipulation. He's graceless and tacky, with a mean streak that's meant to sow divisiveness. Yet Trump supporters choose not just to subject themselves to those behaviors, they encourage it. And participate in it. Some even adopt his traits.

This devotion, regardless of what Trump does, gives meaning and context to the concept of 'cult'—an automatic obedience to The Leader, no matter what he does or says, no matter how it flies in the face of truth and just plain common sense.

Whether Democrat or Republican, conservative or liberal, we're watching this country being torn apart, but it has nothing to do with these labels. Regardless of what we call ourselves, this animosity bordering on hate, this distrust of each other, this tearing apart of families and relationships, is based on whether or not we support Trump.

People aren't ending friendships or fear speaking a political opinion because they disagree with Trump's fiscal or trade policies, or the role of government; all that is baked into the politics of a two-party system. That's just the normal push and pull of policy debates, but that's not what's causing the contentious national divide or driving away thoughtful conservatives in droves.

It's Trump. For Trump and his supporters, compromise and cooperation are relics of a political past. If you publically disagree with him, you will find yourself being mocked and a subject of scorn. His former Republican opponents in the Senate and House are now his lackeys, and it has nothing to do with newly gained respect for him or themselves—they've simply decided the ends justify the means—lowered taxes for the wealthy, conservative judges, a booming stock market— that's enough.

Souls, sold. Costs, huge.

Like most autocrats, Trump himself is easy to manipulate; give him positive attention, compliments and praise; court him like you would an abusive spouse. Meanwhile, he's also a skilled manipulator as politicians learn to walk the thin line, avoiding confrontation at all cost, crossing him at their own risk. Go along to get along. That pretty much defines the Republicans in the House and Senate.

This divided country is the measure of Trump's success. His purpose is to set Americans against each other based on race, religion, country of origin, politics, and now, even gender. Like that abusive spouse who isolates their victim, there is never room for negotiation, compromise, or discussion.

Trump offers his supporters a chance to be just like him, to take on his characteristics, to bask in his glory even if they debase themselves in the process. Here's a small example: men and women wearing shirts that say, 'Grab 'um by the pussy!' Do they really approve of their children and spouses assaulting others? Or being assaulted? Do they really want to throw everyone in jail who opposes Trump? If, as Trump said, Democrats are "dangerous," evil" and "the party of crime," don't criminal and dangerous people belong in jail? The message is clear. Be afraid. Quit protesting and shut up. Or else.

Russia, ISIS, and every enemy who wishes us ill must be ecstatic about what's happening. We are imploding from within and doing more damage to ourselves than they ever could.

Iconic conservatives like Max Boot and George Will are imploring Republicans to vote for Democrats in the November midterm election to provide some constraint on Trump's worst instincts. Two more years like the last two and we may not have a democratic republic left to defend.

The Founders sought to protect us from the tyrannies

that have overcome other democracies, and to avoid the usurpation of power by a person or single group for their own benefit. We need that system of checks and balances. But first, it has to exist and, currently, it does not. That's what this election, in particular, is all about.

There will always be disagreements and divisions in a country as large and diverse as ours, but when we start seeing our neighbor as our enemy, we're in trouble. When we're afraid to state our political views, we're in trouble. When we're attacked because we dare to disagree, we're in trouble. When facts no longer matter, we're in trouble.

But pendulums swing. Maybe this election will provide the nudge leading the country back to a place where decency, dignity, empathy, truthfulness, and concern for others do matter. One can hope. And vote.

28 OCTOBER 2018

WORDS MATTER.
TRUMP'S INCITE VIOLENCE.

"Speech has power. Words do not fade. What starts as a sound, ends in a deed."—A.J. HERSCHEL

Fourteen people targeted for death. Among them: two former Presidents, a former Democratic candidate, the offices of one of the world's foremost news organizations, an international philanthropist who contributes to liberal and Democratic causes, two Congresswomen, a Senator, a former head of the CIA, a former Director of National Intelligence, a former Attorney General, a former Vice President, a film celebrity, an environmentalist, and Democratic donor.

These bombs, these terrorist attacks, these mass political assassination attempts were targeted at high profile Trump opponents; prominent Democrats that Trump has vilified in tweets or at rallies.

These terror attacks are completely predictable. What happened should not surprise anyone.

Trump casts those critical of him as evil, as the enemy— not just of him, but of the country. He revels in encouraging violence. He stokes fear and hatred.

Authorities hunted and arrested a suspect. But no one has to hunt for the cause.

The bully in the White House has inspired and incited violence—"I'd like to punch him in the face," "the audience hit back and that's what we need more of," in reference to fights breaking out at his rallies. Trump told audiences he would pay legal fees if they engaged in violence against protesters and were arrested: "knock the crap out of them," "maybe he should have been roughed up," referring to a protester. Trump said, "any guy who can do a body slam— he's my kind of guy!"—this in reference to a Montana congressman convicted of assaulting a journalist.

Trump has cast Democrats as 'angry,' 'ruthless,' 'unhinged,' 'treasonous,' 'un-American,' 'a mob,' 'the party of crime,' and 'dangerous.' He vilifies *CNN* and any media that disagrees with him as 'fake news.' One caller to *The Boston Globe* said, "You're the enemy of the people, and we're going to kill every fucking one of you." Except for the threat at the end, every word is Trump's.

Trump and the Alt Right, the Nationalists and conspiracy theorists, have had a field day with George Soros, accusing the holocaust survivor of providing signs for all Trump's protesters and paying them to rally against him. No one, not Soros himself, is that rich. Soros was even accused of planting the women in the elevator during the Kavanaugh hearing and funding the caravan heading to the border. Trump offers no evidence for any of this. He never does. Unless you count the phrase, "People are saying… " (fill in the blank).

Trump has managed to conflate his opponents as enemies, and his enemies are the country's enemies. He stokes anger and fear and makes all opponents a threat.

"What you sow, so shall you reap." Trump throws the bombs; it cannot be a surprise when someone picks them up. That is the consequence.

The person who made and mailed these bombs is the criminal, but he acted at the instigation of the President of the United States. The defense is predictable. When the President says these targeted people are evil and a danger to the country, then doesn't any real patriot have a duty to respond?

But who does Trump blame for the pipe bombs? He deflects to The Media. In an editorial in the Miami Herald, Fabiola Santiago writes, "hate speech is the language of this nation's business for this President," and "American journalists risk their lives covering wars and unrest around the world. Be assured: we are not going to be silenced at home…"

The job description of POTUS is briefly summarized by the Oath of Office. Simply put, it's to "preserve, protect and defend the Constitution of the United States." Every time he denigrates the free press and encourages violence against those with whom he disagrees, he is violating his oath. It isn't a stretch to consider the President of the United States as a co–defendant should his hate speech generate the violence he so frequently encourages.

08 NOVEMBER 2018

AN OPEN LETTER TO REPUBLICANS

"Instead of the 'blue wave' that pundits predicted, it's more like a blue tide—rolling slowly, but inexorably in and washing away the Republican Party."—DAVID GRAHAM, THE ATLANTIC

Dear Republicans,

Remember that old line you used when you were trying to break up with someone—"It's not you, it's me." That same line, with a slight modification, applies to the mid-term election results on Nov. 6th. The loss of The People's House has little to do with rejecting traditional Republicans policies. When Trump implored us to vote as if he was on the ticket, a lot of people took him literally. So, in terms of election rejection, that line should read, "It's not you, it's him."

This election was a referendum on the Trump Presidency and had little to do with the Republican Party as it was before Trump. But, it does have a lot to do with the party now.

So, to all those traditional moderate Republicans who went

along to get along, in order to get the tax cut, deregulation, and conservative judges, ask yourselves whether losing the House, along with the respect from so many voters, was worth it.

You've lost seven key governorships—including those that gave Trump his Electoral College win (Michigan, Pennsylvania and Wisconsin). Seven legislative chambers flipped from Republican to Democrat. And, you've lost the House. Here's one interpretation why—you lost respect for the American people. In contorting yourselves into a pretzel to justify your unconditional support of Trump, by ignoring his excesses that go against everything America and the Republican Party have stood for, perhaps you'll realize your voters lost respect for you.

The House of Representatives is the People's House and is the purest political voice of America. This election sent a lot of messages and, in doing so, we elected a record number of women—110 and counting. We elected more veterans, younger and more diverse candidates who actually represent us— the constituents they serve.

They made it clear what we were voting for by focusing on local issues.

And, here's what we voted against:

We voted against Trump's constant lying and his assault on objective truth.

We voted against his fear mongering, his governing by conspiracy theories, his blatant racism, sexism, and xenophobia, his increasingly vicious attacks on anyone who disagreed with him.

We rejected his ignorance and were embarrassed by his actions on the world stage.

We rejected the ubiquitous corruption emanating from this administration.

We rejected his lack of dignity, integrity and decency, his demagogy, his White Nationalism, and his degradation of the Office of the Presidency.

We rejected his basic lack of humanity and concern for others.

We rejected his immigration policy of separating parents and children which is worthy of the most repulsive and repressive authoritarian dictatorships—the low mark of this administration, and a low mark in the history of this nation.

And surprise, surprise! It turns out that it's not just 'The economy, stupid.' after all. The latest *NBC-Wall Street Journal* poll found that 68 percent of those polled approved of the economy, but 58 percent thought the nation was on the wrong track. And that helps explain the results of the midterms.

And surprise, surprise! It turns out character does matter.

Maybe, hopefully, Republicans in Congress, as well as other officials, will recognize one other truth. It's no longer acceptable to ignore, enable, or otherwise fail to provide oversight in exchange for power. Do your job. Represent the best of who we are. Represent all of us.

That's how you make America great.

Sincerely Yours,

America

18 NOVEMBER 2018

THE 2018 ELECTION POSTMORTEM

"Loyalty to the country, always. Loyalty to the government when it deserves it."—MARK TWAIN

"No matter how far the ideological pendulum swings in the short term, in the end the bedrock common sense of the American people will prevail."—CHARLES KRAUTHAMMER

At this point, the election isn't over. Recounts are ongoing in Florida and results are still to be determined in other states. There are positive and not so hot results for both parties, but the big winners are Democrats and democracy.

Although it will be awhile before final numbers are in, more people voted in this election than any other midterm in history. In terms of percentage, 2018 is rivaled only by 1914. At this point, based on data from *Vox*, *The New York Times*, and others, an estimated 114 million ballots were cast—a massive jump from 83 million in 2014. That's a big deal. And, that's thanks to Trump.

Trump drove both parties to the polls. Republicans came out to support him and Democrats came out to vote against him. He wasn't on the ballot but, as he said, "A vote for (fill in the blank) is a vote for me." The voters agreed. He lost.

Here are the key takeaways reported by *Pew Research, Vox, The New York Times, Business Insider, The Cook Political Report,* and others—with the caveat that it's still early and while numbers may change, the results are likely to remain the same.

The results of this election represents our diverse country more than any other before it. More than 200 candidates running for statewide and congressional races were black, Latino, Asian American, Native American, and LGBTQ. More than 80 of these candidates won (*NBC News, Pew Research*). The average age of the newbies in the House is a decade younger than their counterparts, and there are more veterans in Congress than ever before.

There are many 'firsts.' Michigan and Minnesota elected the first two Muslim women to Congress. Tennessee elected their first female Senator, a Republican. Massachusetts elected their first black Congresswoman. Kansas—very red Kansas—elected the state's first lesbian House member, and one of two Native American House members; a woman beat Kris Kobach for Kansas governor—the self-anointed leader in voter suppression. Colorado elected the country's first openly gay Governor. A Democrat won a Senate race in Arizona for the first time in 30 years, and that new Senator is a woman.

105 women were elected to Congress—86 Democrats and 19 Republicans; 42 are women of color and all are

Democrats.

Millennials and Gen Y voted in record numbers going from 17 percent of those eligible in the last election to 40 percent.

Twenty STEM candidates were elected—folks with science, technology, engineering and math backgrounds. Hooray! Let's hope they get assigned to the right committees.

In the first national vote since Trump's election, there were six million more votes for Democrats than Republicans.

Trump endorsed 75 candidates; 21 won. Obama endorsed 74 candidates; 39 won. (*Brookings.edu*)

More than two dozen NRA backed politicians lost their seats in the House. The new majority in the House includes dozens who, like rank and file members of the NRA, support stricter gun laws. This includes a winning candidate from Georgia who lost her son to gun violence.

Seven Governor's mansions switched from red to blue including key states that gave Trump his Electoral College win; **eight legislative chambers flipped to blue.** This compares to an average of 12 chambers that typically change hands during midterms. That a modicum of good news for Republicans.

Democrats gained the Governor's mansion and both legislative chambers in Colorado, Illinois, Maine, New Mexico, New York and Nevada bringing their total number of trifecta states to 14; Democrats busted up Republican trifectas in Kansas, Michigan, Wisconsin, and New Hampshire. Republicans still maintain 22 states where they control both legislative branches as well as governorships. With dozens of races still too close to call, Democrats won at least 370 new state legislative seats nationwide (*Axios*). They have a way to go to make up the 900 lost during the eight years of the Obama administration, but it's a start.

Republican Senators benefited from supporting Trump. They held their two-seat advantage and may expand their majority depending on runoffs and recounts. This will be vital when it comes to fending off an impeachment conviction, securing confirmations on judgeships, and staff positions.

Democrats needed to pick up 23 seats to gain a majority in the House. Their firm number now is 34 with the final count likely to approach 40 seats.

Although it appears Democrats lost the three of marquee races in Florida, Texas and Georgia, two of the three are close enough to require either a runoff or recount. Two of the three are red states and one is purple—but they clearly trended blue in these races.

This was the first nationwide election since Trump was elected and the results represent the Democratic Party's best midterm performance since Watergate. This was not a 'Blue Tsunami,' but it was an ever so slowly building Blue Wave that became a flood.

It's clear that Trump cost his party the House and helped create new swing states.

In terms of future prospects, look to demographics. In general, Democratic voters were younger, more diverse, residing in large cities and suburbs, female, and more educated. These groups are increasing.

For Republicans, their voting strength was in rural areas. Their largest demographic is older white males. This group is decreasing.

So, what are the implications for the future? The answer

to this question predicts the near future of the Republican Party: *Did Trump help or hurt the Republican position with minorities and women?*

And there you have it.

These next two years will determine whether we have a Republic by, for and of the people, or an autocracy. And, whether we have a government with three coequal branches, and not an Executive Branch that runs roughshod over the other two—with their acquiescence.

The people have spoken; time will determine who is listening.

25 NOVEMBER 2018

THE GAMING OF U.S. FOREIGN POLICY

"Political language is designed to make lies sound truthful and murder respectable."—GEORGE ORWELL

Transactional politics. At the most basic, it's *quid pro quo*—you do something for me and I do something for you. Everyone wins. It's like the political version of 'Let's Make a Deal.'

No one gets anything for nothing. But, with the Trump administration, it's a zero sum game. Both sides can't win; there has to be a winner and a loser. And, it has to happen in real time—not over time.

Trump filters diplomacy and interactions between nations based on how much they flatter him, the length of the red carpet they roll out, and personal and financial ties he or his family have. Like everything else, it's about him.

An example of transactional politics and foreign policy

gone wrong is our relationship with Saudi Arabia. If there is a single nation responsible for the rise of Islamic terrorism, it's this country. Fifteen of the 9/11 terrorists were Saudis. But Trump didn't include them in the Muslim ban. Ever wonder why? As Trump said so eloquently during one of his rallies, "I make a lot of money with them. They buy all sorts of my stuff. All kinds of toys from Trump. They pay me millions and hundreds of millions. Why wouldn't I like them?"

Well, here's a reason: they brutally slaughtered a U.S. resident and journalist employed by an American newspaper, and they made progressively ridiculous attempts to cover it up. Trump bought into each one.

Jamal Khashoggi did not leave the Embassy in Istanbul as the Saudis first said. It was not a fist fight that went wrong as they next claimed. It was not an attempt at rendition (i.e. kidnapping) that went wrong—their last iteration. And, there never has been an explanation of why the Crown Prince's bodyguards and forensic surgeon, complete with bone saw, were flown to Istanbul in private jets prior to Khashoggi's appointment at the embassy.

Trump's response? With every new Saudi version of events, Trump offered support for the Saudis—finally, when even he could no longer defend the indefensible, said it was "the worst cover-up ever." Shame on them for all those botched cover-up attempts—but not a word condemning the horrific attack itself. In fact, he continued to praise the Crown Prince's leadership, calling him a 'good man' even after the Saudis finally admitted the murder and dismemberment were premeditated.

Trump is refusing to suspend the proposed $14 billion in

arms sales to Saudi Arabia as a consequence for their actions. Trump inflated that sale to $450 billion and then rounded it up to $500 billion in his latest version. Same with jobs lost in the defense sector which, according to *Politifact,* would not come close to the one million Trump claimed.

What hasn't been as widely reported is that a real estate start-up, partly owned by Jared Kushner, is looking for an investment of "at least $100 million from a private fund backed by Saudi Arabia and the UAE" (*Business Insider,* May 2018). And there's the entire 45th floor of Trump World Tower that Trump Inc. sold to the Kingdom. Groups lobbying on behalf of the Saudis stay in Trump owned hotels in New York and Washington, DC, dropping hundreds of thousands into the Trump coffers (*Politifact.com/truthometer*).

So, now we get to Trump's version of transactional diplomacy. It has nothing to do with what's right or good. It has nothing to do with American values. You can do anything —literally anything—with impunity, as long as there's a potential benefit to Trump.

We've gone a long way from 'the shining city on the hill.'

Trump still wants to sell American arms to the Saudi's, so they can continue to fight a proxy war in Yemen that's killing tens of thousands of civilians and creating humanitarian crises for millions—using the arms we've sold them. Kushner is using the Saudis and they are using us to isolate Iran. Our foreign policy is based on 'the enemy of my enemy,' etc., and Yemeni civilians are in a vice we helped create.

Now the plot really sickens. Turkey has the evidence that finally forced the Saudis' admission of guilt regarding the murder, though illogically, they continue to insist, even now, that Crown Prince Mohammed bin Salman (MBS) was unaware of the plot.

At one point, to bribe Turkey not to release evidence against MBS, Trump considered turning over what Turkey's President Erdogan wants most—a cleric living in the U.S. whom Erdogan blames for organizing a coup against him (*NBC, PBS, The Guardian, Bipartisan Policy Center*). But the CIA preempted that possibility by issuing a report stating, they believe with 'high confidence,' that MBS ordered the killing of Khashoggi.

Trump's response? Meh. A shrug. "There's really no way of knowing." "Maybe they did, maybe they didn't." He chose to believe a ruthless dictator vs. his own intelligence agency and, in doing so, "granted absolution for chopping up a *Washington Post* columnist" (Joe Scarborough, *Morning Joe*, Nov. 21, 2018). Former Ambassador Marc Ginsberg called Trump's reaction a "gut punch to American values."

Trump's response is outrageous. Every American should be offended.

We need to ask ourselves what we stand for if we allow American values to be trumped, not by an outside enemy, but by our own despot-in-training.

There appears to be no limit Trump won't go, or depth he won't sink if, (to cite another game show), 'the price is right.'

It's long past time that Congress and the American people say, "Game over."

03 DECEMBER 2018

A SCORECARD FOR SCOUNDRELS

"Synergy. Noun. The result of interaction or cooperation between two or more organizations... to produce a combined effect greater than the sum of their separate effects."—SIRI

"It's getting late early."—YOGI BERRA

I n 2016 there was a big national game/election, the outcome of which shocked one team who lost, and semi-surprised the other who won. Now there's an investigation (or post-game analysis) of that game. This investigation involves two sets of players—those defending the process (Team Trump) and the other questioning it (Team USA).

Team USA (aka The Good Guys) keeps scoring hit after hit. Team Trump (aka The Scoundrels) continues racking up swings and misses, and error after error. Keeping track of

Trump's players is exhausting; they keep going over to Team USA with inside information about what the Trump Team did, or attempted to do, to rig the big game.

Trump acts as his own Manager. No one else would take the job. And he's looking desperate. In fact, one might say the Team's biggest problem, as well as its major defense, is Trump's ignorance; total and complete ignorance about, well, everything, but especially the rules of the game. Combine that with world class unsportsmanlike conduct, and you could say Team Trump is a national debacle. Some are even talking about throwing the Manager out of the game altogether. Even their fan base is beginning to drift away.

What is especially concerning is evidence, brought forth by Team USA, that confirms a Foreign Investor bought Team Trump and manipulated the game for their mutual benefit. Trump's continual Tweets of 'no collusion' with that Foreign Investor are so predictable, that team members and fans on both sides could write Trump's Tweets for him. Unfortunately, they are unable to mimic his spelling and syntactical errors, and are considering hiring a third grader to accomplish that task to assure authenticity.

Trying to summarize the game is difficult. Team Trump has players who are also compromised by the Foreign Investor. The Manager is pleading ignorance—oops—innocence, but the scouting reports, and Team USA, say otherwise. And, as mentioned earlier, several Scoundrels are sharing their playbook with Team USA. It's been rumored that significant portions of it are in Russian.

So, let's do a play-by-play and see where we are in the postgame analysis.

Team USA documented that the Foreign Investor, via a bunch of intermediaries, lured up to 14 members of The Scoundrels to help them win the Big Game—and they took the bait. Trump and his players lied about that. Between the Manager, key players, and the foreign government, there were dozens of contacts that occurred before and after the Big Game in November 2016.

These major players took meetings, responded to emails and phone calls, and encouraged further contact. In 2015, early in the game when things didn't look promising for Team Trump, a Russian operative offered to provide political "synergy on the governmental level" to help win the game. There were even attempts to sabotage the scoreboard. According to long established league rules, all of these are major no-no's.

Turns out Manager Trump wanted to set up a concession in that foreign country; they also offered to secretly help Trump win the game. In return, the foreign country was desperate for Team Trump to remove sanctions that prevented them from lucrative trades. Every player on The Scoundrels, especially the Manager and their Foreign Investor, had something to gain from this arrangement.

Manager Trump has insisted all of this has nothing to do with him, and that whatever happened occurred without his knowledge. Tapes of conversations, documents, and testimony under oath by those defecting team members contradict him.

Finally, Manager Trump directed and coordinated the payment of significant sums from the team's recruiting budget—another major no-no—to silence two 'players' who were providing very unique and highly personal services for/ to him—so unique and personal that their awareness by fans could have impaired Trump's ability to win the game.

Team Trump was supposed to be owned by the American people but, without their knowledge or consent, its ownership seems to have transferred to the aforementioned Foreign Investor. Fans are not happy; 38 percent, plus or minus, appear to be in an ongoing state of denial. There's continuing talk about ending the game before the final innings are played—or to quote Yogi, "It's getting late early."

The final postgame analysis is still in process. While Team Trump won the game, he appears to have cheated, tossing out the rule book, and lying about what was done with his cooperation and under his direction.

The problem for Trump is that while he denies he ignored the rules, it's up to the umpires and fans to make the final call. It's a good bet that will include his permanent removal from the roster and kicking the Scoundrels out of the league. Players on Team Trump are desperate to be transferred. Alas, so far, the response has been *Nyet.*

It's been suggested that a much needed and appropriate follow-up for Trump might be a shared family getaway to a semiprivate location where all meals are provided—but not by KFC or McDonald's. They won't need to pack; their clothing, finally "Made in the USA," will also be provided, albeit somewhat limited both in scope and color. And, the throne (the one attached to the wall) will, sadly, not be in 24k gold.

22 DECEMBER 2018

TRUMP'S LUMP OF COAL
IN THE TAXPAYERS' STOCKINGS

"I would build a great wall, and nobody builds walls better than me, believe me, and I'll build them very inexpensively. I will build a great great wall on our southern border and I'll have Mexico pay for that wall."
—DONALD J. TRUMP'S PRESIDENTIAL ANNOUNCEMENT SPEECH,
JUNE 16, 2015.

Trump made this promise the foundation of his candidacy. It was his first promise to the American people. He would build a wall, and Mexico would pay for it. This theme was repeated at every rally leading up to and following the election. It became an anthem for his fans. Trump: "We're going to build a wall! Who's going to pay for the wall?" Supporters: "MEXICO!"

This single statement offers a clue into Trump, his character and his Presidency. Even before his election he must have thought himself Master of the Universe. After all, if he could run the Trump organization by demanding others obey him, he could do that as President, too.

Trump forgot he wasn't elected king. He forgot other countries are sovereign—their leaders answerable to their citizens, not him. He forgot that he will be held accountable. Or maybe he just doesn't care. Worse, maybe he believes the public doesn't care.

Remember his famous brag that he could shoot someone on 5th Avenue and his supporters would stand by him? Well, guess what? Even if that were the case, he would still be arrested, charged, indicted, and tried in a court of law. Whether he grasps this concept or not, ultimately, he is not above the law; he will be held accountable for what he says and does, and there will be consequences.

Maybe he thinks his supporters will forgive him if his first promise made as candidate is his first lie told.

Mexico is not going to pay for the wall. They never were—Presidential tantrums be damned. According to *The Wall Street Journal*, while Congress did appropriate about $1.6 billion, it's being used for repairs and replacement of existing structures, design and border security technology; but this doesn't come close to the $33 billion Trump originally demanded.

Now he wants taxpayers to fund the wall, saying he's sure Mexico will reimburse our treasury as a result of money they've saved by renegotiating NAFTA. If you believe in Santa Claus, perhaps you'll believe that, too.

And, now he has shut down the government because he didn't get his way. In fact, he said he was proud to do that. Imagine that! Proud to hold the government hostage, and put folks out of work, because Congress refuses to comply with his demand that we, the taxpayers, pay for his wall. We should change the chant: "Who's going to pay for the wall?" "I AM!" Or, probably the less grammatically correct, "ME, ME, ME!

Consider this: according to *Bloomberg News,* even this partial shutdown means 400,000 employees will work without pay, and another 350,000 will be furloughed. And, the President of the United States is so proud to have caused this.

He can't face that he's already lost. The Marist Poll at the *Marist Institute for Public Opinion* conducted a survey and reported that 57 percent vs. 36 percent say that the wall "is not a particular interest or priority for the country." Democrats, Republicans and Independents also agree, "They don't want to see a government shutdown." Well, they have it—the third shutdown in a year. Imagine that!

Taxpayers do not want to pay for his broken promises. This lie, if Pink Floyd will pardon the analogy, was the first brick in the wall—a massive wall of lies built entirely by Donald Trump.

And, that's the only wall this administration will ever be able to take credit for.

25 DECEMBER 2018

DONALD'S VERY BAD,
MOST AWFUL, WORST WEEK YET.

"Introduce a little anarchy, upset the established order and everything becomes chaos."—AUTHOR UNKNOWN.

Remember those head-spinning scenes from "The Exorcist?" It's been that kind of week. One thing happening after another—sometimes even simultaneously.

This past week before Christmas has been unlike any other in this administration—but it's important to add—thus far. It's also important to note that, by default, no other administration in recent memory can compete with this one when it comes to the unraveling of a Presidency. It's like being on a ship in a storm and constantly feeling off balance.

Even Nixon can't compare. His problems revolved around Watergate and his attempts to cover up involvement in a crime. In Trump's case, it's about the likelihood of multiple crimes by multiple people in his administration and businesses, as well as foreign governments, all revolving around one constant—a very flawed man absent of any self-awareness or sense of accountability.

So, here's a review of the überweek that was:

It became clear that Russians tried to do to the Special Counsel what they did do to Hillary Clinton. There were all kinds of rumors on social media attempting to discredit Mueller and his ability to render fair treatment. *The Washington Post* and *Business Insider* listed multiple examples of Russia's disinformation campaign. Here's just one meme of many that popped up: "Special Counsel Robert Mueller worked with radical Islamic groups to purge anti-terrorism material offensive to Muslims." The discovery of these Russian blogs and posts took care of this right wing media rant. Score one for the good guys.

Michael Flynn, Trump's former National Security Advisor, has been cooperating with Mueller's committee. This week he appeared before a federal judge for sentencing, having pled guilty to lying to the FBI about his communication with Russian officials. Most thought he would escape a jail sentence. The judge, however, was not inclined to let him off so easily, suggested that Flynn might want to postpone sentencing, and sent him back to continue his cooperation deal with Mueller. Maybe as important, the judge asked Flynn, under oath, to comment on right wing media statements that he had been coerced and entrapped by the FBI, didn't know lying to the FBI was a felony, etc. Flynn negated every one of these talking points.

Then, there was the surprise resignation of Defense Secretary James Mattis shortly after Trump announced, by

Tweet, he was pulling all U.S. troops out of Syria. Apparently, the only consultation Trump sought on the matter was from the Turkish President. Mattis, who many described as the last adult in the room—the man holding up the guardrails of this administration—made it clear he would no longer enable this President.

After Trump dropped his demand that Congress appropriate $5 billion for the border wall, and Congress agreed to fund the remaining aspects of government, Trump did an abrupt about-face. Why? Because Rush Limbaugh and Laura Ingraham criticized him, saying his supporters demanded that he keep his promise to "Build the Wall!" A new budget, containing border wall funding, was defeated in the Senate and Trump 'proudly' shut down the government.

The New York Attorney General stated that Trump and his Foundation had acted with an "astonishing pattern of illegality" by using Foundation funds for personal and campaign expenses, and promptly shut it down. Trump used the charity for his own ends, purchasing paintings of himself, among other 'charitable gifts.' Further, the President of the United States and his children are now banned from serving on the board of any New York charity. He has his hands on the nuclear button, but can't be trusted to run a charity. Imagine that!

And, the final cherry on this fruitcake of a week was the performance of the stock market. It ended with the worst December since the Depression, and the worst week before Christmas—ever. Between the uncertainty of tariffs and trade wars, a government in a constant state of chaos, Trump's negative comments about the Federal Reserve chair Jerome Powell—wondering aloud whether he could be fired—this self-induced stock market decline can be laid directly at Trump's feet.

This is not the end. It may not even be the beginning of the end. And, here's even a worse thought: It may not even be the end of the beginning. And, here's a holiday gift to the American people via the President's policy—one more refugee child died in American custody on Christmas Eve, the second such death in a month.

31 DECEMBER 2018

2018:
A REVIEW OF THE YEAR
AND IMPLICATIONS FOR THE FUTURE

"May you live in interesting times."
—PURPORTED OLD CHINESE CURSE

What a day! How many times did we say that this year? Politically, and in reference to that 'Chinese' curse, I wonder how many 'uninteresting' days we've had in 2018. For many of us, way too few.

So here we are, at the end of the year. It's traditional to stop, take a breath and consider what this year has wrought. Time to review some of the events that happened under this presidency and to consider those that will live on long after Trump is gone. So much to choose from. Every day, it seems, this administration overturned norms and altered policies that changed who we are as a country. He accomplished a lot by his standards, but he destroyed a lot by ours. But, not everything. These are just a few of the highlights and lowlights of 2018, chosen, at least in part, for their likely repercussions in the future.

The kids from Parkland—Here's an example of a horrible situation: the murder of 17 high school students in one of the worst school shootings since Sandy Hook. Its impact will endure long into the future. The survivors fought back. They got pissed and they got to work. They took charge of their lives, refused to be victims and committed themselves to change gun laws.

They started a movement ('Never Again'), set a policy goal of stricter gun safety laws and organized a nationwide protest, *March for Our Lives*, in Washington, DC that was attended by hundreds of thousand of young people. They organized students in high schools all over country who conducted local rallies and walkouts in support of comprehensive background checks. They led marches on statehouses, and they did something else— they got high school students, millennials, and post-millennials registered to vote.

According to *pewtrusts.org*, states have passed 50 new gun control laws as a direct result of efforts of Parkland's students. And, at least two dozen members of Congress, who were supported by the NRA, were defeated in November.

They have just begun.

These 'kids' are as savvy as it gets, can hold their own in national news conferences and debates, and have committed their lives to preventing further school shootings. And one of them, one day, may be president. They are changing the country. They are showing us that nothing is intractable or impossible.

The destruction of the EPA—From day one, Trump set

out to neuter this Agency. And he has. He appointed Scott Pruitt, the swampiest of creatures, who decided the EPA was his personal kingdom and proceeded to spend taxpayers' money to feather his nest. Those gory details are provided in an essay dated 3 July 2018.

Trump's promised deregulation of programs and agencies began with the EPA targeting any program that had President Obama's endorsement. According to *The New York Times*, 78 programs dealing with air pollution, drilling and extraction, water pollution, animals, toxic substances, and safety standards—just to name a few—have been scrapped. Celebratory signings of Executive Orders or bills are regularly attended by the industry likely to benefit, for example CEO's of fossil fuel industries.

Andrew Wheeler, the acting administrator appointed after Pruitt was forced out of his job on corruption charges, is a former lobbyist for a coal mining company, and already is escalating a war on children's health, according to EWG (Environmental Working Group). The EPA under Wheeler is fighting to keep a pesticide proven to cause brain damage, to repeal a rule to reduce air pollution caused by mercury, and to repeal major aspects of the Clean Power Act. EDA (Environmental Destruction Agency) is more like it.

The long-term consequences of these, and other actions, will affect the water we drink and the air we breathe. It's sickening. Literally. As things stand now, the impact will be felt for generations to come.

Supreme Court Justice Bret Kavanaugh—This farce of the hearing before the Senate Judiciary Committee culminated in the appointment of a man unfit to judge a dog show. His past statements that a sitting President should be protected from litigation did not affect his participation in the Ken Starr investigation of President Clinton. The concept that no person is above the law apparently has a glaring exception to the rule. But none of that was as disqualifying as his behavior during the hearing. He was angry, emotional and partisan, and one could not help but question his demeanor and character. There will always be an asterisk beside his name, as is still the case with Justice Thomas, because of credible accusations of sexual harassment. Kavanaugh's denial of aggressive behavior toward women, and serious drinking in his past did not agree with allegations of friends and classmates.

He could be sitting on the Court for decades to come; his appointment now makes the Court 5-4 with no one in the middle, and that could have significant impact on women's rights, criminal justice, civil rights, and voting rights for years to come.

The results of the midterm election—While this was a resounding judgment by voters on individual candidates, as importantly, it was also a judgment of Trump himself. He often said during his rallies that even though he wasn't on the ticket, we were to vote as if he were. The people did, and with dramatic results (see essay 18 November 2018).

This was a Come-to-Jesus election that was a culmination of everything that occurred since Trump was elected. Oversight by committees headed by Democrats will assure that Trump no longer has *carte blanche* to run roughshod over the Constitution, or to act unilaterally on issues, foreign and domestic, that change how we interact with each other and the world. Actions that have brought disgrace to our country, like our criminal actions taking place on southern border, can finally be dealt with.

So, here's to 2019. Let's see if lessons have been learned. And, to share a statement that has more that one meaning, 'Hindsight is always 2020.' I'll drink to that!

07 JANUARY 2019

NOT A GREAT START TO THE NEW YEAR

*"An optimist stays up until midnight to see the New Year in. A
pessimist stays up to be sure the old one leaves."*
—BILL VAUGHN

Whether an optimist or pessimist, we're beginning a
New Year with a hell of a hangover.

The stock market seems to know only zeniths and nadirs,
and we're beginning to shrug it off as highs and lows bounce
between hundreds of points—within the same day.

Much of the volatility is caused by Trump himself. We're
in a trade war with half the world, farmers can't sell a soybean,
Trump questions aloud whether he can fire the Chair of the
Federal Reserve, and he threatens to close off the southern
border. His off-the-cuff comments about China, or specific
companies like Amazon, create chaos in the markets. If there's
one consistent characteristic Trump exhibits, besides lying,
it's that he never considers the consequences of his words. Or

anything, actually.

And now we're in the midst of a government shutdown.

The Trump administration has become completely dysfunctional as we enter the third week of a partial government shutdown affecting 800,000 federal workers, uncountable contractors who will not be reimbursed when this is over, and who knows how many tangential workers whose livelihoods depend on all of them. Many services and programs to those most in need, like food stamps and housing assistance, are being curtailed.

Congress is back in session, with a Democratic majority in the House and Nancy Pelosi at the helm. She has made it clear that 'not one penny' is going to be appropriated for a wall, but she will support funding for border security. Meanwhile, Trump is demanding $5.6 billion for his wall—but the definition of what that means shifts, often within the same sentence.

Trump can't decide what it is he'll settle for; his art of the deal seems to have got up and went. First, it was a concrete wall, then a wall that you can see through, then a slatted wall with pointed tips on top, and then it's a steel wall. A steel wall that you can see through? Wonder if he'd settle for barbed wire?

Meanwhile, *The New York Times* disclosed that Trump's golf courses have been routinely and knowingly hiring undocumented workers—and have been actively hiding them from the Secret Service whose job it is to vet people who come in contact with the First Family. Years ago, news of an undocumented worker working for a presidential candidate was enough to force him to call a news conference. These days? Meh.

As an aside, Trump could, on his own, dramatically reduce the number of undocumented workers entering the U.S. if he signed an executive order requiring a big fine and significant jail time for employers convicted of not using E-Verify and hiring undocumented workers. Which, seriously, would go a long way to reducing the number of immigrants coming strictly for financial reasons vs. those applying for asylum.

Actually, for Trump, this could make a perfect test case: If convicted, could he pardon himself since he's employing them? Could a president who broke the law be indicted while in office? Could it be that he's actually above the law? Or, if convicted, could he wait to serve jail time until after he's impeached? Answers to these questions could serve as a dress rehearsal leading up to the findings of the Mueller investigation.

Meanwhile, Trump's behaving like a two-year-old with temper tantrumitus—"if I can't have my way, I'll shut down government!"

And he keeps escalating his threats. Now he's saying the shutdown could continue for months, or even years! As another exclamation point, he said he's also considering declaring a national emergency which would allow him to appropriate funds from the Department of Defense or FEMA, and all without approval from Congress. Of course, not getting funding for a wall is not a national emergency, since just six suspected terrorists on the watch list have been apprehended crossing the southern border in the first half of 2018—not the 4,000 claimed by Trump. Wow! That's a whopper even for him.

All this could end tomorrow if the Senate did their job and passed the bill that had been agreed to earlier by both Houses. If Trump vetoes it, so be it. It would then be up to

Congress to come up with the votes needed to override his veto. Or not. That's everyone doing their job.

But the Senate has surrendered its role as the 'world's greatest deliberative body,' to become the world's greatest sycophant by turning over their decision-making capability to the President. If Mitch McConnell refuses to allow a vote on a bill just because he's not sure the President would sign, he's not fulfilling the Senate's constitutional responsibility.

And Trump is not fulfilling his either. A deal was set prior to the shutdown that would have funded the government, including money for border security. Trump was willing to sign it until unelected talk radio and a conservative TV host shamed him out of it. Imagine that. The President of the United States allowing right wing media hosts to dictate public policy.

One way or another, 2019 will be a milestone year in the history of the country. The Mueller investigation will be completed (probably) as more information about Russia's connection to the Trump campaign and family finances are uncovered. We will finally discover what Putin has on Trump that has made him such a suck-up, and we'll watch as candidates from both parties rise to confront him—or Pence.

This is the year that will determine whether we survive as a Republic.

As they say, 'Buckle up.' We may be in for a rough ride.

10 JANUARY 2019

IMMIGRATION AND
THE GOVERNMENT SHUTDOWN

"The bosom of America is open to receive not only the opulent and respectable stranger but the oppressed and persecuted of all nations and religions."—GEORGE WASHINGTON, 1783

"I would build a wall of steel, a wall as high as heaven, against the admission of a single one of those Southern Europeans who never thought the thoughts or spoke the language of a democracy in their lives."
—GEORGIA GOVERNOR CLIFFORD WALKER, TO THE KLONVOKATION OF
THE KLU KLUX KLAN, 1924

"These aren't people. These are animals."
—DONALD TRUMP, MAY, 2018

Trump proffered his 'wisdom' in his first Oval Office address to the nation, and it was as enlightening and edifying as being locked in a room while the instructor teaches grammar to English Lit PhD students (but in this case the only pronouns he seems to know are 'I' and 'me).' There was nothing we didn't already know—except that so far, he's not declaring a national emergency.

That's almost a joke. We already have a national emergency. He's it.

The House has refused to appropriate money for a wall that's nothing more than an exercise in vanity, and only under discussion because it was Trump's signature rallying cry. And he's still trumpeting it. He shut down a third of the government and now has left himself no wiggle room except to call a national emergency; that would allow him to bypass Congress and access money by taking funds allocated for other purposes. By the time this gets through the courts, even our grandchildren will be dead and gone and the subject moot.

There's this wonderful Shakespearian phrase from *Hamlet* about a fool having been 'hoisted on his own petard,'— loose present-day translation: Shooting oneself in the foot. Wouldn't it be ironic that out of frustration, Trump declares a national emergency which triggers a Constitutional crisis which sets the impeachment process into motion. His rallying cry of "Who's going to pay for the wall?" MEXICO!—which was one of the mantras that got him elected, could be his 'petard,' and one source of his downfall. Now he's saying he never expected Mexico would pay—when he has said it more than 200 times.

Thanks to excellent reporting by *NBC*, *The Washington Post* and others, we know there's no security justification for this so-called emergency. During the first half of 2018, seven times more people on the terrorist watch list were caught crossing the Canadian border into the US (47) than our southern border (6). And, drugs don't enter the states 'on foot' either. The vast majority, according to the government's own data, come through legal points of entry via vehicles.

So, other than the fact that Trump is the President, there is no national emergency. But now millions of people are suffering under their own personal emergency directly caused by Trump's temper tantrum. According to *NBC,* so far 38 million people have been thrown off food stamps and upwards of two million are in danger of possible eviction because they don't have money for rent. These government employees, these public servants, get health care through their jobs—and now they're faced with a loss of that as well. Not knowing what the immediate future holds has got to feel like the greatest emergency of all.

Trump hasn't a clue what this means to families. But the government and Trump are always there to help. The Office of Personnel Management had the *chutzpah* to suggest several ways that furloughed workers, and those working without pay, could weather this financial crisis. One suggestion was to consult their 'personal attorney' for suggestions. Really? A park ranger or lab assistant will no doubt appreciate this helpful response. Other brilliant gems offered by Coast Guard Support included trading off carpentry or painting skills for rent reduction, babysitting, pet walking, and holding garage sales. And, if that isn't demeaning enough, as a last option, the Coast Guard document suggested filing for bankruptcy.

Trump said he was sure people would make adjustments; "They always do." No, they do not. Late payments affect credit scores and incur fees; medications can't be put off, nor can the myriad of consequences resulting from the stress associated with not being able to care for your family.

One can't help but wonder why Trump is demanding money for his vanity wall now, when it wasn't a national emergency during the two years Republicans controlled both Houses of Congress and the votes were there for the taking. It only became an 'emergency' when Democrats took over the House. This is a phony issue. Period.

Trump's shutdown is impacting so much in addition to the needless pain he's causing public sector employees. The FBI Agents Association said that even a threat of a shutdown was a threat to national security. Air Traffic Controllers are working without pay as are TSA agents and the Coast Guard. If Trump declares a national emergency, that will only compound the problems. He's looking at appropriating funds designated for disaster relief for California and Puerto Rico and diverting them to build his wall. It would be stunning if we weren't already in a state of gobsmackedness!

Much of the immigration issue can be solved, not by walls, but by putting the onus on a major source of the problem; U.S. employers ignoring E-Verify and hiring undocumented workers. If mandatory prison sentences and hefty fines were the rule—no exceptions—there would be a dramatic decrease in immigration. Incidentally, that's one way for Trump to see how good he looks in an orange jump suit; his businesses have been routinely hiring undocumented workers for years (*New York Times, Axios, Washington Post, Vox*). And, we need to set up a system that would allow workers to move back and forth with ease across the border based on work demands here. Maybe Trump can tell us how that's done since his use of certain visas (when he's not hiring the undocumented), are his frequent *modus operandi.*

The question has often been asked: What will it take for Trump supporters to say 'enough is enough.'

If national statistics can be applied to the 800,000 workers affected by the government shutdown, about 200,000 voted for Trump. The statistics have held since Trump was elected; about a third of the country support him unwaveringly. But being directly impacted by a Trump policy could be a mind and heart changer. Those 800,000 all have families, and they live in communities that depend on these 800,000 people for their livelihood. That's a lot of people, millions in fact, who are being trumped (as used here, seems like a reasonable substitute for the word starting with 'f').

This time, Trump himself may be paying the greatest cost for a wall that will never be built. As he said, he's proud to have caused the shutdown. Now he gets to own the consequences that follow. All of them.

Seems he might yet be hoisted on his own petard—caught in his own trap.

15 JANUARY 2019

THE MANCHURIAN PRESIDENT?

"No, you're the puppet. You're the puppet."
—DONALD J. TRUMP'S RESPONSE TO HILLARY CLINTON DURING THE
FINAL DEBATE.

*"His brain has not only been washed, as they say,
it's been dry cleaned."*
—DIALOG FROM THE FILM, *THE MANCHURIAN CANDIDATE*

The unthinkable has become impossible to ignore. *The New York Times* published a report that the FBI was investigating whether Trump "has been working on behalf of Russia against American interests."

While the statement is shocking, stepping back, it's a logical conclusion arrived as a result of many separate, but related, events. What follows are some of the questions whose answers fit that conclusion.

Why demand that one—only one—item be changed in the Republican Platform prior to the Convention? NPR and a multitude of other sources reported at the time that the Trump campaign directed a weakening of support for U.S. assistance to Ukraine. Of all the hundreds of items addressed in the platform, why was this deemed worthy of special attention, let alone change? It can't be attributed to Trump's knowledge of foreign policy or current events. Even today, it's a good bet he couldn't locate Ukraine on a map—or maybe even Kansas.

And, why would Trump indicate he might consider recognizing Russia's annexation of Crimea from Ukraine and lifting Russian sanctions imposed by President Obama?

And, why would Trump request; "Russia, if you're listening…" urging Russia to hack and release Clinton's 30,000 missing emails? That same day the Russians made their first attempt to break into her personal servers, according to *The New York Times*. Twelve Russians were eventually charged with election hacking.

And, why was Trump so willing to consider any source for election meddling other than Russia? During the final pre-election debate, Clinton noted that "17 intelligence agencies, military and civilian, have all concluded that these espionage attacks…came from the highest levels of the Kremlin and are designed to influence our election." Trump retorted saying, "She has no idea whether it was Russia, China or anybody else." It took him until July, 2018 to admit that he accepted the consensus of the intelligence community, but added that it "could be other people also." This statement followed a disastrous summit with Putin in Helsinki when he accepted Putin's denial of interference over the word of his own government; the resulting hue and cry forced him to recant but, veering off the written comments, he added the caveat noted above.

Why has he never, not once, given a full throated condemnation of Russia's cyber attack on this country?

Why did Trump host Foreign Minister Sergei Lavrov and Ambassador Sergey Kislyak alone in the Oval Office the day after he fired FBI Director, James Comey? American journalists and photographers were excluded—but the photographer from the Russian state news agency was allowed to memorialize the meeting. According to *The New York Times,* Trump told them that "firing that 'nut job' Comey eased pressure from the investigation". Why would he share that information with the Russians? Why would he allow an adversary in such a sacred space without staff or Secret Service present?

Why would Trump purposely slow the implementation of new sanctions, and consider easing those implemented in the previous Congress, as a response to Russia's attack on the election process? This was the major topic of discussion during the Trump Tower meeting, June 9, 2016 between Donald Trump Jr., campaign operatives, and eight Russians. Trump denied knowing about the meeting, but that has been contradicted by his then personal attorney, Michael Cohen.

It seems whenever an opportunity arises for Trump to side with his own governmental agencies against the Russians and Putin, he passes. Or deflects. Why?

The final bow to Russia and final blow for Secretary of Defense, James Mattis, was Trump's sudden announcement that we were pulling troops out of Syria. That was Trump's Christmas present to Putin. Intense pressure from the Senate and the DoD resulted in cabinet officials picking up the pieces and backtracking on the decision.

And, why would he consider pulling out of NATO? The effect, according to Michele Flournoy, former Under Secretary of Defense, "would be one of the most damaging things any president could do to U.S. interests." Again, a Putin dream.

Finally, why is there's no written record of any of the five one-on-one meetings Trump has had with Putin since the election (*The Washington Post*)? Why would Trump even agree to meet alone with a major adversary who interfered in our election? Given the level of concern and agreement that Russia hacked the 2016 election, and questions about Trump's linkage to that interference, one would think he would want as much transparency as possible when it comes to any interaction with Putin. *The Washington Post* reported that Trump told the interpreters they were not to discuss the meeting or its content with anyone, including those in the administration. In one case, Trump took the interpreter's notes. When asked in a Congressional Hearing, the Director of National Intelligence, Dan Coats, said he's never been briefed on what took place during the most recent two-hour meeting between Trump and Putin. Think about that.

Neal Katyal, the former Acting Solicitor General, said "The only people who don't have witnesses at their meetings are those who are guilty."

The question is, 'guilty of what?'

There are two choices.

The first is that Trump is what Russians fondly call a 'useful idiot.' Trump is enamored with autocrats—especially rich ones who have the capability of making him richer. The Russians and Saudis were purchasing properties and providing loans to him when no legitimate American funding source would. He owes them. They own him. The end result is that he stumbled into being an agent.

The second option is that Trump is, and has been, a knowing agent of a foreign power. Perhaps it's a combination of the two. It really doesn't matter how it happened; the result is the same. Then add the possibility of blackmail—not for money but to prevent damning information from becoming known.

There is no other explanation—and it has the added benefit of being the easiest explanation. Occam's Razor, the principle that states the simpler the solution the more likely it is to be correct, applies here. In this case, it's obvious. Sooner or later, that infamous dossier will come to light and more of the 'whys' will be made clear.

David Laufman, former Chief of the Counterintelligence and Export Section of the Department of Justice, reported on *MSNBC* that Trump represents a 'clear and present danger' to the country, and believes him to be an agent acting against the United States on behalf of a foreign power.

That's the definition of treason. It doesn't get more stunning than this.

Trump's time is running out. How much is left is unknown, but it's surely less than two years. And all this is before the Mueller Report is completed and released.

In *The Manchurian Candidate*, the anti-hero was brainwashed. In this case, all it took was feeding Trump's overwhelming greed and narcissism.

In the end, he is his only allegiance.

25 JANUARY 2019

THE WALLS CLOSE IN
AND THE PLOT SICKENS

"Life is a solitary cell whose walls are mirrors."
—EUGENE O'NEILL

We're being bombarded by events so fast there's little time to recover before the next blast of news hits. This has been an unusual couple of days even by Trumpian standards and, looking back, may serve as benchmarks leading to the end of this fiasco.

This morning we were in day 35 of the partial government shutdown. During this time, we've learned a lot about those who run our government. Multi-millionaire Commerce Secretary Wilber Ross demonstrated just how divorced he is from the people who employ him. He said he doesn't understand why those furloughed or forced to work without pay are going to food banks when all they need do is go to their local bank and get a loan. He didn't mention anything about paying the interest, nor did he provide any suggestions about what people should do while the bank is contemplating their decision. Politico reported that Kevin Hassett, Trump's economic advisor, suggested government employees consider their absence of work (and a paycheck) as a free vacation. Seriously.

Apparently, absence of empathy is a contagious condition. Or maybe it's a job requirement.

Yesterday, two Senate bills failed to pass; Democrats insisted that Trump reopen the government prior to any talks about border security—which still does not include funding for a wall. Trump and Republicans insisted that funding for the wall be assured prior to any negotiations about reopening the government.

But today is a different story. This morning, out of safety concerns, air traffic controllers instituted a ground stop at LaGuardia Airport that impacted incoming and outgoing flights nationwide—including those in and out of Washington, DC. This afternoon, Trump caved to the demands of House Speaker Nancy Pelosi. He announced that the government would reopen with funding secured for the next three weeks. During that time, Democrats and Republicans in Congress would have to come up with a bill to fund border security, to include his vanity wall. After three weeks, if his demand hasn't been met, he can shut down the government again. He also intimated he could call a national emergency.

Where are we? All this angst, anxiety, and real pain for so many government employees, their families, the people in their community who depend on them for their livelihoods, contractors who have lost those paychecks forever— and we are exactly where we were before Trump's hissy fit. The status quo remains. Trump accepted the same deal that was originally offered and agreed to, until Ann Coulter questioned his masculinity. What a waste. So many people hurt, and for what?

Actually, there has been a change; Trump's poll numbers are sinking like a Stone—which brings us to Roger.

Today's story number two began with an early morning raid and the arrest of long time Trump aide, advisor and friend Roger Stone. More than a dozen FBI agents were involved—agents who, ironically, were working without pay because of the shutdown. Karma, as they say, is a bitch.

This arrest brings the ever moving walls closer in on Trump. Stone was indicted on seven criminal charges, including witness tampering, obstruction, and lying to Congress. The Mueller documents carefully lay out Stone's contact with Wikileaks as a go-between and intermediary about releases of hacked material from the Clinton campaign, as well as lying to investigators. The indictment indicates close communication between "a senior Trump campaign official who was directed to contact Stone about any additional releases and other damaging information Organization 1 (Wikileaks) had regarding the Clinton campaign." The indictment is replete with documentation about releasing information concerning Clinton's 'failing health,' an October surprise, and more. It shows coordination between Stone, Wikileaks, and the Trump campaign. This makes six former Trump campaign aides that have been indicted. So far.

The walls move.

Two other events took place in the last couple of days that might be lost given these headlines. They shouldn't be; they may turn out to be as consequential, albeit in different ways, as the arrest of Stone and the temporary ending of the shutdown.

The first was a speech on the Senate floor by Michael Bennet (D-CO) about the government shutdown. It was epic. Lawrence O'Donnell, former Senate staffer and commentator on *MSNBC* said he wished he had been there, "just for this perfect speech by Senator Bennet," to hear it in person. Bennet, known for his calm demeanor, let loose on Ted Cruz, recalling his cavalier behavior during the 2013 shutdown. His speech appeared to be spontaneous and put in words the devastation that shutdowns cause to families only to feed political egos. The speech drew national attention. Perhaps he will be even more visible in the lead-in to 2020.

The second event brought to light astonishing information that should not be seen as merely circumstantial. It was known that Jared Kushner had difficulty obtaining needed clearances when he was first appointed as Trump's senior advisor; he had to make dozens of modifications to the official clearance forms to include foreign contacts that he 'neglected' to include originally. Additionally, according to *NBC News,* the FBI background check "raised concerns about potential foreign influences on him." Two career White House security specialists rejected his application for Top Secret clearance. That decision was overruled by Carl Kline, newly installed director of personnel security in the Executive Office of the President, and a Trump appointee. Kushner also sought even higher security clearance requiring approval by the CIA—they denied it and refused to budge.

So now we have someone who attends the President's Daily Brief and is privy to the nation's top secrets, who career security specialists believed to be 'unclearable.' According to NBC News, "Kushner's was one of at least 30 cases in which Kline overruled career security experts." That number is unprecedented.

The House Oversight and Reform Committee is planning to investigate why the White House would overrule career intelligence professionals 30 times and put the country at risk. Given what else is now known, this is a very very big deal.

These are the walls, moving ever closer, that Trump needs to worry about—these are real; unlike the one he'll never get on our southern border.

A LEGEND IN HIS OWN MIND

"History always repeats itself, first as a tragedy, then as a farce."
—KARL MARX

This essay could just as easily be titled "Arrested Development." Only two-year-olds believe they are the center of the universe, and only teenagers believe they know everything. So, it's deeply troubling that the President of the United States, the person who has the world's most demanding, complicated, and consequential job, manages to combine the traits of both. In this one aspect, he is an overachiever.

What is earthshakingly dangerous is that he believes all knowledge resides in him. Period. Whatever the topic, no one knows more.

Instead of realizing what an awesome responsibility he has undertaken, and that no single person can ever have all the answers; instead of relying on the best minds in their area of expertise to provide advice and assistance, Trump needs no one but himself.

There isn't a sane person on the planet, in or out of government, who would agree that any single person has all the answers about anything—with the exception of Donald Trump. But, then again, the caveat was 'sane person.'

How do we know this? He's told us so. *Politico* reported back in March of 2016, as a candidate, when asked on *MSNBC's "Morning Joe,"* whom he consulted on foreign policy, his response was, "I'm speaking with myself, number one, because I have a very good brain and I've said a lot of things." He added that "My primary consultant is myself and I have a good instinct for this stuff." Stuff?

One would think two years into his term, he would have enough experience to know what he doesn't know, and to rely on people he appointed to provide him with information to make complicated decisions. Instead, his opinion of himself has cemented and fossilized into that of an expert in all areas, not just of governing, but apparently everything. He really believes he knows it all.

And by all, he means all. This is only a sampling of what he has said. "Nobody knows more about taxes than I do and income than I do." "Nobody knows more about construction than I do." "Nobody knows more about campaign finance than I do." "I know more about drones than anybody." "Nobody knows much more about technology than me." "Nobody in the history of this country has ever known so much about infrastructure than Donald Trump." "I know more about ISIS than the Generals do, believe me." "I understand things. I comprehend very well, OK? Better than almost anybody."

"Nobody knows more about environmental impact studies better than me." "I understand the power of Facebook maybe better than almost anybody." "I know more about renewables than any human being on earth." "Nobody knows more about polls than me." "I know more about courts than any human being on earth." "I know more about steelworkers than anybody who's ever run for office." "No one knows more about banks than I do." "Nobody knows more about trade than I do." "I understand the tax laws better than almost anyone."

Hold on, we're just getting started.

"Nobody knows more about trade than me." "I know more about nuclear weapons, believe me." "Who knows more about lawsuits than I do. I'm the king." "Who knows more about offense and defense than they will ever understand. Nobody even understands it but me." "I understand money better than anybody." "Nobody knows more about debt than I do." "I know more about contributions better than anybody." "I understand the other side almost better than anybody." "I know a lot. I know more than I'm ever going to tell you." "Nobody believes in the First Amendment more than I do." "There's nobody bigger or better at the military." "Nobody has more respect for women than I do. Nobody." "Nobody reads the Bible more than me."

Aside from atrocious grammar and syntax, what a litany of BS.

And, now he knows more than the entire intelligence community.

Last week, the people he appointed—the Director of the FBI, the Director of National Intelligence, and the CIA Director, provided their annual Threat Assessment Report to Congress, gave public testimony, and answered questions about key findings. This is the combined work of 17 different agencies and thousand of people around the world. The 42-page report contradicted Trump pronouncements on ISIS ("We beat them."), Iran ("They haven't stopped nuclear"), Russia ("The Russia thing is a hoax"), and North Korea ("We are much safer now that I have such a good relationship with Kim Jong Un").

This isn't new. Earlier, senior briefing officials warned "the President is endangering American security with... a stubborn disregard for their assessments" (*TIME*, Feb. 2, 2019). The President's Daily Brief, according to *TIME*, is rarely daily and in person. Briefers have simplified content, using short sentences sprinkled with graphics, using his name and title often to keep his flea-like attention on the topic. He rarely asks questions or requests additional information.

When asked about the difference between Trump's statements and those of the intelligence community, White House officials declined to comment, but it's clear there's a critical disconnect. Later, Trump spoke for himself Tweeting that 'the intelligence chiefs were "passive and naïve" and suggested "they should go back to school."

John Brennon, former CIA director, said Trump was "blinded by his own arrogance," and that it was "outrageous" that he publically disparaged the findings of the intelligence community.

To square the circle, after gathering with the three intelligence experts in what looked like a Come-to-Jesus meeting in the Oval Office, Trump said, "We are all on the same page and they were misquoted." The only way that works is to admit that you didn't hear what you heard or see what you saw.

Welcome, for the umpteenth time, to *1984*.

Karl Marx got a lot of things wrong. The quote at the beginning of this essay is one more. He has the sequence reversed. First comes the farce, then the tragedy. The farce began when this flawed person announced he was running for President and continued with his election. From that point on, it's been a mixture of both. The perfect example is the farcical promise that Mexico would pay for his wall, which morphed into the tragedy of placing kids in cages, and the forced removal of children from their parents. Trump's farcical temper tantrum turned into tragedy when he shut down the government because he didn't get his wall, impacting more than a million families nationwide. It seems everything he does morphs into tragedy.

Ignoring the Threat Assessment, and disparaging the people working on behalf of all us, could result in the biggest tragedy of all.

Two-year-olds grow up. Teenagers become responsible adults. Usually. But in Trump's case, his narcissistic belief that he knows everything can only lead to tragedy—but it will never ever be his fault. After all, nobody knows more than he does.

17 FEBRUARY 2019

TO IMPEACH OR NOT TO IMPEACH: THE TRAGEDY OF TRUMP, FAILED PRESIDENT OF THE UNITED STATES (WITH APOLOGIES TO W. SHAKESPEARE)

To impeach or not to impeach: that is the question:
Whether 'tis nobler in the mind to let loose the slings and arrows of
•Congress, or take the risk, and pray we the people will do the good
and right deed?

G ood question. Let's start with the goal of getting Trump out of office. Mueller's investigation appears to be drawing to a close, but there are still multiple ongoing investigations in the House of Representatives, the Southern District of New York, and elsewhere. There will be sufficient justification for the House of Representatives to initiate impeachment proceedings. But should they?

If they do, and the House votes to impeach, that's where this ends. Regardless of what the House does, or the evidence presented, the Republican-controlled Senate will not vote to convict. They fear their hard-core base and being primaried. It would take 20 Republican Senators to join the 45 Democrats and two Independents to reach the two-thirds majority required to convict Trump and remove him from office. That's not going to happen. Starting the process with impeachment, but being unable to complete it with a conviction, would result in a wounded animal wandering around the White House, capable of anything.

The other reason not to instigate impeachment proceedings are his supporters. It's reached the point that it doesn't matter what awful thing he does, his supporters will not believe it. Even if they actually saw Trump shoot someone on 5th Avenue, they would say the video was doctored, that it was fake news, it was some Democrat made up to look like Trump, it was self-defense—you name it. It doesn't matter to them what he has done or will do; that hard-core of 35 percent will never accept his being ousted from office before his term is up.

And that's important. After all this is over, the people will be left to pick up the pieces. Trump has damaged the American psyche—who we are at our core, how we see ourselves, and how we're seen in the world. It will take an incredible level of acceptance, forgiveness, time, and hard work to reconcile and return to that aspirational image of a shining city on a hill vs. the "American carnage" Trump described in his inauguration speech—and then proceeded to make real.

So that leaves Trump with two options. If given the choice between perpetual lawsuits, indicting family members, losing his 'fortune,' (and being seen as the world's biggest loser) or leaving office voluntarily, he might choose the latter. But that leaves Pence to serve out Trump's term, and he would surely run

and probably win in 2020. The other choice is the best option—
to beat him completely and thoroughly at the polls.

It's important that the results aren't close, so that no
claim of vote tampering could be seen as credible. His brand of
politics has to be completely rejected by the American people.

Alas, poor Trump, now we know him all too well.

Maybe the most appropriate consequence for our actions is
that we have to endure two more years of Trump, just to pound
it into our collective heads that this must never happen again.

26 FEBRUARY 2019

EVER FEEL YOU'RE LIVING
IN AN ALTERNATIVE UNIVERSE?

"We're all mad here. I'm mad. You're mad."
—LEWIS CARROLL FROM *ALICE IN WONDERLAND*

"The world is a stage but the play is badly cast."
—OSCAR WILDE

Sometimes you just have to stop and look around and, like Alice, wonder in amazement at the rabbit hole we've all fallen into. So much is opposite of what was normal just two years ago but, because of the continual assault on our norms and values, this is what we've now come to expect. Actually, we've come to expect anything.

Nothing is surprising any more. What was gobsmacking a short time ago, we now brush off. But, if we don't stop every now and then and attend to what's happening, we could wake up in a very different world—as foreign as *Alice in Wonderland* and *1984*—and find we're living in both, in surround sound and living color.

The fact is that every day we're living what used to be unimaginable. That's how much has changed.

So, let's play the 'what if' game to see just how far we've devolved.

What if President Obama made no comment for a week about a massive terror attack planned by a self-proclaimed black activist who was going to murder leading Republican politicians and conservative reporters?

What if a former acting director of the FBI said, 'I think it's possible President Obama is a Russian asset?

What if the Obama administration secretly tried to transfer American nuclear technology to Saudi Arabia—the home country of the majority of the 9/11 assassins?

What if President Obama appointed the least qualified people in history to high level staff and cabinet positions, including family members; and what if the Democratic Senate approved them all?

What if President Obama was elected with support and comfort from the Russian government, thanks to help provided by them to his campaign?

What if President Obama tore up treaties and agreements that had been signed by previous Republican administrations, without consulting Congress or other allied signatories?

What if President Obama insulted allied leaders while supporting the Russian agenda to reduce the influence of NATO and other international alliances?

What if President Obama lied over 8,000 times in his first two years in office?

What if President Obama's written messages, that are actually official documents, were often unintelligible, full of syntactical, grammatical and spelling errors, and his expressive vocabulary was comparable to an average 4th grader?

What if President Obama's administration ordered the separation of thousands of parents and children, had no means of tracking them, and made no plans to reunite them?

What if President Obama said some people carrying Nazi banners and yelling anti-Semitic statements "are very fine people?"

What if President Obama held meetings with a leader of an adversarial country on five different occasions, and insisted there be no record of what was said in those meetings?

What if President Obama called the press "the enemy of the people" when they reported facts he didn't like?

What if President Obama instigated the possibility of a constitutional crisis by usurping the power of the House of Representatives to fund a project they had denied?

What if President Obama couldn't be bothered to regularly attend the Presidential Daily Brief?

What if President Obama maintained several White House staff who were denied required security clearances? What if, having been denied security clearances, President Obama granted them anyway?

What if President Obama received his marching orders from left wing media, and altered legislation and actions to meet their demands?

What if President Obama encouraged violence at his rallies saying? "Knock the crap out of them, would you?" "I'd like to punch him in the face." "Part of the problem is no one wants to hurt each other anymore." "Maybe he should have been roughed up."

What if the Obama administration, in its first two years, incurred 36 indictments, seven guilty pleas, three prison sentences, and over 191 criminal charges— thus far.

What if Obama refused to release his tax returns after promising that he would?

There are so many more 'what if's' but there isn't enough time or space to delineate all the norms Trump has broken; that really isn't the point. The point is that had these been actions taken by Obama and not Trump, Congress would have immediately initiated their oversight responsibilities and called for hearings. But Trump is President, and Republicans in Congress apparently do not care. It appears they have taken an oath of loyalty to Trump, not the Constitution.

The intellectual dishonesty of the Republicans in Congress in accepting and supporting the actions of the Trump administration is mind-numbing. But it is more than that. It is treacherous. And profoundly dangerous.

Ethics and decency are the prerequisites for everything else and cannot be conditional based on the party in power. Without a moral framework, corruption fills the void. And, that's exactly what has happened. The Grand Old Party is dead. Its members have opted for power and are complicit in Trump's assault on democracy. All hail to the party of Trump!

Alice asked the White Rabbit, "How long is forever?"

The White Rabbit responded, "Sometimes, just one second."

Imagine how he'd feel after two years of Trump.

05 MARCH 2019

THE MELTDOWN—
A LOSER SURROUNDED BY FAILURE

"Failure isn't fatal, but failure to change might be."
—JOHN WOODEN

You're having a lousy day—or in Trump's case, week. It's when we're under pressure, when things aren't going well, when the best laid plans go awry, and when, like Trump, the entire world watches as you go up in flames—that's when we get a glimpse of what a person is really like.

Most of us tend to respond to pressure and difficult situations by relying on what has worked in the past; individual patterns of behavior that provide a sense of security. At least for a while, we retreat and regress and hold on to those old security blankets before moving on to problem solve. That's been Donald Trump's week—another worst week yet. He just keeps outdoing himself. But rather than learn from what got him there, rather than analyze what and why things go wrong, he returns to what he needs—what gives him solace but, in the end, creates even more problems.

His needs are as simple as he is. Basically, he has just one; like all narcissists, it's adoration.

So, let's dip into Trump's worst ever, embarrassingly awful, failure of a week. While he was making nice with his new love and BFF Kim Jong Un, Michael Cohen was recounting his dirty deeds being Trump's fixit man and, while at it, providing a road map for the House Oversight Committee about where the next subpoenas should be directed.

He began, under oath, by stating "Trump is a racist. He's a con man. He's a cheat." He spent much of his opening remarks providing documentation for these statements. Cohen said Trump knew in advance about the massive email dump from Wikileaks that would hurt Clinton's campaign. Cohen said he threatened individuals on Trump's behalf on at least 500 occasions. He showed a copy of the check, signed by Trump, after he was in office, reimbursing Cohen for paying off a porn star to keep silent about their affair. His final statement was the most disturbing of all—"I fear that, if he loses the election in 2020, that there will never be a peaceful transition of power. This is why I agreed to appear before you today."

Not a single Republican on the Committee questioned the substance of Cohen's testimony.

Instead, they resorted to schoolyard taunts, one of which was actually printed on large poster board reading, "Liar, liar, pants on fire." Yes. Really. In the House of Representatives. You can't make this stuff up. Well, you could, but no one would believe you.

As all this was going on, Trump was in Viet Nam (about 50

years too late) to meet with the head of North Korea. Because of the time change, Trump was able to see Cohen's damning testimony. The following day, Trump abruptly ended the summit, but implied the love affair was still on, and that he trusted Kim. Within hours of his departure, a missile site in North Korea appeared to be reopening. Trump must believe we don't remember that he said North Korea was no longer a nuclear threat.

Trump came home to nonstop coverage of Cohen's testimony, along with news that the House rejected his call for a national emergency to appropriate already designated funds to build his wall, which Congress had already rejected. The Senate is likely to follow.

And there's more. The Treasury Department announced that the budget deficit grew by 77 percent in the first four months in comparison to the same time period a year ago. The trade deficit soared to an all time high— the same deficit Trump promised to end. And the national debt continues to increase each month— more all-time highs. And, it appears Trump ordered Ivanka and Jared be given Top Secret clearance when they couldn't pass the normal vetting process.

His concern for border security pales by the possibilities just down the hall—or by the image in his mirror.

He's a loser surrounded by failure. What to do, what to do? Simple. Have an adoration rally. As luck would have it, he was scheduled to speak at the CPAC annual conference. For two agonizing hours, Trump lied, pontificated, preened, and reiterated the same old tropes he can't seem to let go. It was bizarre and profane. It was illiterate and rambling. It was so over the top that any psychologist could use it as evidence of

Trump's divorce from reality.

Here are some examples: "Right now, we have people in Congress that hate our country." "I have one of the great inventions in history. It's called TiVo." "Every once in a while you have to remove the leaves because they are so…" "And by the way, as of today, probably tomorrow, we will actually have 100 percent of the caliphate in Syria." "The crazy female Senator from the state of Ohio… uh, the state of Hawaii, right?"

He railed against Mueller's 'witch hunt,' saying that a member of the Commission ran the Clinton Foundation, and that they are "all killers." He claimed the Green New Deal would take away Americans' cars and ban air travel. And he revisited crowd size at the inauguration. Again.

Here's another sample of the oratory skills of the President of the United States:

"You know, I don't know, maybe you know. You know, I'm totally off script, right—you know I'm totally off script right now. And this is how I got elected, by being off script. True. And if we don't go off script, our country is in big trouble, folks. 'Cause we have to get it back."

Just imagine the content of Trump's Presidential Library. Oy.

In actuality, the only difference between this and previous speeches was its length. And because of that, there is no way of escaping how deviant from anything approaching normal Trump has become. This is a President who has lost any ability to objectively evaluate his own actions—in fact, he really is his own worst enemy—not Mueller, not Hillary, not the Democrats. It's he who proves he's not fit. It's he who blames others. He has never said, 'I could do better,' or 'I'm sorry.' Nor has he accepted responsibility for his role in anything that goes wrong.

The quote by Coach Wooden is worth a comment. It's not failures, or mistakes, that have long-term impact, but rather their continuation. Trump doesn't believe that he makes mistakes—that he has failed at anything. The blame always belongs elsewhere, so there's no accounting, no self-awareness, and therefore no possible reason for him to change.

He is a failure as a politician and as President, but more than that, he is a failure as a functioning, adapting, rational human being who learns from experience. But, this isn't a reasoned choice that he's making; he is simply not capable of anything else.

And, it's that failure that will be fatal for Trump. Let's hope he doesn't take the country with him.

18 MARCH 2019

QUESTION: WHO ARE WE?

ANSWER: TO BE DETERMINED.

"Most of the power of authoritarianism is freely given. A citizen who adapts in this way is teaching power what it can do. We are no wiser than the Europeans who saw democracy yield to fascism, Nazism, or communism. Our one advantage is that we might learn from their experience."
—TIMOTHY SNYDER FROM HIS BOOK, *ON TYRANNY*

Fifty people were murdered in mosques in New Zealand. Eleven people were murdered in the Tree of Life synagogue in Pittsburgh. Fourteen pipe bombs were sent to politicians, news outlets and public figures in America. These events have one thing in common; the perpetrators in every instance invoked Donald Trump's language.

These are some of the actions/comments Trump has made about Muslims and immigrants:

- He said he would consider surveillance of mosques

(6/12/16).

- He called for a Muslim ban (6/12/2016).
- He said Syrian refugees are "trying to take over our children and convince them how wonderful ISIS is and how wonderful Islam is" (6/13/2016).
- He said under Obama "Muslims can come into this country, but Christians can't" (5/16/2016).
- He said he will "look at" closing mosques (10/21/2015).
- He called for surveillance of Muslim communities (11/16/2015).
- He called Muslims "sick people" 12/13/2015).
- He said, "Islam hates us" (3/9/16).
- He said, "There were fine people on both sides" in Charlottesville—one side carried Nazi banners chanting 'Jews will not replace us' (8/14/2017).
- He called unauthorized immigrants, "animals" (5/16/2018).
- He called Haiti, El Salvador and African countries, "shithole countries" (1/11/2018).
- He said people attempting to emigrate from Mexico were "bringing drugs, they're bringing crime, they're rapists" (6/16/2015).
- He said Nigerian immigrants wouldn't ever "go back to their huts" (12/23/2017).
- He continually refers to immigrants as 'invaders' (3/16/2019).
- He called immigration an "invasion of illegal aliens" (11/2/2018, 3/16/2019).
- He said, "Democrats have become the anti-Jewish party" (3/8/2019).

The New Zealand murderer wrote, "Trump is a symbol of

renewed white identity and common purpose." His 'manifesto' decried the decaying culture of the white, European, Western world, and called himself a White Supremacist and a Fascist. He selected the New Zealand location to show 'no part of the world was free from mass immigration" and called them 'invaders.' Trump has described himself as a nationalist and immigrants as invaders.

An avowed supporter of Donald Trump sent pipe bombs to Trump's 'enemies.' He had posted material online denigrating Muslims. Trump defined and called out what he described as, "enemies out to get him," and has denigrated Muslims as a group for decades.

Before the shooter entered the Tree of Life Temple, the Pittsburgh shooter ranted online that Jews were helping immigrants cross the U.S.-Mexico border as part of the so-called (by Trump) "caravan invasion."

The language of these murderers, and that of the President of the United States, is the same.

We have a problem.

What is clear is that white nationalists, white supremacists, and bigots are receiving what they perceive to be solace from the President of the United States. And, why wouldn't they? This weekend—the weekend following the mass killings in New Zealand, Trump chose to attack a months long dead Senator, instead of condemning the growth of white supremacy and white nationalism. He uses words that earn praise of David Duke, the former head of the KKK. Mass killers use his rhetoric. When *The Daily Stormer,* an American neo-Nazi, white supremacist website that advocates for the genocide of Jews, states "Trump has set us free" (Jan. 19,

2017), we have a problem.

Words matter. Actions follow. The Anti-Defamation League and the Southern Poverty Law Center report that White Nationalism is on the rise. Here are the statistics for just one year— from 2017-2018:

Supremacist propaganda: +182 percent

Racist rallies and demonstrations: +20 percent

Hate groups: +7 percent

It's no surprise that hate crimes were up 17 percent in 2017, and the 2018 statistics are expected to be much worse. And then there's this: *Business Insider* and *The Washington Post* reported studies by the University of North Texas that showed U.S. counties that hosted a Trump campaign rally in 2016 saw a 226 percent increase in hate crimes, compared to similar counties that did not hold a rally. Words matter. Actions follow.

The President of the United States is supposed to represent us. But he does not. This pretense of a man represents the incompetent, the delusional, the greedy, the racists, the bigots, the fearful, the thoughtless, the haters, the pessimists, the insecure, and the scared. While these characteristics mirror who he is as a man, that is not who we are as a nation.

This cannot be acceptable.

We have to continue to fight back. Only then can each of us help determine who we are.

One thing is for sure; we are better than this.

28 MARCH 2019

VICTORY LAP
—UH, NOT SO FAST

"Is this just real life, is this just fantasy? Caught in a landslide, no escape from reality."
—LYRICS FROM *BOHEMIAN RHAPSODY*, BY QUEEN

Tah dah! Finally! After almost two years, the Mueller investigation is over, and the report is made available to Congress and to the citizens who paid for it. That, it turns out, is 'the fantasy'.

Attorney General William Barr only released a summary of three-and-one-half typed pages of what is reported to be about a 400-plus-page report (not counting appendices). This summary sought to answer the two major questions of the investigation—whether Trump obstructed justice, and whether he colluded/conspired with Russia during the 2016 campaign.

Barr said the report found that the Trump campaign did not criminally conspire with Russia, however regarding obstruction, the Special Counsel stated that "...while this report does not conclude that the President committed a crime, it also does not exonerate him..." quoting from the Muller's report.

AG Barr then decided pick up that dropped ball and make the determination himself, concluding that "The evidence developed during the Special Counsel's investigation is not sufficient to establish that the President committed an obstruction of justice offense." Barr provided nothing to justify his determination; no discussion, no evidence, no nothing.

Try to find the logic here. After two years of investigation, Mueller was not able to exonerate Trump, but after a two-day review of 400 pages, plus all those attachments, Barr was able to make that determination.

While that assumption is way beyond Barr's responsibility, from Trump's point of view it served as total vindication accompanied by a multitude of 'I told you so's' and threats of vengeance for those who dared doubt his oft repeated words of "no collusion!"

The AG received the report on Friday, March 22, and released his summary to Congress two days later.

Here are the problems—the 'real life,' making it impossible to accept Barr's summary as written. In addition to distilling 400 pages of evidence and findings into three-and-one-half typed pages, only four partial quotes (42 words) from the Mueller Report are provided and none are contained in complete sentences. It's impossible to know the context, or the words, coming before or after the quotes. On this alone, any first year law student would likely be in deep poop.

And yet, this is predictable. When Barr wrote an

unsolicited 'audition letter' for the AG position to the Justice Department (copied to Trump), he made it clear he believed the President has "absolute" and "all-encompassing" constitutional authority over actions by the Executive Branch. In the memo, Barr questioned the scope of Mueller's investigation, stating that Mueller should not be permitted to demand answers from Trump regarding his pressuring the former FBI Chief James Comey to drop his investigation of National Security Advisor Michael Flynn, or Comey's subsequent firing when he refused.

The House is not going to accept this. They want the entire report, together with backup evidence, and will subpoena the report, the AG and Robert Mueller to get it, if needed.

No escape from reality.

Trump isn't waiting. He decided to celebrate with a victory rally in Grand Rapids, MI, and it was a fantasy romp into his imagination. Trump claimed it was a "total exoneration, complete vindication" and went so far as to label the investigation itself as 'ridiculous bullshit." And then came the blame. "All of the Democrats, politicians, the media also—bad people—the crooked journalists, the totally dishonest TV pundits helped perpetuate "the single greatest hoax in the history of politics"—in an effort to overturn the 2016 election."

The entire report needs to be released to Congress; the Judiciary and Intelligence Committees can determine for themselves what redactions are needed. What is abundantly clear is that Congress, and the people, will not accept Barr's fantastical summary or Trump's wishful thinking.

Bohemian Rhapsody foretells Trump's reality: Eventually,

he'll be saying, although not nearly so eloquently, *Goodbye everybody, I've got to go. Gotta leave it all behind and face the truth.*

We wish. And don't let the door hit you... etc.

15 APRIL 2019

HE'S GETTING WORSE

"If you really want to escape the things that harass you, what you need is not to be in a different place, but to be a different person."
—LUCIUS SENECA, LETTERS FROM A STOIC

"Reality is the leading cause of stress."
—JANE WAGNER

D onald Trump was never an intelligent or thoughtful man, or even someone with normal flaws like the rest of us. For whatever the reasons, the end result is that he's seriously damaged; a warped human being of little consequence—except for his title and the power that goes with it.

He's has few interests outside of himself. He doesn't have friends—he has mutually manipulative acquaintances; it's all transactional, *quid pro quo,* minus emotion and feeling. Trump acts impulsively, seemingly unable to look ahead to see the consequences of his actions. He doesn't learn from mistakes and has no tolerance for anyone who disagrees with him. He hates being told what he cannot do—even if what he wants to do is against the law.

He disregards expertise; no one knows more than he does. Yet, he doesn't read, isn't curious, and has little investment in anything except enhancing and protecting his fragile ego. Max Boot, the conservative writer and historian, described Trump as 'functionally illiterate'—he chooses not to read. Trump has nothing to fall back on in times of stress. Even golf ends at the 18th hole.

A previous essay dated 11 January 2017, titled "The Trouble with Donald," details the characteristics of Narcissistic Personality Disorder from the *Diagnostic and Statistical Manual of Mental Disorders (DSM-5)*. It doesn't take a psychologist to see that he exhibits every single diagnostic symptom/behavior. In this one area, Donald Trump represents perfection.

But, now we see something in addition; we see a man unraveling before our eyes.

There's no denying stress acts as a trigger for most of us; and there's also no denying that Trump is under increasing stress, much of it self-induced—and all of it on world display. But, unlike most of us, he has nothing to fall back on. Everything bad is beginning to come together, and the impact on him is obvious. He is a man alone.

So, let's look at some of the stressors of the past couple weeks.

The release of the full Mueller report is as sure as the sun will rise. The redacted version is due any minute. AG Barr's rendition of absolution will not hold. Members of Mueller's investigative team are 'outraged,' stating that Barr seriously overreached in his conclusion that Trump wasn't guilty of obstructing justice, and they are beginning to grumble out loud.

There remain at least seven ongoing investigations into Trump's activities, and that doesn't include those by Congressional committees. There are reports of a 'small army' of whistle blowers in the government, some inside the White House, documenting events. That can't provide solace for an already suspicious Trump.

The turnover of key staff is historic—a whopping 46 percent according to *The New York Times* and the *Brookings Institution*. One reason for these statistics is that Trump pulls already existing agency heads or other staff to fill vacant positions as acting heads, thus leaving another opening. It's musical chairs in the White House, but in reverse; the number of chairs stay the same—only the players disappear. Acting positions leave voids in leadership and demoralized staff.

At this point, the Defense Secretary, Department of Homeland Security, UN Ambassador, FEMA Director, ICE Director, DHS Deputy Director, Department of the Interior, the FAA head—all unfilled. *The Guardian* lists a total of 15 leadership posts with temporary heads. But, Trump says he likes it that way: "I sort of like 'acting'. It gives me more flexibility." The fact is that qualified experienced professionals see working for the Trump administration as an automatic step into either political oblivion or a court of law—or both. He has fewer and fewer people who want to work for him, and fewer and fewer people whom he trusts.

The House Ways and Means Committee recently requested copies of Trump's tax returns for the past six years—the Treasury Secretary is stonewalling, hoping the next election will take place before the courts rule.

But some states are trumping Trump; they aren't waiting. They're passing legislation requiring everyone running for president release their tax returns as a condition to being on the ballot.

Desperate to change the subject from his latest debacle and to divert attention from the obstruction of justice claim, Trump decided, apparently without talking to anyone in the Senate, that he was going to end the Affordable Care Act— without a replacement. McConnell said 'No.' Oops.

So, then he goes to his go-to: immigration. He threatened, again, to shut down the southern border. When he got massive pushback in terms of what that would do to the economy, he fired everyone with a significant role in the Department of Homeland Security, including the head of the department responsible for protecting him and his family. He says he wants to stop the flow of refugees, but he eliminated foreign aid to the sending countries, which only exacerbates their problems, increasing the flow of refugees here. And, he's verbalizing his wish to rid the system of immigration judges. So, who's really running the Department of Homeland Security—the second largest government bureaucracy? Quoting Trump, "I'm running DHS."

He is spiraling out of control. He called Robert Mueller's probe an 'attempted coup' that amounted to 'treason.' That's beyond the pale, even for Trump.

The stress is showing in his erratic behavior and language. He's exhibiting symptoms of aphasia or, perhaps, dementia—he can't seem to find the right word—for instance substituting what sounded like 'oranges' for 'origins.' He's repeating himself constantly—he makes a simple five-word statement and repeats it, and repeats it again, and then again with maybe a slight variation. He forgets people's last names, even when they're sitting next to him with a name plate; Tim Cook becomes "Tim Apple." He said wind turbines cause cancer. Woo hoo!

Stress is a multiplier. Mistakes cause more stress, which cause more mistakes, which cause more stress. He can't avoid reality, nor can he change who he is. He's stuck. The problem is, so are we.

24 APRIL 2019

THE MUELLER REPORT

"The special counsel investigation that threatened Donald Trump's presidency was born of the commander in chief's rage."
—WASHINGTON POST REPORTERS ROSALIND HELDERMAN
AND MATT ZAPOTOSKY; INTRODUCTION TO THE MUELLER REPORT.

With the issuance of the Mueller Report, day 819 of the Trump Presidency will go down in political history. It marks the beginning of the end—one way or another. Trump will either be impeached as a result, resign as a result, or be defeated in 2020 as a result.

There's nothing nuanced in the Mueller Report; it is replete with specific examples of the words and actions that generated this investigation to begin with—most of them Trump's. It's also specific in its limitations and findings. Further, the Report leaves no doubt that "the Russian government interfered in the 2016 presidential election in sweeping and systematic fashion" in support of Trump and the detriment of Clinton (pg. 1, Vol. I).

Volume I focused on actions by Trump operatives and campaign staff regarding cooperation and conspiracy with Russians. Volume II deals with actions by Trump regarding obstruction of justice.

Volume I details two key Russian interference operations to support Trump's election; "the social media campaign and the hacking and dumping operations" (pg. 9, Vol. I). It also specifies "numerous links between individuals with ties to the Russian government and individuals associated with the Trump campaign..." But the report concluded, "the evidence was not sufficient to support criminal charges" of conspiracy (pg. 9, Vol. I). The standard used to make that judgment was "whether the conduct constitutes a crime and if so, whether the admissible evidence would probably be sufficient to obtain and sustain a conviction..." (pg. 8, Vol. I).

It should be noted that the vast majority of redactions in the Report occur in Vol. I, with 'harm to ongoing matter' being the primary reason. The question of conspiratorial activity and coordination of Trump operatives with Russians may not be over.

Volume II of the Report deals with obstruction of justice. The introduction to this volume stated the investigators declined to either initiate or decline to prosecute, due to an opinion issued by The Office of Legal Counsel. That opinion states, "the indictment of a criminal prosecution of a sitting President would impermissibly undermine the capacity of the executive branch to perform its constitutionally defined functions..." and would violate the separation of powers (pg. 1, Vol. II). Because of this determination by the Justice Department that a sitting President could not be indicted, the report leaves it to Congress to act on the 10 examples of possible obstruction of justice enumerated in Volume II.

So, why did Mueller even bother to consider obstruction if no decision, either way, was going to be made? The answer (pg. 2, Vol. II), was to "preserve the evidence when memories are fresh, and documentary materials when available." The report further noted that while prosecution in office was not possible, "the President does not have immunity after he leaves office." (pg. 1, Vol. II).

And, finally, the kiss of death. "…if we had confidence… that the President did not commit obstruction of justice, we would so state… however we were unable to reach that judgment." "Accordingly, while this report does not conclude that the President committed a crime, it also does not exonerate him" (pg. 2, Vol. II).

Here are some interesting facts gleaned from this 448-page report (*Vox, The New York Times*).

- About 500 witnesses were called and 2800 subpoenas issued during this investigation.
- About 10 percent of the Report is redacted, according to *The New York Times*. The vast majority is are Vol. I and involved ongoing investigations and grand jury material.
- There have been 34 indictments resulting from the Mueller investigation.
- Trump declined to be interviewed in person. He responded with "I don't recall," or variations thereof,

37 times in his written testimony. In other instances, "his answers were "incomplete or imprecise" (pg. 1, Appendix C).

- Mueller and his team made 14 referrals to other prosecutorial offices—12 of which had not been made public before and continue to remain unknown.
- 'Real news' outlets such as *The New York Times, The Washington Post, CNN* and others were cited 203 times as sources of verified information.
- There were 140 separate instances of communication between the Trump campaign and the Russians/ WikiLeaks.
- At least 100 pages of the Report contained information about Russian interference in the election.
  Mueller and his team listed at least 10 episodes of possible obstruction of justice; these are summarized by *Vox*.

1. Trump asking James Comey to let Michael Flynn go.
2. Trump's reaction to the continuing Russia investigation and AG Sessions' recusal, asking White House counsel Don McGahn, and others, to convince Sessions to unrecuse, saying he wanted an AG to protect him.
3. Asking the Director of the CIA and the Director of National Intelligence, among others, to publicly dispel the suggestion that Trump had any connection to the Russian election interference.
4. The firing of James Comey and Trump stating that would end the investigation.
5. Efforts to oust Mueller. Trump told advisors Mueller's

appointment was "the end of his presidency" and told White House attorney McGahn that Mueller must be removed and to call him after he had done it. McGahn refused.

6. Attempts to prevent public disclosure of evidence related to the Trump Tower meeting with the Russians.

7. Trump's continued attempts to get Sessions to take back control of the investigation.

8. Trump told McGahn to deny he wanted the special counsel removed, and to create a false record to that effect.

9. Trump's team attempted to get Flynn to share information illegally during the time he was testifying. During Paul Manafort's prosecution, and while the jury was deliberating, Trump praised Manafort publicly, said he was being treated unfairly and declined to rule out a pardon. He added that 'flipping' ought to be outlawed.

10. Trump's changing behavior toward Michael Cohen. Trump went from praise to castigation when Cohen became a cooperating witness. He sent private messages to him to be strong and 'stay on message.' When he began cooperating, Trump publically criticized him, called him a 'rat' and suggested his family members had committed crimes.

No summary can substitute for reading the real thing. The Report is long but a relatively easy read with much of the corroborating details in footnotes and appendices. As further investigations proceed, it would be helpful to have the full report as a reference.

What is clear is that Russia intervened to aid Trump win the election. There is no way of knowing how, and to what extent, this influenced voters and the voting process itself. But what is beyond question is that this was an attack on the country. The FBI and the Director of National Intelligence, among others, have made it clear Russia is continuing its inroads into election interference in the lead-up to the 2020 election.

What is also clear is that the President of the United States has yet to condemn this attack by Russia, or to make it clear that further intervention on their part will not be tolerated.

When it comes to outside foreign influence in our elections, Trump has done nothing. It's his current inaction that may be the most impactful and impeachable offense of all.

19 MAY 2019

TOO MANY POTS;
TOO MUCH HEAT

"Human beings and frogs are the two creatures in nature that have tremendous power to adjust. What kills the frog is not the heat but its own inability to decide when to jump out of the pot."
—SATISH KUMAR

M ost days it seems we're the proverbial frog swimming in a pot of water that's gradually getting warmer and warmer. Events no one would have considered possible in 2016 are now just everyday occurrences—no big deal; we hardly notice. Just like the frog. Had it been dumped in water at the current temperature, it would have hotfooted it out of the pot immediately, but it's amazing how we, like the frog, can adapt to change if acceleration occurs incrementally and continually over a long period of time.

Too many of us have acclimated to what used to be abhorrent, but now is, well, normal. After all, normal is what happens all the time.

But, if we could stop increasing the heat and look at where we are, it's clear we now have a more autocratic government, with extravagant power usurped by the Executive Branch, and a President adept at deflecting attention away from that fact. It's also clear that the Democratic candidates for president and Congressional oversight committees are forcing us to attend to the temperature, to take notice of how much this country and its government have changed.

The release of the Mueller Report was another event that forced us to attend to the temperature by refocusing on actions by the Trump organization. It's no longer possible, even for Trump, to ignore its outcomes or invent results. The report is itself a key variable affecting Trump's current actions, even as it depicts those of his past.

Trump said the report exonerates him. It does not. It delineates 251 contacts between Trump's team and Russia-linked operatives, including at least 37 meetings. None of these were reported to authorities; in fact, the Trump team tried to cover up every one of them. Further, in Vol. II, at least 10 incidents of obstruction of justice by Trump were detailed.

To draw attention away from its content—to draw attention away from the administration's refusal to comply with legitimate Congressional oversight requests for documents and testimony—Trump has chosen to start another pot of water. It seems finally, at least some frogs are beginning to check the condition of their hind legs.

By necessity, this water is already hot, but this time, the administration may have gone too far too fast. This time the world is focused on the rapidly rising temperature emanating from the White House. The sabers are rattling as hawks, eager to finally achieve their fondest dream, try to provoke Iran, and give the U.S. an excuse to retaliate.

John Bolton's mustache is twisting in anticipation of finally being in the position to instigate an attempt at regime change in Iran. *Axios* reports he said the U.S. will respond to any provocation with "immense force."

Trump, in continuance of dismantling all things Obama, started this fire by pulling out of the Joint Comprehensive Plan of Action—aka, the Iranian Nuclear Deal—in May 2018, even though Iran had met every recertification requirement. Having done that, the U.S. reinstituted sanctions. But the U.S. also said sanctions would apply to any country trading with Iran, including our allies. That was the first of many steps leading to increased tensions with Iran, egged on by Saudi Arabia and Israel. And, the timing is perfect for Trump, by conveniently taking public attention away from the temperature in one pot and focusing it on another.

But this time, it's Trump who is playing with fire. In an article in *The New York Times,* Wendy Sherman, former Under Secretary of State—and one of the architects of the Iranian Nuclear Deal—wondered whether Trump was trying to goad Iran into war, or just hoping that increased tensions would make an accident leading to war more likely. Either way, the result would be the same.

The State Department ordered a partial evacuation of the U.S. embassy in Baghdad, responding to what Secretary of State Pompeo said was "related Iranian activity," and issued a warning to avoid Iranian air space. The Acting Defense Secretary presented plans for 120,000 U.S. troops to be deployed to the Middle East in the event of an Iranian attack. This pot is heating up fast—enough for our allies, and even Republicans in Congress, to take notice and question intent. Trump's threats are out of control; his latest Tweet on the subject: "If Iran wants to fight, that will be the official end of Iran. Never threaten the United States again!"

When asked if we were heading to war with Iran, Trump said he 'hoped not.' But he is turning up the heat, and now he has allowed Pompeo and Bolton to take over the temperature controls; they will mightily resist giving them back.

Like everything Trump does, there is no long-term planning or consideration of consequences, unintended or not. This is no way to run any entity, large or small, let alone a government. Things are heating up. Water is simmering in multiple pots. And Trump has given away the temperature controls.

What could possibly go wrong? Let us count the ways.

01 JUNE 2019

A CURE FOR WHAT AILS US

*"National service can bridge the gap between the social challenges
we face and the resources needed to overcome them."*
—TAE YOO, SENIOR VICE PRESIDENT OF CORPORATE AFFAIRS,
CISCO SYSTEMS, INC.

Trump did not cause the distrust, the bigotry, the fear, the racism, the xenophobia—all the elements of hate and just plain meanness—that now seem to politically define too many of us; but he is the result. What had been there all along, seething away below the surface, Trump gave permission to air out loud; if the President of the United States could condone hate and say there are good people on both sides, then that served as license to be just like him. After all, who wouldn't want to emulate the President of the United States?

He gave value and standing to ignorance and fear.

However this Presidency ends, the real test for the

nation will be whether we transition peacefully to the next administration as we pick up the pieces from this one. The problem is that one of the biggest pieces has been badly shattered—the basic assumption that we are the *United* States of America.

We are a nation of immigrants that want to lock the door on everyone else—especially those who aren't white and don't come from European countries. The Declaration of Independence says we're equal, but we're treated unequally and in turn, we do unto others. We say we want citizen involvement in government, but we pass legislation or institute procedures making it essentially impossible for certain citizens to be represented—like state instituted gerrymandering and restrictive voting laws.

Then there's this. We've self-segregated into communities of people that look and think like us. We have less and less contact with those from different backgrounds, religions, races, cultures, education, social and economic status. We live in pockets of self-imposed segregation, rarely venturing out. And, that kind of isolation can promote distrust. It's easy to fear people we don't know; Trump encouraged and took advantage of that by providing traditional scapegoats for whatever problems exist. That may be the most damaging aspect of his Presidency— that it's now OK to be like him—ignorant, bigoted, and fearful.

We seem to have forgotten that the default foundation for all successful relationships is trust. No government can succeed without it, nor can any relationship. But, it's hard to trust people we don't know, haven't met, or maybe never even seen—especially when someone in power tells us not to.

There is a solution, and it's one that has been discussed

and modeled, but not acted on to the fullest extent possible.

It wasn't that long ago when national service was defined by enlisting in the military, but once the draft ended, so too did the personal benefits that occurred as the result of serving. Even then, women rarely served, and a variety of exemptions were allowed. Now, according to the Veterans Administration, active and reserve forces are less than one percent of the population.

When all the people who represent this country have to work together and depend on each other to accomplish goals, inconsequential differences fade, and lifelong friendships develop. People get to know each other as individuals, who they are, what they value. People experience interacting with others whose backgrounds are entirely different and would likely not have encountered in their daily life, but now have to rely on to achieve their own success. People learn and earn trust and respect. That experience is a powerful life lesson that endures—just ask any veteran, or current military member, how they feel about their compatriots.

But national service need not be limited to the military. The nation's needs go far beyond that. Choose any community and there will be unmet needs—in schools, hospitals, day care centers, nursing homes, in infrastructure, and technology. Fires need fighting, natural disasters need cleanup, trades need apprentices, and the homeless need homes. And there's so much more.

AmeriCorps, created in 1993, provides Americans with opportunities to serve in non-profit organizations that mentor and tutor kids, rebuild communities, help veterans, and alleviate poverty. Over two million of us provide community service each year through AmeriCorps and its sister programs. But the needs are massive, especially as programs for those in greatest need are cut or eliminated.

Some of the Democratic Presidential candidates are beginning to talk about national service as a two-year requirement for everyone between the ages of say, 17 and 24. Joining the military would continue to be an option. For every year served, in addition to a stipend, one year of tuition at a community college, trade school or state university would be paid for.

But, here's the really important requirement. Everyone, no exceptions, between the designated ages must serve— including those with bone spurs. Regardless of social or financial status, English speaking or not, immigrant or not, disabled or not, male and female, LGBTQ, everyone must serve. If we believe everyone has worth and we know there is work to be done, then there cannot be exceptions except for those individuals needing ongoing care. No person would be able buy or bribe their way out.

The Oxford Dictionary classifies 'patriotism' as a noun. But for the word to be meaningful requires action. What could be more meaningful than helping to meet needs that otherwise would go unmet, to help others, to support professionals while learning from them, and to work with others—no exceptions—to achieve mutual goals? In the process, patriotism becomes a verb, defined by activity that results in learning about the richness of our country—and the citizens who represent all of us in the United States— while helping to meet those critical unmet needs.

President Kennedy said, in reference to the Peace Corps, "The wisdom of this idea is that someday we'll bring it home to America." Now is exactly the right time, and 'someday' could be now.

05 JUNE 2019

THE IMPEACHABLE OFFENSE IS—
A LACK OF DEFENSE

"He is simply a shiver looking for a spine to run up."
— PAUL KEATING

"To be led by a fool is to be led by opportunists
who control the fool."
— OCTAVIA BUTLER

To sit by, doing nothing while your house burns with loved ones inside, is unthinkable.

To sit by, doing nothing while your country is being attacked, is also unthinkable. And yet...

The Mueller Report made it clear that a foreign adversary systematically intervened and interfered in the 2016 election to benefit Trump. Russia's goal was to sow discord and distrust by promoting lies about other candidates on social media, and demonizing political, racial, ethnic and religious groups. Trump reinforced it all. 'Likes' and 'shares' took care of the rest. If there is a single word that best describes the politics of the past three years, it's 'fear.' If there's a single activity that best describes the politics of the past three years, it's 'instigating fear'.

Rather than seeking to unite, Trump sought to divide, with Russia sowing the seeds of fear and distrust. and Trump and his campaign provided the daily watering. He even had his own propaganda outlet in the ultra–right wing sound machine.

Trump has never, not once, condemned Russia's action, or threatened retaliation if they continue their attack. A couple of days ago, Trump had an hour-long telephone conversation with his BFF, but when asked if he told Putin not to "meddle" in the 2020 election, he said he did not.

They discussed the Mueller Report—whose major finding in Vol. I was that "the Russian government interfered in the 2016 presidential election in sweeping and systematic fashion"—but somehow Russia's role never came up in the conversation. Last week, the FBI Director, Christopher Wray, said that the 2018 midterms was just a "dress rehearsal" for Russia's election interference at the 2020 election. But Trump didn't think that was a topic worth discussing.

That's the ultimate impeachable offense. The house is burning, our country is being attacked. and Trump is watching the house go up in flames. He has wrapped his warped ego around the concept that the Mueller Report is the work of the Deep State, run by Obama and others from the previous administration, and that the Report was actually an attempted "coup"—they were "trying to infiltrate the White House" (Trump, 4/26/10).

People have searched for the justification behind Trump's obsequious behavior when it comes to Putin. What is it that Putin has on Trump? Is it those rumored salacious tapes? Is it financial? Maybe it's just the obvious; Trump wanted to win, and Russia offered to help—with a few caveats thrown in. It could be just that simple.

And now, he has to win again. But this time he has a problem. His current approval rating is 39 percent, and that's with a booming economy. This time he'll have an opponent that Democrats will wholeheartedly support. As Trump feels more threatened, he will become more defensive and erratic. If his approval rating sinks below 30 percent, Republicans in Congress may not find it beneficial to hitch their wagon his falling star. If that happens, and supporters no longer support, what will he do?

The scariest scenario is that Trump will instigate a real national emergency just before the election. Something awful will happen, and only he can save the burning house— the one he himself set on fire. This is his standard practice. He instigates (like separating parents and children at the border), and then intervenes and takes credit for solving the problem, (by ordering the separation policy to stop) that he himself created.

So, there's no question Trump has, and will, continue to commit the impeachable offense of doing nothing to protect this country from a foreign adversary. Congress has to do their constitutional duty, provide oversight, conduct hearings under oath, continue to seek the truth, and educate the American people. Then consider impeachment.

Not since the Civil War has our nation and our Constitution been so sorely tested. Only time will determine if both survive.

13 JUNE 2019

TRUMP IN A NUTSHELL
—WITH SO MUCH SPACE LEFT OVER.

"Jealousy is bred in self doubt. When self doubt turns to certainty, the passion either ceases or turns to absolute madness."
—FRANCOIS DE LA ROCHEFOUCAULD

A nutshell. A small protective container that's tossed away when empty. Colloquially, it's also used to indicate a short summary or brief description. In Trump's case, when it comes to listing his virtues, a wee pea pod would serve as a more appropriate container—and even then...

Trump is a simple man. There is no nuance or depth of character. He is defined by his ignorance and needs. Praise him, never cross him, don't exceed or outdo him in anything, don't denigrate him, and don't challenge him. It's all personal, and it's always about him, especially when it isn't. He functions transactionally; there must be a winner and loser in every interaction, and he must always be seen as the winner, especially when he's clearly not. That's Trump in a nutshell—with room to spare.

If any person personifies the opposite of Trump in terms of life choices, it was and apparently still is, John McCain.

McCain volunteered to serve in Vietnam and was a war hero. He was tortured and held in captivity for five years. He refused freedom until prisoners captured before him were released.

Trump avoided the draft by lying via a doctor who responded to a request as a favor to his landlord, Fred Trump about a nonexistent medical condition (*USA Today*, Dec. 27. 2018; *The New York Times*, Dec. 26, 2018). This was a purposeful act; he refused to serve. McCain volunteered. Trump said on the Howard Stern Show in 1993, and repeated again in 1997, that trying to avoid a sexually transmitted disease was "my personal Vietnam," adding "I feel like a great and very brave soldier."

When interviewed during his recent state visit to the UK, Trump said he would have liked to have served in the military, but not during the height of the fighting in Vietnam, "because I was never a fan of that war." "...I thought it was very far away... " and "...at the time, nobody ever heard of the country." OK. Good enough.

Shame it wasn't 'good enough' for all the solders who also didn't like the war, and the prospect of dying in a place they never heard of. Ah, well.

Beginning back in 2000, when Trump was considering a presidential run, he criticized McCain in an ABC interview questioning whether being captured qualified him as a hero. In 2015, when McCain told the Arizona Republic he disagreed with Trump's comments about Mexicans being criminals and rapists, Trump said McCain was "weak on immigration" at a rally in McCain's home state. McCain, in an article in the New

Yorker, said Trump "Fired up the crazies;" Trump responded by calling McCain a "dummy."

In July 2015 Trump uttered the oft-quoted statement questioning whether McCain was a hero because he was captured. Mr. Bone Spurs added, "I like people who weren't captured.

McCain announced he wouldn't be attending the Republican National Convention where Trump was due to accept his party's nomination. A former candidate for president, refusing to attend his party's national convention, was an unmistakable statement, and one not even Trump could mistake.

The final blow for Trump occurred when McCain achieved what no Democrat could; he assured the Affordable Care Act would not be repealed by voting 'thumbs down' on Trump's second biggest campaign promise—to repeal Obamacare (outdone only by building a wall that Mexico would pay for).

McCain died in August 2018. The feud continued unabated—apparently Trump not realizing it was one-sided. Or, maybe that's why it continued. After McCain died, Trump initially refused to lower the flag, recanted for two days following an outcry, but then raised it. Within hours he was forced to lower it again in response to veterans' groups and others, who vehemently criticized Trump's response. It remained lowered until McCain's burial, as tradition dictated.

As late as March 2019, seven months after McCain's death, Trump was still obsessing. According to *USA Today,* he complained at a rally that he didn't get a 'thank you' "for giving McCain the kind of funeral he wanted, which as President, I had to approve. But I don't care about this."

Wanna bet?

There's so much more to this now one-sided jealousy-fueled feud, but it culminated during Trump's recent trip to Japan. The Navy said in a statement, "A request was made to the U.S. Navy to minimize the visibility of the USS John S. McCain during President Donald Trump's recent state visit." The Wall Street Journal said it more succinctly, saying the order was that the "USS John McCain needs to be out of sight" during Trump's visit. There were reports of tarp being used to hide the name, as well as excluding McCain sailors from attending planned events.

Congressman Ruben Gallego from Arizona sent a letter to the Chief of Naval Operations stating, "It is appalling to hear the *USS JOHN S. MCCAIN* was ordered to slink into the shadows to avoid upsetting a fragile president... " and asked him to explain "How you will ensure that the Navy protects its greatest heroes against petty White House whims... "

In a nutshell, Trump is a petty, jealous little man, obsessed by the need to be adored. And, woe to anyone who dares to contradict his narcissistic view of his own perfection. Trump's jealous reaction to McCain is an exemplar of his fondest wish—to have that same level of esteem, not based on the fear of his wrath, but based on earned respect. Yet with every Tweet and every statement containing lies, he assures that will never happen.

The concept of 'service over self' is as foreign to him as the English language.

Meanwhile, at least 60 percent of the country is looking for just the right nutcracker. So far, 25 people; 24 Democrats and one Republican, are auditioning for the job.

27 JUNE 2019

TRUMP'S PROGRESS REPORT

Svengali—originally a character in a novel who exploits and dominates, now used to denote a person who exercises a controlling influence over another, especially for a sinister purpose.

While there's overwhelming evidence of Putin's influence over Trump, including Trump's unmistakable invitation to meddle again in the 2020 election, we haven't heard lately from Trump's other puppet master, Steve Bannon. While Trump may well owe his Presidency to Putin, it's Bannon who set his political agenda.

Or put another way, Putin provided access, Trump walked through the open door and Bannon provided the to-do list.

Steve Bannon was the White House chief political strategist until August, 2017. Used to setting policy at Breitbart News, it seems others on the Trump team weren't so eager to turn everything over to him. In fact, Bannon seemed to have difficulty working with just about everyone, including Chief of Staff John Kelly, the National Security Advisor H.R. McMaster (who convinced Trump to remove Bannon from the National Security Council), and most importantly, Jared Kushner (*The New York Times, The Washington Post, Politico, Newsweek*). Seems the final blow came when *Time* magazine featured Bannon on their cover calling him "The Great Manipulator," and giving him credit, rather than Trump, for the election victory.

After Bannon was fired, he returned to the Alt-Right publication, Breitbart News where he served as the executive chairman, but that only lasted a few months. It seems Bannon, in a rare pique of honesty, shared his view of Trump Junior with Michael Wolff, author of the tell-all Fire and Fury. Bannon incurred the wrath of the Trumps after he described Don Jr.'s attendance at the 2016 meeting with the Russians as "treasonous" and Ivanka as "dumb as a brick" (*The Guardian*, Jan. 9, 2018).

Bannon's full throated support for accused pedophile, Alabama Republican Roy Moore—who lost Jeff Session's Senate seat to a Democrat—didn't help. The final blow came when billionaire Rebekah Mercer, the major financial and ideological support behind Bannon and Breitbart, threatened to pull her funding unless he was removed.

As to Bannon's impact on the Trump Presidency, his presentation at the Conservative Political Action Network (CPAC) conference in February, 2017, shortly after Trump's inauguration, provides a rare glimpse into the Bannon agenda.

There are the three pillars to the Bannon plan:

1. **National Security and Sovereignty**—These benign sounding words translated into shutting our borders to certain Muslim countries and to refugees escaping war-torn areas in the Middle East. Even today, visa overstays continue to be ignored as the administration concentrates their efforts on keeping black and brown refugees and migrants out of the country. This policy has resulted in horrendous and dehumanizing conditions at the southern border. At the same time, Trump has stopped foreign aid to Guatemala, Honduras and Ed Salvador as punishment for not stopping their citizens from leaving—making the situations there worse—thus increasing the flow of refugees from these countries. It's almost as if Trump wanted more migrants coming here—it's certainly the predictable result. These horrendous actions have been a hallmark of this administration, and a black mark forever on America. There are now more illegal crossings than ever, in spite of Trump's bluster. This has also got to be the biggest failure, by Bannon's standards, of the Trump administration.

2. **Economic Nationalism**—Bannon rebirthed the 'America First' strategy, (which harks back to German nationalism), resulting in a series of controversial decisions that removed the U.S. from international organizations and agreements. *The Boston Globe* provided a list and it's substantial. They include the Paris Climate Accord, the Iran Nuclear Deal, the nuclear arms control treaty with Russia, the Trans-Pacific Partnership, The North American Free Trade

Agreement, UNESCO (the United Nations cultural organization), and UNHRC (the United Nations Human Rights Council). The Trump administration also withdrew funding from a United Nations program that, for decades, helped Palestinian refugees. The Boston Globe reported that, "Several times over the course of 2018, Trump privately said he wanted to withdraw from NATO." This was so concerning that Congress introduced legislation preventing Trump from withdrawing from the organization without Senate approval. 'America First' has become America Alone. Mission Accomplished.

3. **Deconstructing the federal government**—Bannon spoke of Cabinet appointees as the implementers—the people whose job would be to dismantle their agency, regulation by regulation. The blatant corruption of Tom Price at Health and Human Services, Scott Pruitt at the Environmental Protection Agency (nicknamed by employees as the Environmental Destruction Agency), and Ryan Zinke at Interior, finally forced their resignations. Conflicts of interest continue to plague Betsy DeVos (Department of Education), Mick Mulvany, acting Chief of Staff (only for as long as he doesn't cough in the vicinity of Trump), and a multitude of others in Trump's government accused of misuse of public funds, self-enrichment, working for foreign governments, violating ethics rules, and on it goes (*Bloomberg News*). *The Huffington Post* confirms their replacements are no better in terms of conflicts of interests; the new head of

the Department of Interior, David Bernhardt, is a former lobbyist for the oil and gas industry. As acting secretary, he's credited for erasing a chapter on climate change from department's handbook, and has advocated rolling back the Endangered Species Act and methane rules for oil and gas companies (*NPR*). Alex Azar, a former pharmaceutical executive, now heads Health and Human Services, Andrew Wheeler is a former coal lobbyist and heads the Environmental Protection Agency; recently resigned Acting Defense Secretary Patrick Shanahan was a former Boeing executive. Bit by bit, regulation by regulation, institutions that have been the bulwark of government—by, for and of the people—are becoming institutions by and for business, without restraint and plagued by corruption. Two more years and their purpose for being may no longer exist. Mission Almost Accomplished.

Two of the three Bannon goals have been, or are being, accomplished. But the *raison d'être* for this Presidency, building a wall that Mexico would pay for, to stop refugees and migrants at the southern border, has not been met. From Trump's viewpoint, that isn't all bad. After all, he needs unfinished business to justify a second term.

And what better to strike fear and loathing into the hearts of Americans than little children and their desperate parents.

In a recent book, *The Best People: Trump's Cabinet and the Siege on Washington,* author Alexander Nazaryan reports that Bannon may be back to guide Trump's re-election campaign. The author's interview with Trump in February 2019, as reported by *The Guardian*, confirmed that all it takes a little praise to get back in Trump's good graces. The author quoted Trump saying, "I watched Bannon a few times... Nobody says anything better about me right now than Bannon... there is nobody that has been more respectful of the job I'm doing than Steve Bannon." The Great Manipulator, aka Svengali, may be back for a second act.

Well, there you go. A little praise. That's all it takes. And, there's a big to-do item that still remains; so many more desperate families to confront. So many more children to terrorize.

04 JULY 2019

AMERICA:
THE FOURTH OF JULY, 2019—
THE ULTIMATE CONTRADICTION OF VALUES.

"The bosom of America is open to receive not only the opulent and respected stranger but the oppressed and persecuted of all Nations and Religions; whom we shall welcome to a participation of all our rights and privileges."
— GEORGE WASHINGTON

"No one leaves home unless home is the mouth of a shark."
— WARSAN SHIRE

"Fist in the air in the land of hypocrisy..."
— RAGE AGAINST THE MACHINE

As Trump celebrates this holiday with a military parade and fireworks he's throwing in his honor, and our expense; as hotdog eating contests take place, and families and friends gather to celebrate our birthday in backyards, beaches and parks—thousands of adults and children, including infants, sit/lie in filthy cages, sleep on concrete floors, sick and scared, away from their families, away from people who love and care for them.

That is happening here. And now. Being done by our government in our name.

An article in *Esquire* by Andrea Pitzer, who is a historian of concentration camps, wrote the United States has created a "concentration camp system." By her definition, a concentration camp exists when there is "mass detention of civilians without a trial."

When Representative Alexandria Ocasio-Cortez used the term 'concentration camp' to describe the conditions, all hell broke loose. Masha Gessen, in her article in *The New Yorker* wrote that because we can't imagine the camps in Germany, because we say, 'never again,' that it quite literally can't happen again. So, it's unimaginable that it's occurring here. At home. In America. Now.

But, it is clear whatever term is used to describe what is happening, it's beyond awful. Kids are taking care of kids. One doctor compared the camps to 'torture facilities' (*ABC News*). Law professor Warren Binford visited the camp in Clint, TX, where 350 infants, toddlers, and preschoolers were being housed in "horrendous" lice and flu-infected conditions, in space meant for 100 children. The youngest child there was two and one-half months old. While the law states that children are to be in these facilities for no more than 72 hours, some have been there for up to seven weeks; she talked with one child who had been there for nine months.

Six children have died in our custody. Michelle Goldberg of *The New York Times* calls this "a combination of incompetence and malice." But Jason Johnson of *The Root.com* disagrees;

he believes this is one more example of purposely making government chaotic, to tear it down, and that it's working—by not working—exactly the way Trump and his puppet masters want it to.

This is criminal. Literally. It's child abuse at the hands of the United States government. Child abuse is a crime, regardless of who commits it. According to the United Nations, taking migrant children from their parents or relatives without their permission is illegal in the first place (*The New York Times*). It's called kidnapping.

And, it may also be fraud. Private detention centers are charging the U.S. taxpayer $775 per day per child, according to the Department of Health and Human Services. Yet somehow, these centers are unable to provide edible food, blankets, soap or the luxury of a toothbrush.

The center in Homestead, Florida houses 2,700 children. It is run by Comprehensive Health Services, which is controlled by the private equity firm DC Capital Partners. Members of their advisory board include former Trump Chief of Staff John Kelly; Richard Armitage, former U.S. deputy Secretary of State; Michael Corbin, former ambassador to the United Arab Emirates; Michael Hayden, former director of the CIA, and other former top employees of government agencies (*Bloomberg News, Miami Herald, Miami New Times, CBS, The Hill, The New York Times. NPR, PBS Newshour*). This past weekend, several members of Congress were denied entry into these facilities—facilities paid for by taxpayers, and therefore subject to congressional oversight.

It is so bad that Save The Children, an international nonprofit organization established to improve the lives of children and to provide emergency aid to failed nations, is now providing services to some migrant children in our care—because clearly, the United States government could care less. An organization whose focus is helping children in war zones like Yemen, is now helping these children, because the United States government won't.

Trump has instituted actions not to solve the problem of immigration, but to exacerbate it. He needs this. He needs a reason to energize his base. And, the more cruel and heartless the situation, the better his supporters like it. Given the following situations, they are no doubt ecstatic:

- At the El Paso facility, there are four showers for 756 children who are housed in camps at five times their capacity (Inspector General's report obtained by *NBC News*).
- *BuzzFeed News* obtained a different Inspector General's report from two other border stations in the Rio Grande Valley. They report adults being held in standing room only cells for more than a week. "Cell 1 had signage for a capacity of 35 but a head count reflected around 155 actual adult alien males…" Most hadn't had a shower in more than a month. The report added that "Cell 3 had signage for a capacity of 12 but a head count reflected around 76 actual female aliens in standing room only conditions." The report describes these people as 'aliens'—as if from outer space, not like us. Perhaps it's a convenient term used to justify or excuse the government's inhumane treatment.
- In Clint, TX the guards told women who were thirsty to

drink out of the toilets.
- And more. So much more.

People who have seen these camps remark about how cruel the conditions are, as if they are a side effect of internment and a result of mismanagement. But Richard Stengel, former Under Secretary of State, disagreed, saying "Cruelty is the point of it" (*MSNBC*, July 2, 2019).

And now *ProPublica* has uncovered a secret Facebook group of current and former Border Patrol agents, consisting of about 9,500 members. The content is disgusting at best; it includes joking about the deaths of migrants, throwing burritos at "these bitches" (female members of Congress visiting a detention facility in Texas), and vulgar sexual memes depicting and degrading a female member of Congress. Faulted for mistreating children and adults under the care of CPB (Customs and Border Patrol), Daniel Martinez, on the staff of the University of Arizona, described the comments and memes as "clearly xenophobic and sexist" and reflecting what seems to be "a pervasive culture of cruelty aimed at immigrants..."

While everyone is tsk tsk-ing over these disgusting findings, least we forget what the President of the United States said in May 2018, "We have people coming into the country, or trying to come in—we're stopping a lot of them—you wouldn't believe how bad the people are. These aren't people; these are animals." Hardly any wonder then that CPB treats them as such.

So, happy Fourth of July! Maybe the incongruity of the over-the-top celebration in DC, with tanks in the streets of our capital, juxtaposed by the inhumane conditions and cruelty at the border, conducted and condoned by government officials, will give some Trump supporters pause. Or perhaps, like the President, they will see this inhumanity as punishment earned.

George Washington would be ashamed. As should we all.

15 JULY 2019

TWO PLUS TWO = RUSSIA...
BUT WHO GIVES A DAMN?

"Future election interference will likely take three tracks: spread of disinformation intended to discredit candidates, disruption of election infrastructure, and the undermining of public confidence in the electoral process after the election takes place.

— FROM THE SUMMARY OF THE STUDY *SECURING AMERICAN ELECTIONS*, STANFORD UNIVERSITY;

MICHAEL MCFAUL, EDITOR, JUNE 2019.

According to the FBI, it never stopped. Russia is continuing its attempts to meddle in US elections. Director Christopher Wray, at the Council on Foreign Relations (April 26, 2019) said "Russia is a malign foreign influence" that presents a "significant counterintelligence threat" to the United States, adding that "we are viewing 2018 as a kind of dress rehearsal for the big show in 2020."

Every federal intelligence agency, including the CIA, FBI and the National Security Agency, has stipulated that Russia interfered in the 2016 election and to quote the Mueller

Report, did so "in a sweeping and systematic fashion." The Republican Chair of the Senate Intelligence Committee, Senator Richard Burr (R-NC) agreed saying, "There is no doubt that Russia undertook an unprecedented effort to interfere with our 2016 elections."

The Mueller Report provides all the gory details. Through various proxies, the Russian government carried out attacks to magnify already existing divisions in American society, sow distrust in the democratic process, and incite conflict. Social media accounts generated by the Russian Internet Research Agency (IRA) reached millions of Americans. It set up individual accounts meant to impersonate Americans, built an audience for content around divisive social issues, focused on anti-Clinton posts, and even bought ads. One site alone had over 300,000 followers. And there were hundreds of sites on multiple platforms. Cyber attacks included hacking carried out by the Russian military intelligence agency (GRU) and, finally, infiltrating the Trump campaign itself (summarized in testimony by Alina Polyakova, *Brookings Institution*, in June 2019 before the House Judiciary Committee).

At the time of the election, the IRA "had the ability to reach millions of voters through their social media accounts" (Mueller Report). And, they did. To magnify the impact, as if 'likes' and 'shares' weren't enough, Fox News was an eager dupe—or if you prefer—dope, and serving as Russia's mouthpiece, repeated the propaganda. Conspiracy theories became the stuff of their commentaries. *Yahoo News* put a spotlight on one of dozens of Russian generated 'bulletins;' this one became known as the Seth Rich Conspiracy.

They report that *FOX* host Sean Hannity, "obsessively

covered the death of Seth Rich, a staffer for the Democratic National Committee." He claimed Rich leaked the DNC emails, (he didn't; an arm of the Russian government hacked into the DNC) and it was "very suspicious he was killed" (in an apparent robbery attempt) shortly thereafter. It was just a hop, skip and jump to conclude Hillary had a vengeful hand in his death.

Fox News perpetuated this lie almost nightly for a month, which was then magnified through social media. This is one of thousands of examples of weaponized disinformation campaigns designed to discredit Clinton. All of this is stated in the Mueller Report.

But none of this is acceptable to Trump. He has continually labeled the Russian investigations as a "hoax." He denied any attempt to obstruct justice, or of a conspiracy between Russia and his campaign. The Mueller Report documented 272 contacts between Russians and Trump's campaign leading up to the election. Mueller also documented at least ten instances of attempts to obstruct justice.

The only time Trump publicly 'chastised' Russia for their involvement was in response to a reporter's question at the G20 Summit. When asked if he had warned Putin not to meddle in the 2020 election, Trump turned to Putin with a smile and said, "Don't meddle with the election, please." Putin grinned back. It was as if they were sharing a private joke. They were. The problem is that the joke is on us.

Face it, Trump gets more agitated swatting away mosquitoes than condemning this adversary who attacked America.

If Trump doesn't care, at least we the people can count on Congress to address the problem. Uh... not so fast.

While Congress has the responsibility to enact legislation to reduce the impact of foreign influence in the election process, Republicans in Congress can read tea leaves—which clearly is easier and preferable to the many who haven't bothered to read the Mueller Report.

In an effort to curtail Russian interference, Senator Ron Wyden (D-OR) reintroduced the PAVE Act (Protecting America Votes and Election Act) designed to protect elections from foreign interference, by mandating hand-marked paper ballots and setting new cyber security standards for federal elections. A major outcome of this bill would "give voters the confidence they need that our elections are secure," Wyden said. Key provisions ban Internet, WiFi and cellular connections for voting machines, and give the Department of Homeland Security the ability to set minimum cyber security standards for voting machines, voter registration data bases, and other electronic reporting. Funding would be provided to local governments for secure ballot scanning and other equipment. The PAVE Act has been endorsed by a variety of non-partisan organizations as an important step in securing America's vote.

Who would not want to do that? Well, according to @ *powerpost,* a publication of *The Washington Post* that focuses on cyber security, just about all the Republican decision-makers who could make it happen.

Peter Swire, former chief counselor at Office of Management and Budget, and a former member of the government's Review Group on Intelligence and Communication Technology said, "Deterrence depends on a credible promise to take stern action" adding, "it's impossible for the world to believe that this president will take stern action against Putin." Christopher Painter, the State Department's former top cyber security diplomat stated, "When the President casts doubt on whether Russia is responsible... that sends the message that Russian malign activity in cyberspace is okay—not deterring them but encouraging them to do it again since there are no costs for doing so."

And, what has happened to the proposed PAVE Act? Nothing. In languishes in purgatory. Mitch McConnell has decided not to bring any election security bills to the Senate floor for a vote. Last year he stopped the Secure Elections Act from advancing. Why? Why would any member of Congress refuse to consider legislation to help secure our elections? The answer is that Trump will not sign any bill involving cyber security, so there's no point in pissing him off when the end result is a forgone conclusion.

The 2020 election will be a repeat of 2016, but on steroids. Here's why. Although it is illegal for a campaign to knowingly accept help for a foreign entity, Marsha Blackburn (R-Tenn) blocked an effort to pass a bill requiring campaigns to report offers of foreign assistance. Wonder if that has anything to do with Trump saying publically that he might want to listen to what a foreign country had on a political rival. That's an open invitation.

Then, there's the recent closed door "Social Media Summit." Facebook, Google and Twitter management weren't invited. The attendees did include conspiracy theorists and other conservative tech critics who echo Trump's complaints about the liberal media (*Fortune Magazine*). They all are Trump supporters whose posts in the past may well have served him, and the Russian bots well.

So, while this time we know foreign interference is a sure bet, there is little or no protection in place. In fact, it's open season; the prey is the American voter. And, there doesn't appear to be a Republican anywhere who gives a damn.

24 JULY 2019

MEET DONALD TRUMP: RACIST, XENOPHOBE, DESPOT AND, (OH, BY THE WAY), PRESIDENT OF THE UNITED STATES.

"Go back to where you came from."
—DONALD TRUMP'S TWEET TO FOUR CONGRESSWOMEN, JULY 14, 2019

"Send her back! Send her back! Send her back! Send her back!..."
—CHANT AT TRUMP RALLY, AIMED AT REP. ILHAN OMAR,
GREENVILLE, NC, JULY 17, 2019

"We are heading full speed ahead to a very dangerous place."
—JOHN HEILEMANN, JOURNALIST

Those most attuned to the dog whistles—the racists and xenophobes—heard them from the beginning. David Duke, former Grand Wizard of the Ku Klux Klan heard them. White nationalists, anti-Semites, white supremacists, Holocaust deniers, and American Nazis heard them. Those on the receiving end heard them too—directed first at Mexicans, then Muslims, Central American immigrants, refugees,

African Americans, and Hispanics —anyone of color, anyone non-Christian, anyone different. Those hating, and those hated, knew. For the rest, it took a slap across America's collective face.

Simple words really. Short and to the point. **"Go back to where you came from."** Translation: 'You aren't wanted here.' 'You are unworthy.' 'You are less than.'

No one was happier with Trump's statement than avowed white supremacists.

"This is the kind of White Nationalism we elected him for." (*The Daily Stormer*, July 15, 2019).

"With a single Tweet, Trump was able to win back the sizeable portion of the disaffected Right... " this from Richard Spencer, who declared "Heil Trump" following the 2016 election.

One commentator on *8chan*, described as "the internet's most dangerous message board," (*Daily Dot*), said "It is OK for him (Trump) not to want brown scum that clearly despise him, that these invaders have stepped well outside the line... the jewish (sic) media is right to be terrified..."

Jonathan Greenblatt of the The Anti-Defamation League said, "It's hardly surprising that we've seen white supremacists, neo-Nazis and other extremists celebrating Trump's outbursts. To bigots, they are a bullhorn validating their beliefs".

This week, the dog whistle became an unmistakable bullhorn.

The four Congresswomen, Ayanna Pressley, Rashide Tlaib, Ilhan Omar, and Alexandria Ocasio-Cortez are avatars for Trump's disdain. They are everything Trump hates. They are women. Of color. One, now an American, was born in a 'shithole' country and came here as a refugee. They are smart. They are liberals. They are Democrats. They overtly disagree with him. They detest what he stands for.

They have plenty of company.

In addition to being a bigot, Trump is taking the additional steps common to a despot. He is adding those who disagree with him to his list of 'unpatriotic' enemies. Senator Lindsey Graham, apologist extraordinaire, apparently prefers his dear leader be labeled an autocrat rather than a racist. He said, 'Go back to where you came from.' is not a racist statement because "if you're a Somali refugee wearing a MAGA hat, he doesn't want to send you back." Doubtful a MAGA hat on top of a hijab would be sufficient for the Trump crowd, but the essence of the comment was that **out loud dissent will not be tolerated.** Graham went on to call the four Congresswomen "communists and anti-American" (interview on *Fox and Friends*, Jul 15, 2019). One more epithet to be hurled by trumpers.

All else being equal, or more accurately unequal, color comes first on Trump's list of hate based priorities. His history is replete. His history is ugly. Racial resentments characterize his adult life (*Vox.com* Jul 15, 2019; *Huffpost.com* Jul 15, 2019; *The Atlantic.com*, Jun, 2019).

So now, Trump has added one more group to his hate list—anyone who dissents—anyone who disagrees with him. To cite Trump yet again, they "can't get away with" criticizing the United States. His statement further declared that no one should criticize the United States while he is President (*The Washington Post*). He is conflating love of country with unquestioned loyalty to him. For him, they are inseparable. He added, "I think it's terrible when people speak so badly about" the United States and, "in my opinion, they hate our country." And, by that, he means anyone who hates him, who speaks against him, hates America. Ergo, if you want to be an America loving patriot, you must not speak badly about him. Loyalty to him is valued above all else.

And then, as if to exemplify that conclusion, he doubled down on his racist/despotic view, Tweeting, **"I don't believe the four congresswomen are capable of loving our country."** Not capable? Why? Because of their color? Because they disagree with him? Because they're Democrats? Because they have the nerve to defy and criticize his loathsome language and behavior? Answer: All of the above.

So, there you have it.

Trump will assure the 2020 election is race based. He will demand allegiance, not to the country, but to himself. Those who do not comply are unworthy and unpatriotic. What will be the consequence for those who do not toe his line? Seriously. What will be the consequence?

In a chilling statement made to Turning Point USA's Teen Student Action Summit on July 23, 2019, Trump said, **"I have the right to do whatever I want as President."** He thinks he has no limits.

It will be a very long, very dangerous, and turmoil filled 16 months until the election. This is going to get worse. Much worse.

30 JULY 2019

HE'S GETTING WORSE—AGAIN!

Problems are not the problem; coping is the problem.
—VIRGINIA SATIR

Narcissist (n): a more polite term for a self-serving, manipulative, evil jerk with no soul or compassion.
—AUTHOR UNKNOWN

Trump is not having a good time. Neither is anyone else. He seems progressively less able to deal with daily frustrations inherent in the job. What is stressful to him (to mangle the Rolling Stones lyrics), is that not only can't he get what he wants, poor Donald can't even get what he needs. What he needs is universal acceptance and adoration.

He has only one response to criticism and that is to hit back verbally or by Tweet. But he doesn't know enough to attack the policy that's being challenged, so he attacks people personally and, often viciously. While his intent is to hurt the subject of his Tweets, it almost always backfires. He's in a circular firing squad, except the squad consists of one person; he continually sabotages himself, usually by his favorite method of communication. His asinine Tweets will eventually lead to his own inevitable virtual demise.

Trump has no ability to roll with the punches, to sit back and analyze, to consider, to put things in perspective, to think before he responds. It's so easy to push his buttons—he has so many of them. Here are a few: Obama, Mueller, Obama, being seen as weak or a loser, the size of his crowds, the margin of his win, criticism, minorities, questioning his intelligence, Obama, the press, Fox News when they show him 10 points behind Biden, subpoenas, minorities in power, smart people, strong women, fact-checking, Obama, everyone who goes against him, anyone questioning his statements, House investigations, any negative comparison with Obama, Russian involvement in the election, the idea his win may not be legitimate, Obama... the list goes on.

In a nutshell, Trump lacks effective coping skills. And, as he becomes angrier and more frustrated, he hits back, creating more problems for himself. It's a vicious circle that he has created, and he's in the middle of it.

The past week has been right up there in terms of aberrant behavior. *Axios* and a review of his recent Tweets and statements provide a sampling:

He continued attacking the four Democratic Congresswomen of color, Tweeting that they were a "very Racist (sic) group of troublemakers" and "not very smart." Talk about projection!

He derided Robert Mueller both before and after his testimony, saying he did "a terrible job." Probably because Mueller's testimony confirmed Trump's culpability and Attorney

General Barr's misrepresentations—aka, lies.

He told an audience of teenagers that the Constitution said, "I can do whatever I want as President." No doubt sending gobsmacked Civics teachers heading for the wine.

He continued to attack reporters who had the *chutzpah* to ask his reaction to the Mueller testimony, calling them 'fake news' and 'untruthful.' His way of dismissing uncomfortable questions is to attack the questioner.

He is attempting to stop asylum seekers from entering America by making any migrant who travels through a third country ineligible for asylum (*The American Prospect*). A nation built by refugees and asylum seekers is attempting to shut the door on refugees and asylum seekers.

He angered Afghanis by saying that if he wanted to win the war, Afghanistan would be "wiped off the face of the Earth." So much for America's goal of securing peace in the region. Surely Afghanis will sleep well knowing how much our Commander in Chief values them and their nation.

He said President Obama's book deal should be investigated. "Let's look into Obama the way they've looked at me... Let's subpoena all his records." He cannot let his nemesis go. He cannot accept that a black man won the White House. Twice. Without Russian help. He has made it his mission to destroy every treaty, regulation, law, and policy Obama supported. Destroying his legacy is his goal. It may be his ultimate goal.

He denied a *Washington Post* article that he had a set of talking points on various lawmakers, even though there is a photo of Trump holding them. Just one more example that truth and facts have no value. He once said, "Just stick with us. Don't believe the crap you see... Just remember, what you are seeing and what you are reading is not what's happening."(speech to Veterans of Foreign Wars, July 28, 2018)

He said that undocumented immigrants "vote many times, not just twice, not just three times." He still cannot accept he lost the popular vote. There is no evidence, none, that any undocumented immigrant has committed this felony even once, let alone multiple times.

He ended the week by attacking House Oversight Chair Elijah Cummings of Baltimore, calling him a bully and stating that facilities at the border were cleaner and better run than "Cumming (sic) **District "which is a disgusting, rat and rodent infested mess... a dangerous and filthy place... where no human would want to live."** In response, an editorial in *The Baltimore Sun* said... (Trump is) *the most dishonest man ever to occupy the Oval Office, the mocker of war heroes, the gleeful grabber of women's private parts, the serial bankrupter of businesses, the useful idiot of Vladimir Putin and the guy who insisted there are 'good people' among murderous neo-Nazis."... Trump is "not fooling most Americans into believing he's even slightly competent... or that he possesses a scintilla of integrity. Better to have some vermin living in your neighborhood than to be one."*

All this, and more, in just one week. Trump is spiraling down. Every time he says or does something antithetical to who we are and aspire to be, the sense is he has reached bottom. But this is the one area in which he overachieves; for Trump, there appears to be no bottom.

None of this is normal. This is a test. The final exam is 16 months away.

03 AUGUST 2019

AMERICA'S VOTE HIJACKED

"We wonder if the shoes that follow us around the Internet will
someday, with the click of a distant mouse,
look like the jackboots of old."
—RICHARD COHEN

"The Russian government interfered in the 2016 presidential
election in a sweeping and systematic fashion... first, through a
social media campaign that favored candidate Donald J. Trump...
second... computer intrusion operations..."
—THE MUELLER REPORT, INTRODUCTION TO VOLUME I, PG.1

It's stunning. Our government, in the form of the Senate and the Executive Branch, is handing over the future of the United States to any country, or group, most effective at influencing, and perhaps determining, the results of the next presidential election. It could be Russia, Iran, China, or an internal force like QAnon—who knows? More to the point, who cares?

Democrats in the House and Senate care. And, so do many Republicans in both Houses. Senate Leader Mitch McConnell (R-KY) and Donald Trump do not. In fact, based on their actions, it appears both welcome it.

The Mueller Report and in-person testimony before the House Judiciary and Intelligence Committees, made clear that (a) Russia intervened in the 2016 presidential election, (b) that the intervention was to the benefit of Trump, and the determent of Clinton, (c) that members of the Trump campaign welcomed and supported that intervention via meetings and shared information and (d) finally that Trump engaged in at least ten acts designed to obstruct the investigation into Russian involvement in the election.

At the hearing, Mueller made clear that Russian intervention was ongoing "as we sit here" and will continue into the 2020 election.

Just one day after Mueller's testimony, the Senate Select Committee on Intelligence released their report on Russian election interference. They too concluded "the Russian government directed extensive activity, beginning in at least 2014 and carrying into at least 2017, against U.S. election infrastructure at the state and local level." The Committee added that Russia's malign influence should result in "renewed attention to vulnerabilities in the U.S. voting infrastructure," and that the "U.S. must create effective deterrence" to prevent this from happening again.

Senator Richard Burr, Republican Chair of the Senate Intelligence Committee, concurred. "In 2016, the U.S. was unprepared at all levels of government for a concerted attack from a determined foreign adversary... since then, we have learned much more about the nature of Russia's cyber activities, and better understand the real and urgent threat they pose."

The report substantiates that it's likely the Russians scanned election-related systems in all 50 states.

If Russia's goal was/is to undermine faith in the sanctity of the vote, they are succeeding. Combine that with disinformation spread through right wing conspiracy theorists and Russian bots via social media, and a foreign actor could take over the most critical aspect of our democracy—the right of the electorate to choose their own leaders—and all without a shot bring fired.

Given this dire warning, it's clear that legislation is needed to combat these malicious activities. But bipartisan Senate bills have gotten nowhere, thanks to Leader Mitch McConnell. House bills passed with bipartisan support are also lying dormant on McConnell's desk.

McConnell has shut down votes on at least four security measures designed to shore up outdated state election systems, including requiring paper ballots as a backup in every state, assuring machines and voting data are not connected to the internet, instituting mandatory sanctions on any country caught meddling, and blacklisting and blocking assets of Russians who participate in nefarious activities. Other bills would have made it a crime for a campaign not to report contact and offers of help from a foreign power. Another seeks to set fair and reasonable guidelines for online advertising and hypertargeting.

What is clear is that the election process is vulnerable on a variety of levels and across media platforms. What is also clear is that the federal government is leaving it up to the states to decide what, if anything, is to be done to protect the vote. The problem is lack of funds and in some states, lack of will. And some issues, like consequences, can only be implemented by the federal government.

Should anyone think this is an esoteric concern, an 11-year-old was able to hack into a replica of the Florida state election website in under 10 minutes and *change voting records.* This was not a one-off. DEFCON 26, a convention for hackers, included kids for the first time in 2018; the youngest was eight. Turns out "more than 30 children hacked a variety of other similar state replica websites in under a half hour," (*PBS.org*) and were able to change voter information, such as names and addresses.

Matt Blaze, a professor of computer and information science at the University of Pennsylvania, and an organizer of the convention, said "It's not surprising that these precocious, bright kids would be able to do it because the (state) websites are vulnerable. What was interesting is just how utterly quickly they were able to do it."

Then there's all the misinformation on social media, designed with care, to target just the right people to assure a multitude of 'shares.'

And yet, the legislation sits.

As to why, the first explanation is that any mention of improving voting security sends Trump over the edge. He has yet to acknowledge that interference even occurred because to do so would place the legitimacy of his election in doubt. But that may not be McConnell's only reason.

He recently earned the nickname "Moscow Mitch" for refusing to allow these bipartisan bills to be brought to the Senate floor for consideration. But the rationale may be more self-serving than preventing a Trump temper tantrum.

The Louisville *Courier-Journal* reported that Oleg Deripaska,

Russian oligarch and pal of Vladimir Putin, could be helping to fund a $1.7 billion aluminum plant on an old strip mine in Kentucky. Rusal, a Russian aluminum company, had been barred from doing business in the U.S. because of their connection to Deripaska and another Russian oligarch. In April, the Trump administration lifted that sanction, with McConnell voting to support sanction relief.

And there's more. *Newsweek* reports that one of the bills would impose "the two largest electronic voting machine vendors with new regulations and financial burdens." These make up about 80 percent of the voting machines used in the U.S. Both companies have contributed to McConnell's campaign.

The result is that, finally, McConnell is taking incoming that hits home and hits hard. The nickname is sticking. He is being called everything from a "Russian asset" (Dana Milbank, *The Washington Post*), "to aiding and abetting Putin's ongoing attempts to subvert U.S. democracy" (former Republican Representative Joe Scarborough).

Perhaps the August recess and contact with fellow Kentuckians, along with some interesting challenges for his Senate seat, may convince McConnell that he would be better off protecting America's votes than to go down in history as 'Moscow Mitch,' protector of Trump, and avatar for *quid pro quo*.

07 AUGUST 2019

GUNS + TRUMP = A TOXIC BREW

*"There's a big overlap between conspiracy theorists, racists, gun
nuts… they all have one thing in common:
they feel like oppressed underdogs."*
—OLIVER MARKUS MALLOY

*"…democrats don't care about crime and want illegal immigrants,
no matter how bad they may be, to invade and infest our Country… "*
—TWEET BY DONALD TRUMP

Invade—*enter a country or region so as to subjugate or occupy it.*
Infest—*live in or overrun to an unwanted degree or in a troublesome
manner, especially as predatory animals or vermin.*
—MERRIAM-WEBSTER DICTIONARY

No country on the planet does this better than the United States; we kill more of our people with guns, per capita, than any nation on earth.

This is the 219th day of the year. During this time, there have been 251 mass shootings as defined by four or more victims

(*Snopes.com,* The Gun Violence Archive). Last year, 39,773 died as a result of shootings in the United States. This weekend, in less than 13 hours, 31 human beings were killed, and 40 more injured in two separate mass shooting attacks.

There are more guns in the United States than there are people. According to the *Graduate Institute of International and Development Studies,* there are 120.5 guns per 100 people. The nearest contender is Yemen with less than half that rate. And, they're at war.

Owning a gun is supposed to make us safer. Given that assertion by the NRA and gun manufacturers, (NRA Institute for Legislative Action), we should be the safest country on earth. We are not.

After every mass shooting, the usual culprits get assigned blame. This time is no different, with Congress members and Trump blaming violent video games and mental illness. But international research, as reported by *The New York Times,* found that mass shootings cannot be explained by violent culture, video games, mental illness, or racial divisions. In all of these areas, we are not exceptional. Different cultures and countries experience all of these things.

What does make us exceptional is easy access to guns. It's so easy that someone on the 'no-fly' list—in other words, a suspected terrorist— can purchase one or 10 or X number of assault rifles.

And now, we have one more element to throw into the mix that increases the toxicity of the national brew. It served as inspiration for the El Paso killer. That element is the abhorrent rhetoric by the President of the United States.

The motivation behind the mass killings in Dayton, Ohio is still under investigation. But there is an accomplice to the mass killings in El Paso, Texas on August 3, 2019.

He didn't pull the trigger, but he sure as hell provided the ammunition.

The killer in El Paso left a screed on the internet which pays homage to Trump, literally using his language. According to *The New York Times,* he used the words "send them back"—a rallying cry during a Trump rally that followed a Trump Tweet urging four Congresswomen to "go back to the totally broken and crime infested places they came from." The killer also wrote:

> *"This attack is a response to the Hispanic invasion of Texas. I am simply defending my country from cultural and ethnic replacement brought on by an invasion."*

Trump's ads in Facebook used the word 'invasion' in reference to immigration more than 2,000 times since May 2018, according to *Newsweek.* Add thousands more uttered by Trump himself in Tweets and at rallies. He has now added the word 'infestation' to his meager vocabulary—not just in reference to immigrants, but also to define America's largest cities, i.e. cities with majority black population.

Trump uses the language of white supremacists and White Nationalists. He and *Fox News* can deny that, but hate groups take solace from their words. Tucker Carlson, one of the most virulent of *Fox's* commentators, and one of Trump's favorites, often talks about 'replacement theory'—that browns and blacks are taking over this majority white country and destroying white culture. The El Paso killer used that as a rationale for his attack (see the quote from the screed above). Remember one of the chants at the "Unite the Right" rally in Charlottesville: "Jews will not replace us." There's that word again.

Hate groups heard Trump loud and clear when he said,

"There are good people on both sides."

When Trump proffers a Muslim ban, calls African nations 'shithole countries' and Mexicans 'criminals and rapists,' he is using, by definition, the language of hate groups. What these groups have in common, according to the *Southern Poverty Law Center*, are "beliefs and practices that malign an entire class of people, typically for their immutable characteristics." According to the *Southern Poverty Law Center*, there were 1,020 hate groups in the U.S. in 2018, and that number has been increasing year upon year.

There's a connection between mass shootings and far-right terrorist attacks, according *BostonGlobe.com*. White supremacists call it "acceleration—an imperative to sow chaos and societal disruption in order to bring about a race war, apocalyptic end times... " They report that "within hours of the shootings, extremists were celebrating on social media with phrases like 'it's happening!' and 'the fire rises!'"

So, the ingredients for this toxic brew are almost complete. The main ingredients are white supremacists and nationalists, who demonize immigrants from Mexico and other Northern Triangle countries (and others not white). Add the President of the United States, who uses the same language that legitimizes their hate using words like 'invade' and 'infest.' This provides a rationale to protect the country from the dirty, diseased and unwashed hordes. Now, add the key ingredient: easy access to guns. Mix them all together, bake in anger, fear, and chest-beating fake patriotism and voila! You have a recipe for disaster.

We may not be able to rid the country of hate, but we can take away the key ingredient. The Senate can pass the universal background check bill sitting on McConnell's desk. Once and for all, pass legislation outlawing assault rifles. The murderer in Dayton managed to kill nine people and injure 16 in under a minute because this was his weapon of choice. Imagine what he could have done had police not been on the scene. Pass a Red Flag law to allow intervention if it's apparent an individual is a danger to themselves or others. Finally, pass legislation that gives domestic terrorism the same level of national priority, funding, personnel, and support that is provided to prevent foreign terrorism.

The historian, Jon Meacham, recently said, *"Because of the spoken word, people can do unspeakable things."* The eloquent Toni Morrison said the same thing in a different way; *"Oppressive language does more than represent violence; it is violence."* El Paso serves as proof.

As if to put an exclamation point on all of this, *Amnesty International* has just issued a travel advisory for visitors to the United States because of "rampant gun violence, which has become so prevalent that it amounts to a human rights crisis."

Trump isn't going to change. Hate groups are not going away. But Congress can make us all safer by passing gun control legislation, and assuring the FBI and other law enforcement agencies give these hate groups the focus and attention they warrant.

It may be important to note, as a sidebar, that Trump will not be eager to sign bills that decrease the impact of supremacists and nationalists and other hate groups. They are, after all, his most strident supporters.

18 AUGUST 2019

<u>SO</u> MUCH SUCCESS

"Fascists... create(d) a drumbeat of propaganda that aroused feelings before people had time to ascertain facts. And now, as then, many people confuse faith in a hugely flawed leader with the truth. Post-truth is pre-fascism."

—TIMOTHY SNYDER FROM *ON TYRANNY*

He has done nothing *for* this country, but he has done so much *to* it.

Nothing that follows is unintentional, a mistake, or a miscalculation. All of it is on purpose and meant to be. Had that not been the case, Trump, or someone in his administration, would have made an attempt at correction. He didn't. No one did. These must be what he and his followers would call 'successes.' What follows is only a small sampling of what he has wrought,

He has succeeded in making our most dangerous enemies 'friends,' even as they increase their nuclear potential, threaten our allies, ignore UN resolutions (North Korea), and continue to attack us by interfering in our elections (Russia).

He has succeeded in making our traditional friends anxious about the reliability of our alliances; NATO and other allies voice concern about the unpredictability of this once trusted relationship. He has removed the U.S. from almost every treaty or pact without consultation or notice to co-signers. His 'America First' policy has resulted in disengagement from the rest of the world.

He has succeeded in increasing distrust in government by making thousands of statements, important and inane, that are verifiable lies, and has made no attempt to correct them. He undermines truth on a daily basis, and with that, respect for the office of the Presidency and respect for this country. To be blunt, he's an embarrassment every time he opens his mouth.

He has succeeded in establishing a state propaganda network which also serves as a source of public policy and, in turn, is a feedback loop that supports those same policies he then implements.

He is accomplishing Grover Norquist's wet dream by gradually destroying the federal government; the Cabinet Secretaries he appoints are slowly dismantling the agencies they are running. Examples include the EPA, the Department of Education, Health and Human Services, the State Department, HUD, the Department of Energy, the Department of the Interior, the Department of Justice, and more. These heads are typically former lobbyists who fought against the agencies they now lead. Once on board, they cut staff and eliminate critical regulations. Some, like Attorney

General William Barr, are just sycophants.

He has succeeded in serving as inspiration for extremists who have conducted violent acts. A review by *ABC News* documented "at least 36 criminal cases where Trump was invoked in direct connection with violent acts, threats of violence or allegations of assault." Further, investigators could not find a single criminal case in federal or state courts where violence, or the threat of violence, was made in the name of Presidents Barack Obama or George W. Bush. Importantly, those 36 instances that established that link to Trump were in court documents and police statements—and made "under penalty of perjury or contempt."

Here's a first for the United States. It's now official. Our country is a dangerous place. In spite of assurances that he would 'do something' after the Parkland, Florida school shooting, no changes have been made in gun laws other than banning bump stocks. Background checks have not been expanded, and assault rifles and high capacity magazines continue to be legal. Following the killings in El Paso and Dayton, Amnesty International issued a Travel Advisory "to exercise caution and have an emergency contingency plan when traveling throughout the USA... in light of ongoing high levels of gun violence in the country." We've made this list for the first time, ever. Japan and Uruguay, among others, also issued travel warnings. Another American 'success.' So much winning.

And, speaking of that, he succeeded in coming up with a new definition of 'winning.' He said tariff wars "are easy to win." But America's farmers are experiencing bankruptcy at an alarming rate—the highest in a decade (*The Wall Street*

Journal). Trump has also come up with a new application for 'socialism' by paying out billions to farmers to cover some of the costs of his folly. But that has not been sufficient to prevent many small farmers, who have lost their traditional markets, from giving up. For them, Trump's easy-to-win trade war has become a life-changing loss.

He succeeded in increasing the budget deficit this fiscal year (thus far) to $866.8 billion, and the national debt to $22 trillion (*Committee for a Responsible Federal Budget*). If he were to be reelected, heaven forbid, the national debt is projected to be $29 trillion before the end of his second term. His tax cuts have dramatically reduced revenues by lessening tax liability for top earners. It has not had a trickle-down effect, unless stock buybacks, and salary increases to CEOs and board members count. They don't.

He has resurrected concentration camps from the wretched past. In our name, he has treated asylum seekers, migrants and children exactly how he has described them—as animals and criminals. He is shaming who we say we are. He is demeaning us in the eyes of the world.

He has succeeded in taking ignorance to a whole new level. A book could be written on this topic alone. Here are a few pithy examples. He resurrected Frederick Douglass saying, he's "an example of somebody who's done an amazing job..."; said raking prevents forest fires; said the killings in Ohio took place in Toledo (it was Dayton); gave a thumbs-up in a grinning photo with a baby whose parents had just been murdered in El Paso; said wind turbines cause cancer; said he thought he was "actually humble... much more humble than you would understand;" claimed to have one of the highest I.Q.'s; defined

Puerto Rico as "an island surrounded by water, big water, ocean water;" and his first, biggest, and go-to in terms of inane comments—"Mexico will pay for the wall." His limited vocabulary is comparable to a fourth grader (*Newsweek*). He describes himself as a "stable genius." He is neither.

He has successfully turned the Constitution on its head by ignoring the concept of checks and balances. The Republican Senate, in the form of toady Leader Mitch McConnell, has stopped all legislation passed by the Democratic House by refusing to bring more than 100 bills forward for discussion or vote. Trump's administration has refused to submit documents and ignored subpoenas from various House committees. He has intervened in determining how money appropriated by Congress is spent—an exclusive responsibility of Congress. To get around it, he declared a 'national emergency.' It wasn't.

He has succeeded in finding full, if not gainful employment for members of his immediate family, thus taking nepotism to a new level. Neither Ivanka nor Jared had any experience or training in government, public policy, or diplomacy; neither had given a day of their lives to public service prior to their relative selecting them as advisors—something they have in common with the relative who hired them.

Other random successes include eliminating human rights as the fundamental core of American values, making racism and xenophobia a component of domestic and foreign policy, playing golf a record 225 times (as of Aug 17, 2019) since becoming President— that's 22 percent of his days in office (*thegolfnewsnet.com*)—and, thus far, has avoided payment to a multitude of cities for costs incurred related to his political rallies (*USA Today*).

He has also succeeded in eliminating the need to vet potential candidates for senior positions (he thanked the press for doing that for the White House; everything else they write is 'fake news'). He has avoided the burdensome step of Senate approval by making many key positions 'acting'—14 as of July 12 (*npr.org*). Trump's turnover rate for his "A Team"— which doesn't include Cabinet secretaries—is a whopping 75 percent with 33 percent having undergone serial turnovers (*Brookings.edu*).

Trump has succeeded in making us all experts in what DSM-5 (*Diagnostic and Statistical Manual of Mental Disorders*) describes as 'Narcissistic Personality Disorder.' His self-aggrandizement knows no bounds.

He has also succeeded in the most devastating way; he and his enablers have torn the nation apart—us vs. them. We are not united, either in fact or fiction, about anything. We've lost a sense of community; that we are all in this—whatever 'this' might be— together. We have lost our moral purpose and, with it, our standing in the world.

The vow on the Statue of Liberty is a poem by Emma Lazarus, which reads in part: "Give me your tired, your poor, your huddled masses yearning to breathe free, The wretched refuse of your teeming shore. Send these, the homeless, tempest-tost to me, I lift my lamp beside the golden door!" Trump has succeeded in turning that precious Statue into virtual rubble.

Timothy Snyder, in his pocketbook of truth and reason titled *On Tyranny*, writes that one way to be a patriot is to "Set a good example of what America means for the generations to come. They will need it." That means living up to the ideals so beautifully stated in the Declaration; striving to be our best selves by attending to our "better angels." It means refusing to compromise on universal values and always striving to do better.

What is clear is that none of us can afford to be bystanders. Not anymore.

28 AUGUST 2019

A SEAT ON THE *TITANIC*

"I am the king of the world!"
—SAID BY JACK BEFORE THE SHIP HIT THE ICEBERG.

Just when you think he can't get any worse, he does—but that's been written before.

The English vocabulary ought to include the word 'worser,' even if it only applies to Trump. There seems to be no bottom to which Trump will not descend. That, too, has been written before. His actions match those of a befuddled and evil dictator and appear limitless.

The impetus behind this past week's meltdown appears to be the economy. It has been the single driving force of his Presidency that has kept otherwise skeptical Republicans and Independents with him. Their response to Trump's Tweets, his careless comments, his racist policies, his lies, and his self-induced chaos has been, "Yes, but the economy... "

That's beginning to change. There are indications that the economy is weakening—mostly thanks to Trump himself. His tariff war with China is seriously impacting farmers, manufacturers, and other countries who contribute to our supply chains; that domino effect impacts an already nervous world economy. All this uncertainty is making inroads in consumer confidence and spending. Self-fulfilling prophesies take over as folks move out of stocks and into safer investments. Markets react like rollercoasters with 800-point losses in a single day, followed by gains of hundreds the next.

The trigger for a lot of these losses is comments made by Trump himself, which often appear to be off-hand and casual. Some are reckless. This past week, he Tweeted, "Our great American companies are hereby ordered to immediately start looking for an alternative to China... " Stocks sank to session lows, and the biggest daily decline this year, immediately after that Tweet.

"Hereby ordered?" Seriously?

The end result is financial anxiety and uncertainty and that creates volatility. Trump has always touted the markets as the measure of his 'great economy' and great administration. But when things go south, his *modus operandi* is to change the subject or blame others. This past week is a sad example of Trump frenetically attempting to do both.

Here are the 'change the subject/blame others' lowlights:

Trump accused American Jews who vote Democrat of "great disloyalty to Israel and the Jewish people." The trope that Jews have mixed loyalty, or none at all, to any nation other than 'The Promised Land' is a symbol of anti-Semitism that has been used for centuries. It's disgusting coming from the President of the United States. Frank Schaeffer, a former evangelical, provided another interpretation: that Trump is planting the seed; that it will be the 'disloyalty' of Jews that will cost him the election, adding, "He's put a target on their back."

Trump re-Tweeted conspiracy theorist Wayne Allyn Root saying, "Jews in Israel love Trump like he's the King of Israel. They love him like he's the second coming of God." Root is the same guy who likened President Obama and members of Congress to "the druggie who abandoned his spouse, kids and job to snort crack cocaine 24 hours a day." He asserted that Obama blackmailed Chief Justice John Roberts so he would be forced to reaffirm the constitutionality of the Affordable Care Act.

Apparently, Trump took that Tweet literally. When responding to a reporter's question about the trade war, he said none of the previous administrations took on the Chinese, looked up to the heavens and proclaimed, "I am the Chosen One."

But apparently, he was not 'chosen' by the Danish government as a prospective purchaser of Greenland; the Prime Minister rejected Trump's absurd proposal calling it, well, 'absurd.' Trump promptly cancelled his state visit to Denmark because of her response, even while saying Greenland wasn't at the top of his list anyway. That's so reminiscent of a pouty five-year-old losing something he really wanted, then saying, "I didn't want it anyway."

More head spinning as Trump yet again changed his mind about the cause of gun deaths. After mass killings in Florida, and now in El Paso and Dayton, he said that background checks needed to be expanded. And as before, he changed his mind after talking with NRA's Wayne LaPierre; seems existing background checks are sufficient after all and that the real gun safety issue is the mental health of the gun owner—which a comprehensive background check just might uncover.

Trump's wacky pronouncements help create diversion from a faltering economy. And, what could be wackier than opining that hurricanes might be broken up by dropping a nuclear bomb in the eye. And in case you hadn't heard, spoiler alert—you haven't—Trump said he received the award as Michigan's Man of the Year—an award that doesn't exist. Ditto, Log Cabin Republicans. No award.

It's as if he makes up one lie in order to divert attention from a previous one.

As luck would have it, the G7 meeting took place in France over the weekend—which could have served as the perfect diversion for the sliding American economy—except that so much of it was focused on the world economy, all the while coddling Trump in hopes of preventing a blowup.

In order to hype the markets while at the G7, Trump said that he had received two calls from the Chinese eager to negotiate a trade deal—except China said no calls were made. White House staff were forced to admit that no call had been received. Trump also announced a trade deal with Japan. There is none. He just makes this stuff up.

And, he didn't hesitate to involve his wife in his political fantasies. While at the G7 meeting, he claimed Melania would agree with him about his view of the North Korean dictator Kim Jong Un, since she "has gotten to know" him. Problem is they've never met. A *ménage a' trois* only in Trump's mind.

I apologize for any lingering mental image.

Then there's the already iconic picture of the G-7 climate meeting that Trump was too busy to attend, because he was meeting with the German Chancellor and the Indian Prime Minister. The picture, however, shows only one empty chair at that meeting and it's Trump's; Merkel and Modi were both in attendance. He's such a lousy liar.

In a stunning statement, Trump compared his handpicked Federal Reserve Chair, Jay Powell, to China's Chairman Xi. He blamed the woes of the U.S. economy on the Fed because they won't lower interest rates on his command. In a Tweet he said, "My only question is, who is our bigger enemy, Jay Powel (sic) or Chairman Xi?" Actually, the bigger enemy is the man asking the question.

Finally, as a salute to white supremacy and tyrants everywhere, Trump sent an email through his re-election campaign: "The President is calling on you at this critical time to remind AOC (Representative Alexandria Ocasio Cortez) and Democrats that "this is our country, not theirs." This was in response to a Tweet written by AOC that the time had come to abolish the Electoral College. Think about that. "This is our country, not theirs." What?? By this standard, does he plan to deport all Democrats?

So, the economy may not be the projectile needed to guide him into his second term after all. What to do? The answer is obvious; go back to building the #@%* wall. He has kept few of his promises (not that his followers care), but the one item they might not forgive is the missing wall, which he insists is being built. It isn't. Existing sections are being repaired and renovated, but as of this date, there is no new wall. Trump told officials to redouble their efforts and, if they have to break laws in the process (like take property without consent of the owner) not to worry. He will issue pardons. Several current and former officials provided this information to *The Washington Post*. Trump called this fake news.

Bret Stephens, conservative writer for *The New York Times* said, "Trump is either mentally unwell or morally unfit." But these are not mutually exclusive. There is enough evidence, in just his past week alone, that he is both.

So, here's the question. Is there anything Trump wouldn't do to win the election?

Even asking the question is acknowledging we all have a seat on the Titanic. We know there are so many icebergs, all dangerous and all created by Trump, but barely acknowledged by his enablers and supporters. We also know we have a spoiled, self-serving teenager at the helm who thinks he can do no wrong.

How do you spell SOS?

03 SEPTEMBER 2019

HEROES AND VILLAINS

"What really matters is whether we use the alphabet for a declaration of war or the description of a sunrise. What really matters is whether we use numbers for the final count at Buchenwald or the specifics of a brand-new bridge."
—FRED ROGERS

In the stream of American history, we may be living in the most dangerous time since the Civil War. Maybe the '60's comes close; there was the divisive Viet Nam War, racial animus, riots, protests, cultural changes and assassinations. The country was in turmoil, but there is a difference between then and now. Then, no one wondered whether the nation would survive as a democratic republic. Now, it's a question mark.

As the nation tries to cope with all the Trump-induced chaos, it's important to recognize those who step up and speak out—to alert the public to Trump's assault on accepted norms, values and laws, as he continues to spiral downward.

These people endure put-downs, name-calling and constant threats—verbal and physical. These are the people of proven character and integrity, who have placed the country and truth above partisanship, and even their own safety. They rise against this mutant presidency and deserve acknowledgment. They are heroes.

At the top of the list are members of America's press—especially those from the mainstream media assigned to the White House. They call out lies, are the target of massive abuse from Trump, have had their press passes suspended for assertive reporting and pushing back against untruths, are ignored as punishment for asking questions that counter the White House narrative, and called names from 'punk' to 'liar' to 'enemy of the people' when they push for truth.

Listing any, risks omitting many, but it's important to at least make a stab and acknowledge newspapers like *The Boston Globe, The New York Times, The Washington Post, The Los Angeles Times,* and *The Miami Herald;* so too *CNN, Bloomberg News, NBC, ABC, CBS, NPR, The Economist, Associated Press, BBC, PBS, Business Insider,* and so many more. And, add online news sources *Politico, Slate* and *Axios* to the list. Magazines like *Vanity Fair, The New Yorker* and *The Atlantic* have devoted space and time to in-depth stories that provide readers with background and details on issues impacting the country. So many reporters, investigative journalists, opinion writers, cartoonists, and editors have refused to be intimidated. All together, they are the lifeline to reality for the rest of us as Trump goes off the deep end.

Trump fears the free press, across its various platforms, more than any single entity. And lucky for us, he has good reason. They are the documenters. They are the truth tellers. They remind us to be shocked. They are saving the day—and perhaps the republic.

Fact-checking sites earn every penny, especially given the ubiquitous conspiracy theories, Russian bots, and the sheer number of just plain lies. Politifact, Snopes, FactCheck. org., and Google Search are among the best.

There are those who have put their political career on the line—Justin Amash (R-MI), the only Republican in the House, so far, to support impeachment; Senators Jeff Flake (R-AZ) and Bob Corker (R-TN) lost any chance of re-election after frequent rebukes of Trump. Bill Kristol, a 'never-Trumper' and longtime editor of the prestigious conservative magazine, *The Weekly Standard,* watched as the publication he helped found closed its doors after 23 years. Max Boot, David Frum, David Jolly, George Will, Joe Scarborough, Steve Schmidt, Jennifer Rubin and Nichole Wallace are just a few of the leading conservatives who not only left the Republican party, but are speaking and working against Trump; they continue to publically disown his agenda of racism, purposeful lies, studied ignorance, and feckless governing.

There are a few people who actually report the news at *FOX* and deserve special mention, especially given the political environment that worships at the altar of all things Trump. Shepard Smith, Chris Wallace and, lately but rarely, Neil Cavuto go against the tide, opt for truth and honor their profession. There is the sense that others may soon follow.

Robert Mueller and his investigators are heroes by any standard. So too is James Comey, who refused to trade his ethics for a job; he became the whistle blower that resulted in the appointment of the special counsel. Jeff Sessions, oddly, also qualifies for not caving under constant insults and bullying from Trump. George Conway, Kelly Ann's husband, deserves a medal! There are so many people who put their careers (and marriages) on the line to do the right thing.

Then there are the anonymous sources in the White House and other governmental agencies who risk so much to provide the truth and serve as 'deep throats' for journalists.

At the opposite end are the villains. They are the enablers, the corrupt and the greedy, whose fortunes in wealth and power depend on Trump's good favor. His toughest Republican critics before the election became his strongest enablers afterwards.

They moan, complain, and roll their eyes off the record in the Senate cloakroom, but genuflect and pander the moment they leave. Marco Rubio, Ted Cruz, Lindsey Graham, and Mitch McConnell are exemplars. They could have been leaders and stopped the worst of Trump's behaviors. Instead they did the opposite. Here's hoping their political careers are over. They chose not to honor their oath to protect the Constitution, but instead chose to serve and protect a flawed, dangerous, empty, pathetic, excuse of a man.

Then there's Attorney General William Barr. He stands alone. He assured the public that the Mueller probe found Trump innocent of conspiracy and obstruction of justice. He lied. The AG knowingly lied to the American people. His fawning behavior is shameful. He continues to be Trump's stooge; that is his living legacy.

Speaking of enablers, *FOX* commentators/hosts deserve the booby prize. They have promoted and demonstrated arrogant ignorance and massacred the truth. Tucker Carlson, Sean Hannity, Laura Ingraham, and others act as Trump's kitchen cabinet. They set policy, reinforce the worst of Trump's behaviors, get the easily led to buy into anything, manufacture, and spread conspiracy theories.

The Trump administration and *FOX* trade staff back and forth. Trump uses *FOX* as an employment agency, while serving as the next career step for former Trumpers demoted to public sycophancy. *FOX* is the state propaganda machine; an extension of Trump and the White House. And he insists on fealty. To prove the point, he was upset that a *FOX* news anchor had the *chutzpah* to interview the communication director for the Democratic National Committee and treat her as a professional. Trump Tweeted, "We have to start looking for a new news outlet. Fox isn't working for us anymore!"

Wayne LaPierre and the National Rifle Association have been, and are, villains. LaPierre manipulates Trump as easily as does Putin. Turns out, these two may not be that separate from one another—the NRA admitted accepting funds from a Putin ally. And, the Russian government supports social media content via bots and conspiracy theories—aided and abetted by *FOX*—and at every rally. Through Tweets, Trump provides the enemy list to white supremacists. LaPierre's guns provide the means; circle complete.

The villain list has to include evangelicals. While there are a few defectors, especially among the young, their allegiance to Trump is mind numbing. They have traded their values for idolatry of someone they view as a fighter for their cause. Here's a quote from Jerry Falwell, Jr. that sums up their support of Trump: "Conservatives and Christians need to stop being 'nice guys'... the United States needs street fighters like @realDonaldTurmp at every level of government b/c the liberal fascists Dems are playing for keeps..."

Evangelicals have yet to learn that the only cause Trump fights for is his own.

Here's another quote from evangelical Jim Bakker. "The first horse of the apocalypse has started to ride! God spoke to me the other night and said 'I put Donald Trump on Earth to give you time to get ready." They view Trump as heralding in the Rapture and claim any opposition to Trump is the devil's work.

And let us not say, 'Amen.'

None of us is Mr. Rogers... well, except Fred Rogers. He was a hero. And, as his quote suggests, we are all capable of choices that make us heroes or villains. To varying degrees and at different times, maybe we're combinations of both. But these are not normal times. They require us to make choices.

It can't be that hard to be responsible; to choose to do what's morally right, and objectively honest.

Can it?

Again, to cite Fred Rogers: "We live in a world in which we need to share responsibility. It's easy to say 'It's not my child, not my community, not my world, not my problem.' Then there are those who see the need and respond. I consider those people my heroes."

We could sure use a lot more heroes—and a lot fewer villains.

12 SEPTEMBER 2019

WHAT WENT WRONG?

"Nearly all men can stand adversity but if you want to test a man's character, give him power."

—ABRAHAM LINCOLN

What went wrong? Good question. So much seems to have failed. Maybe individually the system could have coped, but together these multiple failures threaten the Republic.

The Founders were well aware of the dangers of a tyrannical government. It was what they feared most. They set specific duties, responsibilities and contingencies to prevent that from happening. These are well defined in the Constitution and affirmed by 243 years of experience. But, these fail-safe mechanisms have... failed.

Turns out we are a lot more fragile than we thought. So, what has gone wrong?

We elected a flawed person as President.

Aided and abetted by Russia, made possible by the Electoral College, and 107,000 votes in three states, Trump became the 45th President of the United States. He started off without a mandate, almost three million votes short of his opponent. He was/is fixated on destroying his two nemeses—Hillary Clinton and, especially, Barack Obama. He did nothing to build the needed bridges with Democrats. Instead, literally from day one, he exacerbated the divisions.

Trump's psychological problems are described elsewhere. It's their manifestation that has turned the country, and the world, upside down. He has demonstrated a lack of knowledge or interest in our history, norms, good governance, or the Constitution. He has chosen self-seeking grifters and adorers as advisors and agency heads. He has turned the Presidency into his own unlimited bank account and continues to profit from it financially. He persists in kowtowing to the world's autocrats and dictators while brushing aside, in one case literally, historical allies. He makes policy by Tweet, chock full of grammatical and spelling errors; his Presidential Library will be a testament to ignorance and self-absorption. He cannot admit to making a mistake; instead he doubles down.

He has usurped roles constitutionally assigned to Congress. He has caged immigrants and refugees in inhumane conditions worthy of the world's worst dictators. He has tried to make the free press the enemy of the people. He has promoted division rather than unity and has made lying an art form which he practices daily. He shows no empathy for anyone. He has neutered governmental institutions. He has eliminated environmental, energy. and consumer regulations at an alarming rate. He is demolishing trust in government. He has promoted racism, sexism, anti-Semitism, xenophobia, and yes, violence. And more. So much more.

The Senate isn't doing their job.

We no longer function under the requisite three co-equal branches of government. While the current occupant of the White House moves to extend his power and usurp the authority of Congress, there is no pushback from the Senate under majority leader Mitch McConnell (R-KY). The House has passed 170 pieces of legislation since January 2019. They are sitting on McConnell's desk and include everything from prescription drug reform, protecting the vote, gun safety regulations, and campaign finance reform.

McConnell's job is to bring these bills up for discussion, possible amendments and a vote. If they fail, so be it. But, to do nothing is abdicating the Senate's constitutional responsibility. The Republicans in Congress have been Trump's staunchest enablers. What they wouldn't have tolerated from Obama, they accept and support from Trump.

The best examples that demonstrate this hypocrisy are fiscal: tax cuts for the rich and massive increases in military spending have resulted in an annual budget shortfall this year of more than $1 trillion. Since Trump took office, $8 trillion has been added to the national debt, which now tops $22 trillion for the first time in history (*thebalance.com, cbsnews.com*). But the Senate does not care. Under McConnell, they rubber-stamp whatever comes from this administration.

The best example of McConnell's abject failure is his refusal to bring any bill to a vote unless Trump assures him beforehand that he'll sign it. That isn't how it's supposed to work. Trump can veto any bill presented to him, the Senate can vote to override, or not. McConnell is allowing Trump, the Executive Branch, to dictate what the Senate, part of the Legislative Branch, will even discuss, let alone bring up for a vote.

The House is trying to do their job.

But they're not trying hard enough. Many of the new House members were elected in 2018 to, among other things, provide oversight of an administration run amok. The Mueller Report detailed a myriad of examples of the administration's attempts to obstruct justice, as well as other possible crimes outside the jurisdiction of the Special Counsel. The Judiciary, Ways and Means and Oversight Committees in particular, have attempted to secure testimony and documents from the administration, and have been rebuffed every step of the way—with the blessing of the Attorney General who appears to have one client; and it's not the American people.

With very few exceptions, committee chairs have been forced to seek judicial interdiction to get needed information. The process is slow and tedious, with every request resulting in a lawsuit. If the goal is to educate the public, and present them with justification for moving forward with impeachment—or at the very least, justification for voting Trump out of office—it's happening too slowly. When it does happen, the committees often settle for whatever they can get at the moment—which may be testimony behind closed doors. That is not educating the public.

Testimony by everyone should be under oath and in public. All told, there are about 60 different investigations into suspected misconduct by the Trump administration. These need to be televised as they occur—and not just on C-SPAN. Noncompliance with subpoenas and documents need to be met with hefty fines and contempt charges. It's time to get serious.

Congress is not working.

Trump is trying to seize more and more power away from Congress, including the power of the purse, taxation and the use of troops to deal with domestic issues; and he's succeeding. He ordered money appropriated for the military and homeland security transferred to build his wall when Congress specifically said 'No.' He violated a law when he sent military troops to the southern border to deal with domestic issues. It's also been argued that Trump's decision to impose increasingly punitive tariffs is "tantamount to a national federal sales tax on consumers which constitutionally he does not have the power to impose" (Andrew Napolitano as reported by Newsweek). Lawsuits on these power grabs, and others, are pending.

The Judiciary? To Be Determined.

So much rests with these ultimate decision makers. As Trump pushes and exceeds the limits, it will eventually be up to the courts to determine what is legal under the Constitution. Whatever the decisions of lower courts, the other side will appeal. Eventually, it will be left to the Supreme Court to determine whether Trump's actions have been constitutional. Given the makeup of the Court, Chief Justice Roberts will likely be the tiebreaker. The survival of the Articles and Amendments which make up the Constitution, and the legacy of the Court itself, could well depend on this one person.

The Constitution is a remarkable document that has been

the envy of the world, but it is only precious as the guiding document to those in government who live it.

The introduction to the Declaration of Independence and the Constitution, published by the Cato Institute declares "...*no constitution can be self-enforcing. Government officials must respect their oaths to uphold the Constitution; and we the people must be vigilant in seeing that they do... it is up to us, to each generation, to preserve and protect it for ourselves and for future generations.*"

It's time we the people got to work.

16 SEPTEMBER 2019

IMPEACHMENT—THE ONLY OPTION

"We the people are the rightful masters of both Congress and the courts, not to overthrow the Constitution but to overthrow the men who pervert the Constitution."
—ABRAHAM LINCOLN

"The only conduct that merits the drastic remedy of impeachment is that which subverts our government or renders the President unfit or unable to govern."
—CHARLES RUFF, FORMER WHITE HOUSE COUNSEL

"Impeachment is not about punishment. Impeachment is about cleansing the office. Impeachment is about restoring honor and integrity to the office."
—LINDSEY GRAHAM, 1999

The hesitancy of the House of Representatives to initiate impeachment proceedings had nothing to do with the lack of evidence and justification, but with the certainty that the Senate would never vote to convict. In addition, Trump has demonstrated he becomes more irrational and erratic when under pressure or being criticized; an impeachment inquiry would be sure to result in even more unpredictable and unhinged behavior.

Another consideration was the certainty that impeachment would increase divisiveness in a country already being torn apart; therefore, the best way to remove Trump from office would be for the people to vote him out. The counter argument is that impeachment proceedings would provide the public with information they need to make a fully informed decision—information that now is being withheld.

Trump himself is forcing the House to act. The administration's refusal to provide documents, as well as ignoring congressional requests to testify in public and under oath, is preventing the House from performing their responsibilities under the Constitution. Refusal to comply with House requests for information was the basis of one of the articles of impeachment under Nixon.

Trump has become an institutional menace. He just keeps piling on blatantly illegal acts and weird behaviors. Those who have questioned the political consequences of impeachment are now saying the time has come.

It's no longer an option; it's a necessity.

There are two Articles in the Constitution that apply to impeachment. **Article II, Section 4 reads:**

"The President, Vice President and all civil officers of the United States, shall be removed from Office on Impeachment for, and conviction of, Treason, Bribery, or other high Crimes and Misdemeanors."

We know Trump is an unindicted co-conspirator. His former personal attorney pled guilty to making illegal campaign payments (hush money to keep two former mistresses silent prior to the 2016 election) "at the direction of a candidate for federal office." That attorney is now serving a three-year prison term. That candidate was Trump.

We know the Mueller Report stipulates at least 10 impeachable offenses by Trump. Included were attempts to obstruct justice by trying to intervene in the Mueller investigation, and multiple abuses of power including possible bribery by offering the possibility of pardons for those who didn't 'flip' and testify against him.

We know Trump did not divert or turn over his businesses to a blind trust.

We know there are domestic financial dealings that could amount to anything from abuse of power to fraud. According to *Rolling Stone,* as of June of this year, taxpayers have paid $105.8 million in reimbursements to properties owned by Trump during his administration. In the most recent example, the Air Force used a non-military airport (a critical hub used by guests to get to a Trump property) to gas up planes instead of using far less costly and easily accessible military bases. This arrangement provided an additional $11 million to an airport that was struggling before Trump's deal with them in 2014 (*The New York Times*). Since that time, the number of Air Force refueling stops near Trump's Turnberry Golf Resort went from 95 in 2015 to 259 so far this year (*The New York Times*).

We know conflicts of interest have been a concern from the beginning of this administration and may be best personified by another temporary residence on Pennsylvania Avenue. The Trump International Hotel (*aka* The President's Hotel) has hosted lobbyists and influence peddlers, foreign and domestic. According to Robert Maguire, the research director of the Center for Responsibility and Ethics in Washington (*CREW*), a nonpartisan ethics watchdog, "It is becoming harder and harder to figure out where the Trump administration ends, and the Trump organization begins." Another example involved the use of Trump's Doral Hotel outside Miami. For the past two years, the payday lending industry held their annual convention there. This year they could celebrate the proposed gutting of a crucial rule requiring lenders to assure that after paying back loans, borrowers would still be able to cover their basic living expenses—which is hard to do with annual interest rates of around 400 percent. The head of the Consumer Financial Protection Bureau, who proposed this change, had been recently appointed by Trump (*wnycstudios.org* and *ProPublica*).

We know Trump 'mishandled' classified information on several occasions (Tweeting a classified photo of a failed Iranian satellite launch, sharing highly classified information with Russian officials in the Oval Office, refusing to give up his use of unsecured smart phones).

We know Trump and his staff reportedly attempted to force Ukraine to investigate Joe Biden and his family by threatening to cut off U.S. military aid (*Vox, Reuters*).

We know Trump granted top level security clearances to family members after professional investigators, tasked with carrying out investigative reviews, refused.

We know membership fees at Mar-a-Lago doubled within days of his election.

We know that, thus far, 101 members of Congress have spent campaign funds at Trump properties since his election (*CREW*).

We know that Trump Organization properties have made almost $6 million from political groups since Trump took office. Prior to Trump's run for office, his businesses never made more that $100,000 a year from these same organizations (*CREW*).

We know Trump is personally profiting from his presidency.

Article I, Section.9, Clause 8 reads in part:

"...no Person holding any Office for Profit or Trust under them, shall, without the Consent of the Congress, accept of any present, Emolument, Office, or Title, of any kind whatever, from any King, Prince, or foreign state."

We know the Foreign Emoluments Clause prohibits Trump from accepting any benefits from foreign states unless he first obtains the consent of Congress. He has never sought or received consent. An emolument has been defined as 'anything of value.'

We know Trump has accepted benefits in the form of rents from foreign governments at Trump owned hotels and buildings both foreign and domestic.

We know Trump has refused to release his tax returns. These would be useful in determining whether and to what extent, he has financial dealings with foreign governments.

We know that high ranking administration officials are using Trump properties at Trump's suggestion at an increased cost to taxpayers (The Vice President stayed at a foreign Trump owned resort 180 miles from meeting site; getting there required helicopter transport).

We know that Trump promoted Mar-a-Lago as the site for the next G7 meeting. That could amount to millions of dollars from foreign governments paid to the Trump Organization.

We know *CREW* found that, as of August 2019, 111 foreign officials have made over 130 trips to Trump properties.

It's suspected that much of Trump's finances and properties are tied to relationships with foreign governments. Not separating his foreign entanglements from objective decision-making, constitutes potential conflicts of interest.

This isn't meant to be a complete listing of what may amount to high crimes and misdemeanors, and emolument clause violations. But it's a pretty good start.

If Trump doesn't meet the standard for an impeachment investigation by the House, then who would?

If it's true that in this country no person is above the law, then the House has no choice but to initiate an impeachment inquiry and proceedings which may, or may not, lead to the impeachment of Donald J. Trump.

Doing nothing is no longer an option.

IT'S ALMOST OVER.
NOW WHAT?

"In politics, being deceived is no excuse."
—LESZEK KOLAKOWSKI, POLISH PHILOSOPHER

"When you're finished changing, you're finished"
—BENJAMIN FRANKLIN

Scattered throughout these essays are random thoughts about how and why we elected such a flawed, incompetent and insufficient human being, and what can be done to prevent it from happening again. If we're honest, Trump is the result, not the cause, of policies we put in place. These, along with actions that devolved out of control over time, gave us Trump. This has been a long time coming. But no country that espouses government by, for, and of the people— one that proclaims to be constantly striving for a more perfect union— can tolerate someone like Trump as its leader and survive as the Founders and Constitution intended.

Plato said that democracies always become dictatorships.

As of now, we have one of the longest lasting democratic republics on the planet, but we are on notice.

We've seen the fragility of American institutions. Elect and appoint the wrong people, blindfold or bribe Congress—and progress in civil and human rights, protecting the environment, improving public education, implementing sensible and humane immigration policies, providing a system that promotes equal justice, assuring health care as a right, modeling ethics and decency at all levels of government, providing thoughtful leadership at home and in the world—it can all disappear in the blink of an eye.

It's been stunning to see how easy it is to destroy what we thought was indestructible; it's going to be harder to repair the harm because, in addition to governmental and social institutions, real damage has been done to our political psyche—how we see ourselves in relation to our fellow Americans and how we treat one another. Trump almost destroyed that. Almost.

We need to reconsider what we've become, and how the system allowed someone like Trump to rise from the muck to be elected president. That requires looking in the mirror, and then picking up the broken pieces.

Let's start with a given. Too many citizens have come to hate politics and politicians. Over time, more and more of us have disengaged; way less than half bother to vote. More people stayed home than voted for any presidential candidate in 2016. Ask why and you'll get responses like "they're all corrupt, they're all bought and paid for, they only care about lining their own pockets, those with the most money win, so my vote doesn't matter, I live in a blue (or red) state so my vote is worthless." They'll say they're sick of the never-ending campaigning instead of people doing their jobs.

Perception is reality. It's also often true.

The disaster that gave us Trump provides the rationale to revisit the system and correct what, over time, has turned politics into a fraudulent enterprise that depends on too much money while ignoring what's moral, ethical, or right.

So, how do we start to address the issues that gave us Trump, and what is seen by many as a dirty enterprise unresponsive to voters. Here's a suggestion:

Convene a 9/11 type blue ribbon commission with the goal of improving the process and procedures of elections. Members should be independent and non-partisan, with the authority to produce recommendations and suggest legislation to Congress. They should include former presidents (with the obvious exception), vice presidents (not this one), attorneys with special background and experience dealing with ethics in government, constitutional scholars, retired judges and other former public officials whose knowledge, reputation and experience would contribute a valuable voice and provide immediate credibility. Provide full transparency via interim reports to the nation, and publish a final report detailing findings and recommendations.

Their mission would be two-fold.

First: codify in law or regulations additional requirements for the presidency. Clearly, age and place of birth are not sufficient. Here are just a few ideas.

Require top secret security clearance. The process would begin as soon as candidates announce their intent to run. If it's required for top level staff, it should also apply to the president.

Candidates must have experience in public service and answering to a constituency, be they voters, citizen groups, stockholders, or benefactors.

Candidates must pass a physical and mental health exam conducted by recognized professionals appointed by an outside panel of experts and unknown to the candidates.

Tax returns for at least the past 10 years must be made available to the public.

Second: The Commission would consider systemic changes and make legislative recommendations to increase voter participation and reduce the influence of money in politics. Now comes the hard part. Here are some ideas to consider.

Set term limits for the House (6 terms, 12 years) and Senate (2 terms, 12 years) with no back and forth between the two.

Institute a lifetime ban on professional lobbying after leaving Congress.

Find ways, including legislation, to end Citizens United and SuperPacs which allow unlimited campaign contributions.

Disallow contributions by corporations to any federal, state or local campaign.

Set a maximum of, say, $300.00 for an individual contribution to any one candidate.

Ban all contributions of any amount, at any time, from registered lobbyists.

Reduce the election cycle to a specific time period of

a few months. Any announcing or campaigning prior would result in hefty fines.

Allow only public funding for presidential elections by providing a tax credit up to a certain amount to be spent on the candidate of their choice. This would be tax deductable on current year's taxes.

Assure equal television access by national networks via donated time to presidential candidates.

Review the election process itself. Consider ways to reduce the possibility of outside hacking and influence, voter suppression, and gerrymandering. Review current best practices and develop a consistent nationwide system.

Eliminate caucuses, create uniform presidential primary procedures among states, and hold all presidential primaries on the same day.

Develop plans to encourage voter participation—a national holiday, stamp free mail-in ballots which provide a paper trail, online voting, automatic voter registration.

To assure every vote matters, eliminate the Electoral College by Constitutional Amendment or though state action by assigning electoral votes to the winner of the national popular vote.

Mostly, because of money, we've reached a crisis of confidence in politics and the election process. Combine that with an absence of any meaningful official qualifying requirements to become president, and we have the recipe for disaster.

That's not hyperbole. That's exactly where we've been and where we are. But, this also provides a great opportunity to fix the problems that got us here.

HOW TO MAKE
A MORE PERFECT UNION

*"Leaders build bridges and seek common ground to unite. Small
people build walls and invent excuses to divide."*
—MAMUR MUSTAPHA

The Wall is the perfect metaphor for the Trump Presidency. He began his candidacy railing against immigrants. He tried to stop immigration from certain Muslim countries. He shut down part of the government throwing 800,000 government employees and hundreds of thousands of contracted employees out of work because Congress refused to grant funding for his wall. When that didn't work, he declared a 'national emergency'—all for a useless wall that he promised Mexico would pay for.

Trump tried and succeeded in building walls between his supporters and everyone else. He appealed to the worst of human faults and, by providing a model, encouraged knee-jerk fear of 'the other'—blaming any group for whatever problems exist. And, if a problem didn't exist, invent one, or two or ten. He had to have internal enemies in order to survive.

The problem was, and is, those enemies are us: Fellow Americans, our neighbors, members of our own family, and our closest friends. The enemy is anyone who is 'different'— brown, black, non-English speaking, non–Christian and (here it comes) Democrats, and even worse, liberals. These walls are as real as the one Trump wanted to build to separate us from Mexico and, like that wall, these are penetrable as well. Not by tunnels or ladders or saws, but by truth and reconciliation.

There are a lot of quotes throughout these essays, mostly at the beginnings. Many were chosen because they help confirm that what we've experienced with this presidency, has been experienced before in different times, with different people. And we're still here. But, maybe because Trump is so recent and caused so much damage to us as a nation, this time seems so much worse. But, there has to be a place to begin finding that truth and achieving that reconciliation.

Lao Tzu, sometime back in the 4th Century wrote:

> "A great nation is like a great man: when he makes a mistake he realizes it.
> Having realized it, he admits it.
> Having admitted it, he corrects it.
> He considers those who point out his faults his most benevolent teachers."

We need to realize we made mistakes, then admit and correct them. We need to find ways to come together. Mistakes were made, through commission, by voting for and then supporting a president who systematically tore down, or attempted to, all the norms of civility, trust, decency, respect, and concern for others—mistakes empowered by greed and sustained by power. And, there are the sins of omission, by not standing up, and standing out to decry what was happening.

The Trump Presidency was fed by greed and manufactured fear of the 'other,' and sustained by the need to retain power. That's about it in a nutshell.

It seems that the divisions in the country are as massive as the walls that separate us—but that's not true. We have so much more in common than the differences that divide.

We all love this country. We all want the best for our kids. We all want to live in a world at peace. We all want to be safe in our schools and neighborhoods. We all want the best that education can offer, for the needs of today and the world of tomorrow. We all want to be able to meet our family's needs. We all want the pride of decent pay for the job we perform. We all want to breathe clean air and drink clean water. We all want to live in a country where people value its magnificence and beauty. We all want the opportunity to make the best possible lives for ourselves and our children, and to achieve the self-respect that comes from that. We all want our kids to learn the value of honesty, empathy and decency in their interactions with others. If we want these things for ourselves, shouldn't we want our leaders to have these same values—not just for themselves, but for the people they serve?

These should be what we all are working to achieve, while knowing—and respecting— there are different ways of getting there.

So, what can be done to tear down the walls of uber

partisanship and fear? What could be done structurally to help make this a more perfect union? Here are some ideas.

Each political party needs to make a conscious, overt decision that the other is not the enemy. At the DNC and RNC level (the National Committees of each party), each political platform should address this. The enemy cannot be each other; instead the internal enemies are those who want to tear down and tear apart those values we all hold dear.

Maybe a good place to start is each party's platform asserting those common values we ALL hold—like the ones noted above and then develop a plan, based on those tenets, to assure each is addressed. Voters could compare and contrast using the same metrics.

Blurring the hard edges of both parties could be enhanced by doing something once considered radical. Each presidential candidate could choose their running mate from the other party. It almost happened when John McCain considered putting Joe Lieberman on his ticket. It's likely the choice of each party, almost by necessity, would be a moderate —another positive factor. Think about the advantage this person would have working on the Hill to get legislation passed. Think about what it would feel like for a Democrat or Republican voting for a presidential ticket that includes a member of the opposing party. Yes, it would get some getting used to, but it would be an immediate way to break down the 'wall' that exists between the two major parties. Every person voting for a Democrat for President would also be voting for a Republican and vice versa. Republicans and Democrats would be talking to each other in the White House every day, modeling collaboration, cooperation, and compromise. Imagine that.

The seating arrangement in both Houses of Congress needs to change so that Republicans and Democrats sit next to each other—there would no longer be 'their side of the aisle.' That 'wall' would cease to exist. Such a logical and simple thing to do.

The concept of Red and Blue states would fade in importance if more of them signed on to the National Popular Vote Interstate Compact. Those that have, pledge that once there are a sufficient number of states in the Compact to total 270 electoral votes, they would instruct their electors to vote for the winner of the national popular vote. As it is now, if you are a Democrat living in Alabama or a Republican from New York, your vote will be lost in the landslide of that state's major party. If the Electoral College was no longer a factor, every vote would be worth the same and every vote would be meaningful, regardless of the state of residence.

The Electoral College is long past its sell-buy date, but because of parochial interests in swing states, and those with smaller populations, it is unlikely Congress would rid itself of this anachronism. And, even if they did, ratification by three-quarters of the states would be close to impossible. The Compact is a work-around that assures all votes would be worth casting. This would likely increase turnout, especially in those states we now think of as Red and Blue. Another wall—gone.

While we're at it, why should Americans declare themselves a member of any political party when they register to vote? While some states have a closed system that only allow party members to vote in their primary, that's becoming more of an exception than the rule. The fact that Independents/

Non-Party Affiliates are the fastest growing political group in the country testifies to a reluctance to declare. So, let's rid ourselves of that self-imposed dividing 'wall.' And, why not have one national primary day with all candidates of both parties on the ticket? Yes, all this sounds radical and way outside the box, but what we're doing now sure isn't working.

Then there's the question of facts. We have become a nation of conspiracy theorists and people who simply make up stuff, because they can. We currently have a model in the White House who is unbeatable at that. There are at least five reputable fact-checking organizations that do this full time. We've got to come up with a system that assures that the news and information we receive is accurate—and if it isn't, it has to be called out in real time. Information is the basis on which all of us make decisions. It needs to be accurate.

Another systemic change that would help break down walls separating Americans would be to require national service for everyone, with no exceptions. Aside from giving back to a country that has given so many opportunities to its citizens, national service provides the opportunity for people to work together to achieve common goals, to learn from and rely on each other, to achieve together while working with people representing different economic and educational levels, cultures, ethnicities, religions, and life styles. Stereotyping and demonizing will never be the same as a result; nothing changes minds and hearts like having learned through experience. If there is one single change that could affect the heart and soul of a nation now and for generations to come, this is it.

A Congressional committee, or some other entity, could

surely come up with more and better ideas than these. But what is for sure, is that we have to deal with the divisions in our country that have been prodded and poked, encouraged, magnified, and ignored for too long. They are slowly destroying the fabric of America. We have to come together. We have no choice if we are to survive as a democratic republic.

Historian Jon Meacham said it best in his book, *The Soul of America:*

> *"For all our darker impulses, for all of our shortcomings, and for all of the dreams denied and deferred, the experiment begun so long ago, carried out imperfectly, is worth the fight. There is, in fact, no struggle more important, and none nobler, than the one we wage in the service of those better angels who, however besieged, are always ready for battle."*

We are all in this together.

We are, after all, still and so far, the *United* States of America.

EPILOGUE

THE FINAL ACT —
STARTS WITH *THOUGH*
AND ENDS WITH THE ANSWER TO *WHY.*

From the beginning, Russia and Ukraine have played an outsized role in relation to the Trump administration. And now, here they are again, as we head toward the finale.

A word spoken at the end of a sentence, ushered in the final act of this corrupt and incompetent administration. And the answer to a question would help explain Trump's treasonous behavior. Russia and Ukraine are involved in both.

The word 'though,' uttered by Trump in yet another transactional foreign policy action, was the start of his official downfall and the beginning of the end of this national nightmare. It served as the impetus for the inquiry in the House of Representatives that will result in the impeachment of the 45th President of the United States.

To summarize: U.S. military aid, granted to Ukraine, struggling in their fight against Russian incursion, turned out to be conditional and dependant on the Ukrainian government providing dirt on Trump's leading Presidential opponent.

Speaking to the Ukrainian President, following his request for funds, Trump said the magic words that will lead to his impeachment: **"I would like you to do us a favor, *though.*"**

Days after the whistle blower's summary of this call was made public, as if to put an exclamation point on his middle finger raised high, Trump publically asked China to do the same thing.

According to the Federal Election Commission, "It is illegal for any person to solicit, accept, or receive anything of value from a foreign national in connection with a U.S. election."

What Trump asked for, in trade for foreign aid, had nothing to do with American policy or security and everything to do with a personal favor to help his re-election campaign.

The President of the United States broke the law. Again. And again. First Russia, then Ukraine, then China. Three strikes and you're out.

As important, there is a fundamental, but as yet unknown truth underlying policies and actions, foreign and domestic, of much of this corrupt administration. It is the answer to this question: **Why is Trump so beholden to Putin?**

There is nothing, literally nothing, about Trump that is redeeming—not personally, not ethically, not morally. That lack of character, some would say 'soul,' assured his failure at a job that required all three. This absence of character and his need to be seen as a winner, made him vulnerable to Putin's machinations. But why was Trump made vulnerable? The answer to that question is key to understanding Trump's presidency.

Here are just a few of the events where Putin's influence impacted American policy:

Trump's Campaign Chair (now federal prisoner) Paul
Manafort, led the fight to soften U.S. support for Ukraine
in the 2016 Republican platform as a response to Russian
incursions. (*Politifact,* Aug.4, 2016). *Why?*

For the first time in American history, two top level
Russian diplomats were invited into the Oval Office, to meet
alone with Trump the day after he fired FBI Director James
Comey. That action alone was a breach of national security.
Aside from expressing relief the investigation into Russian
interference would shortly end, Trump shared highly
classified information with them (*The Washington Post,* May
15, 2017; *The Guardian,* May 15, 2017; *The New York Times,* May
16, 2017, *Reuters,* May 16, 2017). *Why?*

Trump discounted all 17 U.S. intelligence agencies
who agreed Russia interfered in the 2016 election on his
behalf. *Why?*

Within days of his inauguration, Trump indicated he
might consider recognizing Russian's annexation of Crimea
from Ukraine and rolling back sanctions on Russia. *Why?*

Trump never chastised Putin for Russian election
interference or warned him not to do it again. *Why?*

Trump never supported, in word or deed, legislative
actions that would reduce further foreign interference in
U.S. elections. *Why?*

The contents of every one-to-one meeting between Putin
and Trump, and there have been at least five, remain secret, not
just from the public, but from *everyone.* Trump even went so far
to assure translator's notes were destroyed. *Why?*

Trump took no action following Russian forces seizing
three Ukrainian ships and Putin's threats to dismantle

Ukraine as an independent nation. *Why?*

Trump's personal attorney, Rudolph Giuliani (his previous one is in prison and Rudy may soon follow), made multiple trips to Ukraine trying to implicate the Bidens in a non-existent scheme to funnel money into the 2016 election to support Clinton (*The Wall Street Journal*, Oct. 10, 2019). Seems Giuliani's goal was to implicate Ukraine and absolve Russia from election interference. *Why?*

Finally, almost every significant overseas foreign policy decision Trump has made, including betraying the Kurds—which will result in countless allied deaths, millions of refugees, the rejuvenation of ISIS, loss of trust in the United States, along with his decision to pull troops out of Syria and send troops to Saudi Arabia—all benefit Russia—to the detriment of the U.S. and our allies. *Why?*

The final act will begin when Trump is impeached and perhaps convicted, or when he resigns or is voted out of office. But this tragedy will not end, and the final curtain will not fall, until there is an answer to these questions.

And there is an answer.

Marsha Shearer
September 2019

ACKNOWLEDGMENTS

When I began writing opinion pieces for *Villages-News. com*, a community online news publication, I had no idea they would serve as the impetus for a book. So, my thanks to Meta Minton, owner and publisher, for providing me with a platform to vent—which resulted in feedback—a lot of feedback. Even in this very conservative enclave, some of it was actually positive.

And, I was surprised by comments like, "I look forward to reading your column. Even though I don't agree with a word you say, I love the way you say it." I never thought of myself as a writer; I was just a pissed-off citizen who couldn't tolerate the one-sided Trumpian view of our country's character and politics being circulated in our community. Yet people chose to read, knowing they would disagree starting with the first sentence. What more could a writer ask?

A huge thanks to Chris Stanley for her ongoing encouragement, her techie skills, and her patience at the lack of mine, her superb editing, and valuable advice. This book exists, in large part, because of her. This is the only part of the book she didn't read before publication.

And, thanks and long-distance hugs to Melanie Goldstein whose editing skills and suggestions helped made me a better writer. Doug Hughes provided valuable feedback on all things Constitutional; Mark Welton, Brian Mullady, Jim Ukockis, and Roger Cooper critiqued several essays each; their unique backgrounds helped give me the confidence that reinforced my decision to publish.

Steve Burt, mystery writer and fellow Villager, suggested I talk with writer and designer John Prince, who quickly became a trusted advisor and through his editing and graphic skills, helped essure that the book was attractive and readable. He guided me through the self-publishing process, beginning with the raw essays and ending in the book you are now reading.

With friends and advisors like these, and so many more who provided encouragement and support, I can attest that most anything is possible. It also helps to be an optimist by nature.

I'm also optimistic that, with attention and care, we can fix the "what went wrong" that resulted in Trump's election. We can reestablish and implement the values and principles on which this country was founded. These are—after all and above all—what makes this country great.

ABOUT THE AUTHOR

Marsha Shearer is a retired educator and school administrator. During her career, she helped develop and promote early childhood special education programs throughout the country. Her last position was an administrator with the U.S. Department of Dependent Schools overseas. She has three sons and four grandchildren, and is living the retirement cliché in The Villages, Florida.

Contact her at *America.in.Crisis.Book@gmail.com*, and 'Like/Follow' her on Facebook.